Streamline ALUMINUM TRAILERS
Restoration & Modification

Daniel Hall

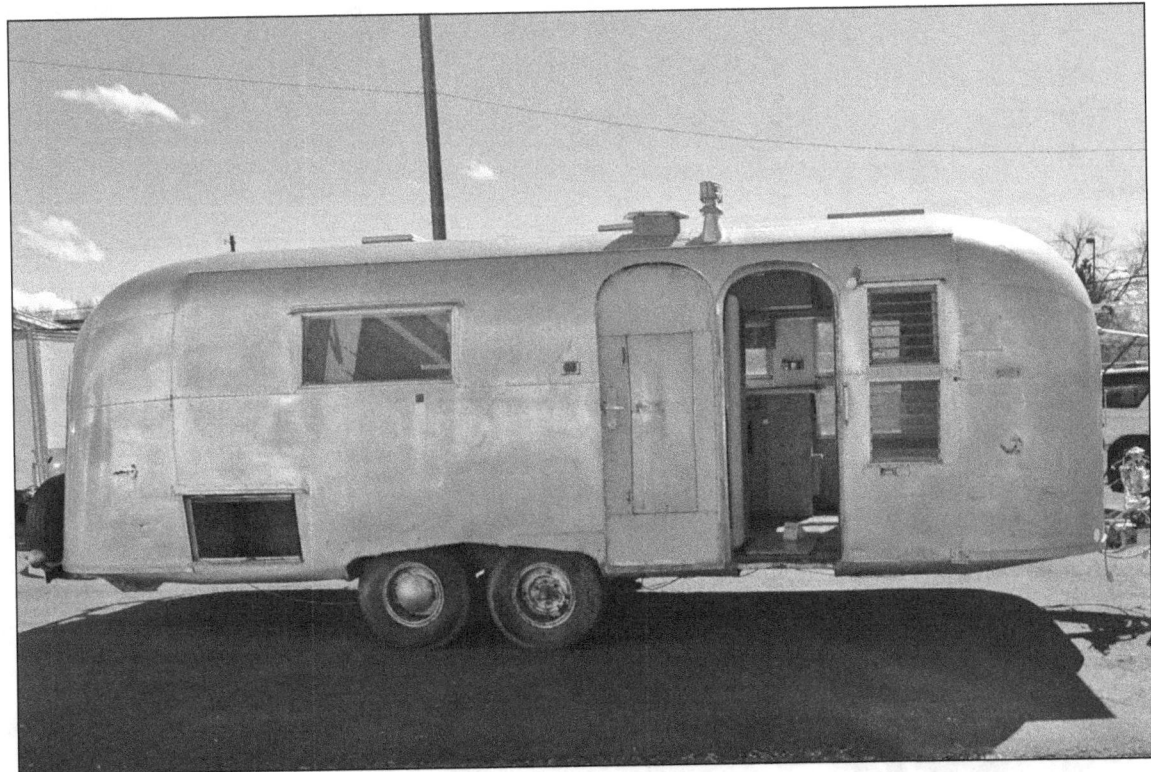

CarTech®

CarTech®, Inc.
838 Lake Street South
Forest Lake, MN 55025
Phone: 651-277-1200 or 800-551-4754
Fax: 651-277-1203
www.cartechbooks.com

© 2017 by Daniel Hall

All rights reserved. No part of this publication may be reproduced or utilized in any form or by any means, electronic or mechanical, including photocopying, recording, or by any information storage and retrieval system, without prior permission from the Publisher. All text, photographs, and artwork are the property of the Author unless otherwise noted or credited.

The information in this work is true and complete to the best of our knowledge. However, all information is presented without any guarantee on the part of the Author or Publisher, who also disclaim any liability incurred in connection with the use of the information and any implied warranties of merchantability or fitness for a particular purpose. Readers are responsible for taking suitable and appropriate safety measures when performing any of the operations or activities described in this work.

All trademarks, trade names, model names and numbers, and other product designations referred to herein are the property of their respective owners and are used solely for identification purposes. This work is a publication of CarTech, Inc., and has not been licensed, approved, sponsored, or endorsed by any other person or entity. The Publisher is not associated with any product, service, or vendor mentioned in this book, and does not endorse the products or services of any vendor mentioned in this book.

Edit by Wes Eisenschenk
Layout by Monica Seiberlich

ISBN 978-1-61325-716-6
Item No. SA344P

Library of Congress Cataloging-in-Publication Data

Names: Hall, Daniel (Daniel Irwin), author.
Title: Streamline aluminum trailer restoration / Daniel Hall.
Description: Forest Lake, MN : CarTech, [2017]
Identifiers: LCCN 2017015469 | ISBN 9781613252277
Subjects: LCSH: Automobile trailers--Conservation and restoration--Handbooks,
 manuals, etc. | Automobile trailers--Maintenance and repair--Handbooks,
 manuals, etc. | Trailers--Conservation and restoration--Handbooks,
 manuals, etc.
Classification: LCC TL297 .H35 2017 | DDC 629.28/76--dc23
LC record available at https://lccn.loc.gov/2017015469

Written, edited, and designed in the U.S.A.
Printed in the U.S.A.

Title Page:
This 1960s Tradewind is rough and dirty but is a good candidate for a smooth restoration because it retains all the original windows, its panels are in great shape, and the chassis, including the coupler, looks straight. This unit does, however, have split rims, so an axle replacement and new tires/rims should be planned.

Back Cover Photos

Top:
This camper is ready for its original skin to be replaced. Before that work begins, the masking is removed and the walls are brushed off and vacuumed to remove any loose foam and particulates to help prevent air-blown debris while the panels are worked into place.

Middle Left:
If your wish is for a fully custom interior, you can often find someone else's abandoned project for cheap. This Airstream arrived fully gutted and ready for a custom interior design.

Middle Right:
The heat shield is in position to check for fit. I did not have a large enough piece to make it out of one sheet. It was constructed out of two and joined using rivets.

Bottom:
A wood-burning stove in this Airstream provides heat and ambiance, a unique feature that you do not find on a production camper. Both the galley and bathroom are split into two sections. There are no overhead cabinets, which lends to the feel of an open space.
(Photo Courtesy Joe Roberts, Abaci Photos)

CONTENTS

Acknowledgments 4
Introduction 5

Chapter 1: Getting Started 10
Models to Consider 11
Where to Find a Project 14
DIY or Outsourcing 16
Tools and Equipment 17
Fasteners 18
Design Modifications 20
Planning Your Work Space 20

Chapter 2: Disassembly 21
Safety First! 21
Animal Contamination 21
Tanks, Stove and Fridge 22
Galley, Bed and Cabinets 23
Interior Skin 23
Insulation 27
Lift the Shell 29

Chapter 3: Chassis 31
Frame Members 31
Coupler 34
Stabilizer Jacks and Bumper Mod 35
Propane Tank and Spare Tire Mount 35
Finish Application 36

Chapter 4: Flooring 37
Material Choices 37
Plywood Template 37
How to Salvage Damaged Wood 39
Subfloor Install 39
Marmoleum Floor 41

Chapter 5: Body 48
Belly Pan 48
Aluminum Bodywork 50
Hidden Components 52
Vents 52
Body Reinstallation 52
Panel Patching 53
Panel Replacement 56
Locker Restoration 59

Chapter 6: Doors and Windows 61
Main Door Disassembly 61
Main Door Reassembly 63
Baggage Door Restoration 66
Window Restoration 71
Rubber Gasket Replacement 75
Screen Replacement 75

Chapter 7: Electrical Systems 78
Volts and Circuits 78
Battery Choices 81
Distribution Block 85
Solar Panels 86
Chassis Wiring 87
Trailer Taillights 88

Chapter 8: Insulation 93
Fiberglass 93
Foil-Backed Bubble Pack 94
Spray Foam 96

Chapter 9: Interior Skin 100
Panel Sanding 104
Endcaps 105
Panel Painting 111
Interior Panel Repair 112

Chapter 10: Interior Cabinets 115
Wood Finishes 118
Woodworking Procedures 121
Aluminum Trim 125
Tables and Bed Lifts 127
Overhead Lights and Lockers 127
Metal Plating 128
Upholstery 129

Chapter 11: Appliances 131
Heater 132
Stove 133
Ice Chest 135
Gas Lamp 138

Chapter 12: Plumbing and Liquid Propane .. 141
Plumbing 141
Propane 148

Chapter 13: Polishing and Brightwork 153
Polishing Tools 155
Small-Scale Polishing 156
Large-Scale Polishing 160
Preserving Your Work 166

Chapter 14: Traveling with Your Trailer 168
Empty the Tanks 168
Towing Preparation 169
Hitching Up 171
Choose a Destination 173
Accessorizing 174

Epilogue 176

DEDICATION

To the memory of Judy's dog, Charles . . .
high fives and biscuits forever, little buddy.

ACKNOWLEDGMENTS

Like restoring or building a camper, producing a book on the methods and concepts involved with a travel trailer is no small achievement. And, even though I work on these things every day, I can't pretend to know everything about the subject matter.

With that said, this book contains a mass of information from the tradesmen and professionals at Camper Reparadise. Camper Reparadise is a restoration shop in Salt Lake City, Utah, that began as a small family business and has since grown large enough to occupy a 10,000-square-foot facility, employ around 12 professionals, and produce more than 20 restorations a year. Among those specialists, a special thanks needs to be given to Bryan Rowe and Chad Nielson for their contributions in the woodworking and polishing sections.

Likewise, Brandon Zinninger, aka the-best-boss-ever, needs a hearty thank you for allowing the time and resources this book appropriated from the needs of a quickly growing business. From photo taking to long hours at the computer screen, the following pages required much of my attention and devotion over the past year, while other significant responsibilities sat on the back burner.

Additional thanks go to Steve and Melanie Zinninger for providing the stepping stone that Camper Reparadise needed to get off the ground. Without them, I wouldn't be where I am today and there would be no avenue to professionally restore campers. Similarly, a special thanks go to the clients who trusted in the shop's ability and commissioned the restorations you see on these pages.

Thanks also to my inspiring group of friends, and thanks to my supportive family, especially my parents, who put a tool in my hand at an early age and encouraged me to pursue my passions. Finally, I thank my wonderful wife, who kept me on track and graciously supported me throughout this whole experience.

INTRODUCTION

Despite Airstream being the first brand to come to someone's mind when discussing shiny vintage campers, there are many alternatives to choose from, like this polished Barth.

It's possible that the perfect camper restoration project is around the corner from where you're sitting right now. But more likely, finding a worthy candidate often leads to traveling thousands of miles to retrieve, such as the Boles Aero featured in this book.

When I started this book, the only camper I planned to include was a 1952 Airstream Cruisette. As soon as writing began, however, it was apparent that more than one restoration should be featured to cover everything you need to know to resurrect an old camper. Besides the Cruisette, I included a 1950s Boles Aero Ensenada and a 1970s Airstream Sovereign.

Boles Aero Ensenada

Pulled from the palm desert where it sat for decades, the Boles Aero Ensenada required a couple of days and a well-equipped tow rig to recover. Sometimes retrieving a camper requires traveling to remote areas and using minimal resources to fix it. Getting this gem from a sedentary state to roadworthy status required jacking it up in the sandy desert to remove the wheels so the dry-rotted and square tires could be replaced. Luckily, it did not have split rims, so the wheels did not need to be replaced.

Finding the proper bolt-pattern wheels for this camper would have been difficult. Just finding a good set of tires took a day to complete. While the wheels were off, the hubs were disassembled and re-greased to ensure that it would make the trip to Salt Lake City. It's always fun disassembling stuff in a dirty environment. If it had been windy, the hubs would not have been serviced because dust would contaminate the bearings.

Trailer lights were run under the trailer and zip-tied to LP lines and frame wheels. Because there wasn't anything ferrous to attach the magnetic trailer light kit to, they were duct-taped to the original light buckets.

The Ensenada was originally a park model, which means that there were no fresh, gray-, or black-water tanks installed on the camper. To make it usable off-grid, holding tanks were added to the unit.

The basic interior layout was retained, but a few changes were made to open up the interior and accommodate modern conveniences. Now a 12-volt electrical system based on two 6-volt glass-mat batteries powers interior electrical components, including lighting and ventilation. When plugged into shore power, the batteries are maintained, and the 110-volt outlets are powered.

STREAMLINE ALUMINUM TRAILERS: RESTORATION AND MODIFICATION

INTRODUCTION

This is how the Boles Aero looked when it arrived at Camper Reparadise. Water damage was pretty rampant, affecting the usual locations, including the vent opening and windows, and some not-too-common places such as the galley.

Some custom cabinetry from a previous owner had taken the place of the original liquid propane heater, but thankfully, the heater was found in a pile of scrap in an adjacent field.

The galley retained its original faucet and the cabinets still had their art deco latches, which are the important bits. Sourcing hardware that matches these originals can be difficult.

Boles Aero Aluminum Trailers

The name Boles Aero carries just as much history as an Airstream but is less of a household name due to the company closing its doors in the 1980s. They are a riveted, lightweight, all-aluminum top-quality trailer that dates back to the post–World War II trailer camper boom. According to Tincantourists.com, Don Boles, the Boles Aero founder, was instrumental in founding the consumer rally and show that by the mid-1960s was the largest RV-related event in the world.

Boles Aero contributed many design features still used today, such as flush vent covers, recessed fillers, and flush door handles for a smooth, aerodynamic profile. Not only that, Don Boles spearheaded setting industry standards for safety and quality that were enforced by various associations. It's estimated that nearly 18,000 trailers of various types and configurations were produced by the Boles factory in Burbank, California.

Adding trailer lights to a vintage camper can be difficult because the light kits are designed to magnetically attach to bumpers. Many early campers, such as this Boles Aero, did not have bumpers. To get this trailer 800 miles home, the trailer lights were taped to the camper's original light buckets.

INTRODUCTION

A quilted stainless-steel backsplash, solid black-walnut countertops, and painted walls give this 1950s Boles Aero a classic yet distinctive look. It also hides many contemporary upgrades, including an LED TV in the galley cabinet (it pops up through the countertop when needed). (Photo Courtesy Joe Roberts, Abaci Photos)

The original restored heater adds to the Boles Aero's history and interior space. A quilted heat shield ties this space into the galley, while the shoe storage by the door is a custom feature. The walnut ceiling and Marmoleum floor go the length of the trailer. In back is a full-size shower and queen-size bed. (Photo Courtesy Joe Roberts, Abaci Photos)

A TV is hidden in the galley countertop, and a modern water heater, range, and fridge ensure that these conveniences operate flawlessly. For the sound system, modern speakers are hidden behind original venting slats. The interior finish is a fresh change from the normal varnished birch common in most vintage campers. Painted walls and cabinets set off the walnut ceiling. Original, refinished cabinet hardware and fastening screws retain the vintage art deco feel.

The floor is finished with Marmoleum, and the walls are insulated with 2-pound closed-cell foam. The result is a vintage camper unlike any other and a great retreat after a long day.

Airstream Sovereign

The other camper that is featured in this book is a 1970s Airstream Sovereign. This restoration arrived as a blank canvas, with an owner ready to try something different. With the goal of off-grid capabilities and fully featured interior accoutrements, I set out to build something special.

As with most of my restorations, 2-pound closed-cell spray foam insulates this camper from the elements. After the exterior was patched and sealed, insulation was sprayed on the walls, ceiling, and belly pan to provide 360 degrees of thermal efficiency and sound deadening. The coach is warmed by an Aquahot system that also heats water for the sinks and shower.

When cabin heat is needed, the hot water is circulated throughout the cabin and fed through heat exchangers until the thermostat tells the system to stop circulating. The result is quiet and safe heat. The system can run on liquid propane or 120-volt

If your wish is for a fully custom interior, you can often find someone else's abandoned project for cheap. This Airstream arrived fully gutted and ready for a custom interior design.

STREAMLINE ALUMINUM TRAILERS: RESTORATION AND MODIFICATION

INTRODUCTION

Even though someone had already installed a new subfloor, it was removed to ensure that there was no rot and to add insulation and new tanks. The endcap, window surrounds, and interior skin still need to be removed.

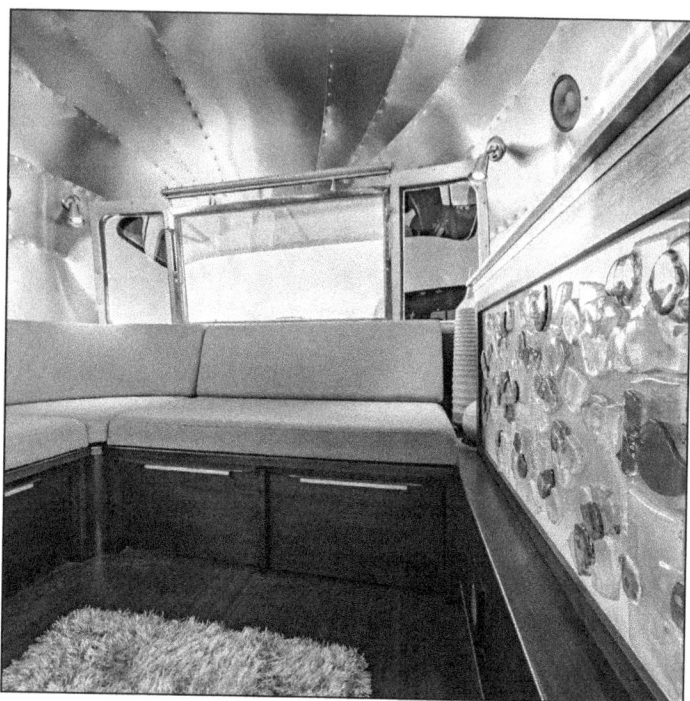

Behind the art glass, a 43-inch TV is hidden and raises and lowers via a remote control. This is a clever way to hide an often-taboo item like a TV in a recreational vehicle. Vents at the front of the TV cabinet provide heat from the Aquahot system. (Photo Courtesy Joe Roberts, Abaci Photos)

A wood-burning stove in this Airstream provides heat and ambiance, a unique feature that you do not find on a production camper. Both the galley and bathroom are split into two sections. There are no overhead cabinets, which lends to the feel of an open space. (Photo Courtesy Joe Roberts, Abaci Photos)

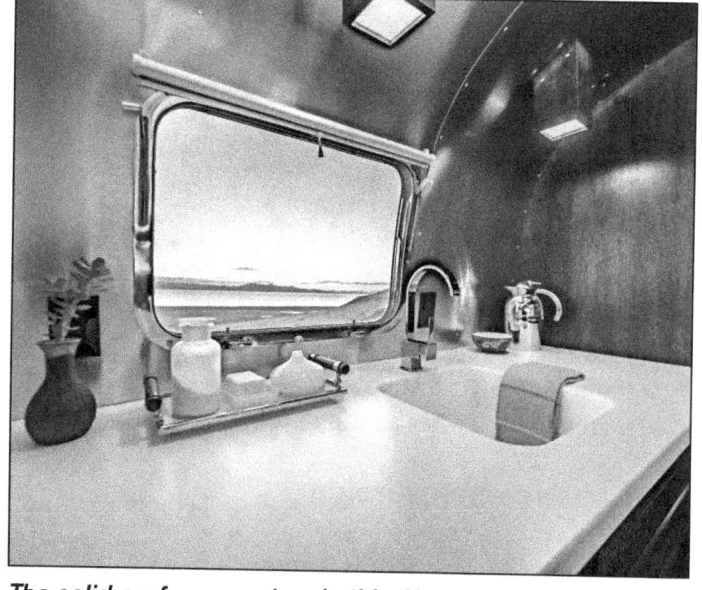

The solid-surface counters in this Airstream are easy to clean and work well with their simplicity. The range is opposite of the sink to increase counter space. Instead of factory plastic knobs on the window levers, custom aluminum handles complement the marine window shades. Another custom feature is the walnut droplights above the countertops. (Photo Courtesy Joe Roberts, Abaci Photos)

electricity. To power the large Airstream off-grid, six 6-volt glass-mat batteries are charged by solar panels and an external generator.

The interior features custom walnut cabinetry, Marmoleum flooring, and new aluminum skin. The front endcap features back-mounted woofers for the sound system, while the tweeters are mounted above the front windows. For entertainment, a 43-inch TV is hidden inside the cabinet by the door. Art glass in the TV cabinet ties into the glass found at the end of the galley, which covers the audio system's amplifier.

Art glass is also used for the shower and bathroom doors. This glass was crafted by a local artist for this project and is intended to represent Aspen trees. The green glass leaves also coordinate with the custom lounge upholstery.

The split galley (sink on one side, range on the other) houses two high-efficiency Engle refrigerators/freezers. Two are used to maximize space. Having two fridges is a common practice on land yachts, where efficiency and space is a priority.

On the sink side, a clothing washer and dryer are housed in the cabinet. This unit is for shore power or generator use only, like the low-profile Dometic A/C unit mounted on top of the Airstream.

The countertops are a solid surface and were produced by a local manufacturer.

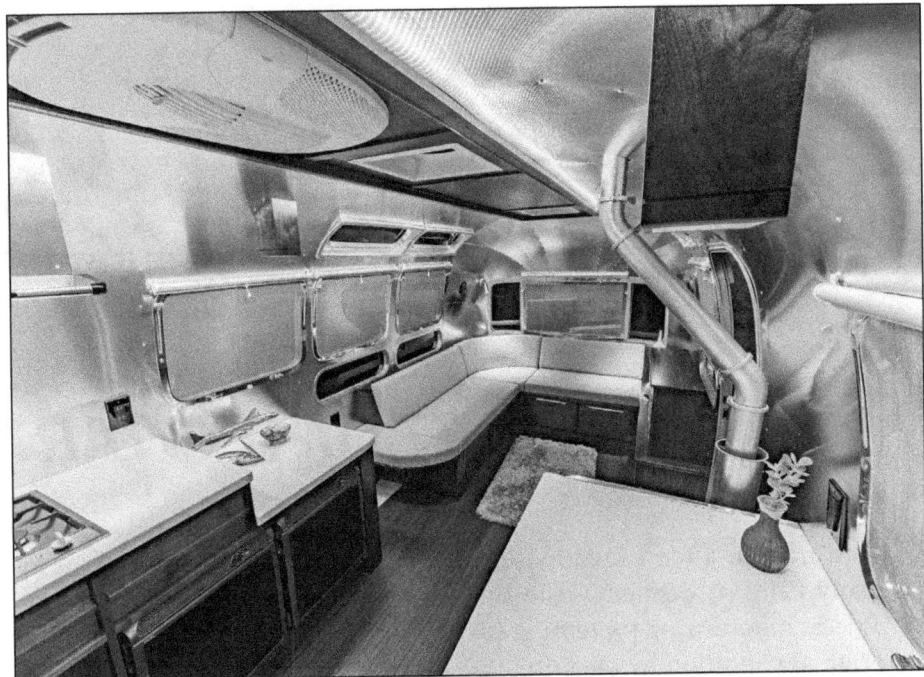

Dual 12-volt fridges help to maximize space, while the drop-down counter and lounge area can do double-duty as a computer workstation. Across from the fridges, a washer/dryer all-in-one unit is hidden in the cabinet. (Photo Courtesy Joe Roberts, Abaci Photos)

The exterior was left as is to ease maintenance, rather than stripping the clear coat and polishing. On top of the coupler is the Aquahot water heating system and a propane tank. (Photo Courtesy Joe Roberts, Abaci Photos)

CHAPTER 1

GETTING STARTED

Restoration, a term used loosely in many fields, is defined as the act or process of returning something to its original condition by repairing it, cleaning it, etc. For vintage campers, returning one to a concours level or to museum quality might not fit your intent or purpose. But some of these campers are treasured pieces of Americana and should be treated as such. That said, retaining the essence of your vintage camper is just as important as making it more habitable than its current, unrestored state.

In one circumstance, you might plan on a museum-piece restoration, where respecting originality and preserving as much as possible is paramount. In that case, cloth-covered wiring and retaining factory split rims are some of the details that are crucial to the camper's originality. Unfortunately, they're both often lost, understandably, in favor of safer, more modern alternatives.

In another circumstance, you might plan to bring the unit up to a usable state by replacing the axles and wheels with modern alternatives. Given the choices available, I like to divide restorations into three categories: the Usable Weekender, the Park Model (an off-grid cottage/rental/mother-In-law version), and the Show Camper (a museum/concours renovation).

The Usable Weekender restoration includes addressing all major systems to produce a vintage camper that can be towed to any destination and provide all the comforts expected of a camper.

A Park Model restoration is essentially building a unit that's dependent on the grid (shore power, city water, and waste-water hook-ups) and not focused on stand-alone systems (12-volt/liquid propane).

A Show Camper restoration carefully retains all original components, materials, and building techniques of the era. And, in some instances, it avoids repainting or upsetting the originality of the unit, only preserving decay-prone materials.

You need to decide what priorities are essential to your goals and plan accordingly.

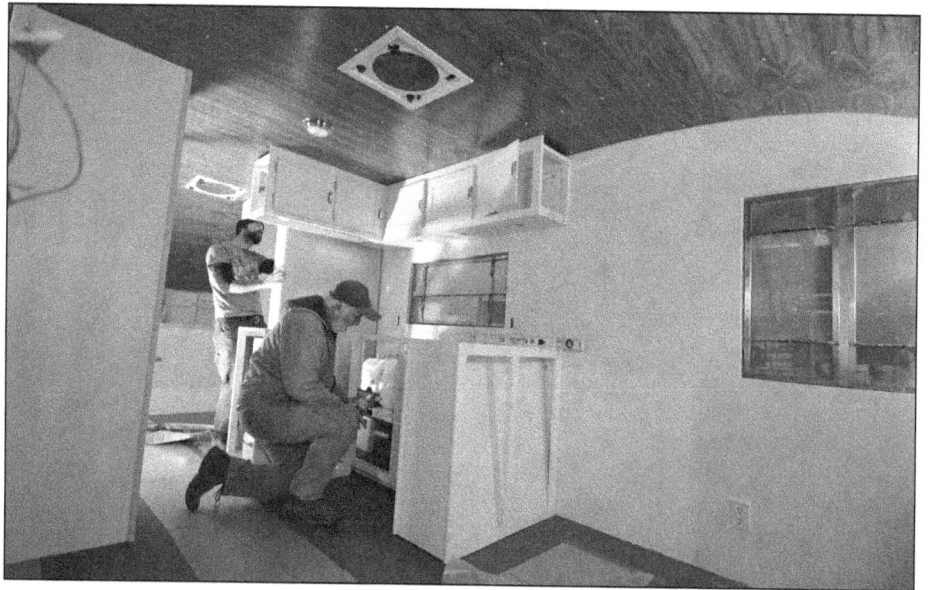
Because camper restoration involves many skills (from metal fabrication to carpentry to upholstery to paint), you need to focus on your strengths and arrange to outsource your weaknesses to skilled professionals for a quality end product.

GETTING STARTED

A Show Camper requires attention to detail and respecting the originality of a vintage camper. But this doesn't mean you can't make improvements to safety or usability without compromising the vintage essence of the camper.

Built in a similar manner to Airstream, this Boles Aero can be a less-expensive alternative due to less brand awareness. The downside is less parts availability. The challenge and reward of finding and creating working solutions makes the restoration process gratifying.

Models to Consider

While Airstream is a household name, many manufacturers from the heyday of interstate travel share general construction techniques. This book focuses on the "riveted" style of fabrication that's favored for its low weight and structural integrity. The process is loosely based on airplane manufacturing and many of the tools are interchangeable.

Silver Streak, Barth, Avion, and Boles Aero, to name a few, all use aluminum ribs riveted to aluminum sheet metal; and, because they're not branded with the Airstream name, prices can be more reasonable. At least half a dozen manufacturers share this construction method, and the techniques used in this book can be applied to many of them.

The downside to a non-Airstream riveted restoration is that these manufacturers have not received the aftermarket love that Airstream has. You may find it difficult to source some unique components for these trailers. But the challenge and reward of finding and creating working solutions is part of what makes the restoration process enjoyable.

Things to Avoid

When shopping for a project camper, there are some important things to avoid that make the restoration go smoother. For example, most aluminum campers of the 1950s and 1960s have panels with distinct patterning or curves that might be expensive to tool and re-create.

Trying to find a unit with endcaps and ornamental body panels in good shape should be a priority. Pretty much anything can be re-created by a metal fabrication specialist, but the cost to do so can easily blow a small budget. With this in mind, dented or creased panels, which are flat, are

As expected of a 60-year-old camper, there are a couple of red flags on this Flying Cloud worth noting. A dented corner panel might jump out, but it's the least concerning. The extended coupler with suspect fabrication accompanied by a non-original curbside front window proved to be difficult to properly address but not an impossible task if you are resourceful.

CHAPTER 1

This 1960s Tradewind is rough and dirty, much the same as the 1950 Flying Cloud. This is a much better candidate for a smooth restoration because it retains all the original windows, its panels are in great shape, and the chassis, including the coupler, seems to be much straighter. This unit does, however, have split rims, so an axle replacement and new tires and rims should be planned.

The interior finish of some panels in this Cruisette had army-green finishes, indicating that it was from the stock of surplus aluminum sourced by Wally Byam after World War II. When planning on panel replacement, you need to consider the difference between vintage aluminum and new stock. Current aluminum matrixes do not perfectly match vintage aluminum when polished.

easier to repair or replace and can be used in your favor when negotiating a price.

Another thing to consider when assessing a candidate for restoration is replacing old aluminum paneling with new paneling. New aluminum isn't the same as the original because the elements used in manufacturing (and suppliers) have changed since the production of the camper. If you're going to replace a large curbside panel, the quality of the polish and finish of the new aluminum will not match that of the original pieces.

Although not a deal breaker for a Usable Weekender, the difference will be noticeable to a trained eye. In the case of post–World War II Airstreams, surplus military aluminum was used extensively and can often be identified by army-green finishes.

Missing emblems are another big hassle. The pot-metal dies are most likely long gone for most vintage campers, and finding the correct ones for your restoration will be difficult. These items define the camper, and while not impossible to reproduce or locate, it will be difficult and time-consuming. Try to find a unit with intact, or at least partially intact, branding (i.e., emblems and decals).

Appliances are another important factor. They do wear out and are often replaced with newer models or scrapped altogether. An original range and fridge or ice chest is important to the restoration process. If you can find a unit with factory-specified appliances, a show-quality or respectful restoration will go smoother. Or, it could dictate what kind of restoration path you're going to take. If you've found an already-replaced or updated fridge and stove, you might go modern and skip the vintage appliances in favor of ease of use. Also, many recreation vehicle appliances are shared across manufacturers, which makes a tasteful, period-correct restoration possible.

A vintage camper with original fixtures and hardware is much more valuable than one that has had its originality lost to a mid-life update or

Broken glass is usually a nonissue, only an inconvenience, with vintage campers. However, do make sure that all window hardware is still intact when shopping for a restoration candidate. Even more important when searching for a restoration candidate is ensuring that no-longer-available cast-aluminum hardware and stampings are still present.

GETTING STARTED

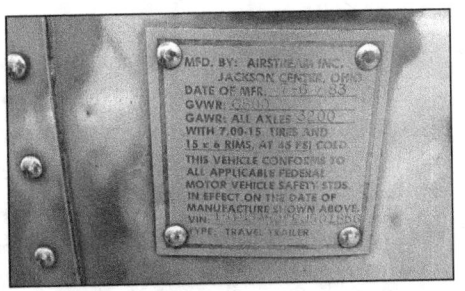

Finding the correct VIN number is essential to registering a camper. Typically, a stamped plaque is mounted near the entrance door, but these are often lost over time. If this piece is missing, you can sometimes locate the number on the A-frame by the LP tanks, but do not confuse this with a serial number stamped on the coupler, as that's related to the coupler manufacturer, not the trailer.

do-it-yourself (DIY) hack. For example, if a potential unit's original tin lights were scrapped in favor of brittle plastic replacements, you should negotiate the price with the consideration of finding period-correct replacements.

Likewise, windows are important. Currently you can service many vintage Hehr windows through vintagetrailersupply.com, but not all windows and pieces have replacement seals and hardware available. It's important that the trailer you pick has intact windows. This doesn't have to include glass, as that's often fairly easy to replace. If a window is missing altogether, however, or has been replaced with a department store alternative (such as on the Flying Cloud), finding a correct replacement may be daunting. But not entirely impossible.

If a title is not present, a bill of sale and Department of Transportation Vehicle Identification Number inspection is necessary. It's best to check with your state's DMV regulations on titling a unit before you purchase a non-titled camper. Addressing this early prevents major roadblocks and headaches down the road. Also, get the camper registered in your name before any of the restoration process begins. It's easier to register/title an unrestored unit than a unit you've already heavily modified.

Things that Shouldn't Deter You

It's a given, unless you've stumbled upon a sheltered time capsule, that a potential restoration has already been through many quick fixes and DIY dress-ups by previous owners. Basic camper restoration is undoing those layers of paint, questionable carpentry, mysterious metal fabrication, and liberal applications of caulk and silicone. A true renovation includes ensuring roadworthiness. It's up to your discretion to guarantee that the chassis is structurally sound, axles are safe, and the body is habitable.

That said, to do it right, taking a camper down to the essentials is often required, regardless of the style of restoration you're considering. For that reason, sometimes a basket-case example, rather than searching long and hard for a garage queen, is a good choice for a project; you can only make it better. You'll be undoing decades of quick fixes, so starting with a neglected unit shouldn't deter you from a potential restoration project.

You want to avoid projects whose price has been inflated by work you're going to undo. Many vintage campers are advertised as restored or partially restored. Although this might be tempting, the owner could be hiding damage, rather than addressing it; so it might not be worth the higher price. Imagine finding a floor fix that is layering wood over a rotted subfloor or new interior walls hiding old wiring and rodent-infested insulation. If you're going to restore

Sometimes, a basket case is a good choice for a project. You can only make it better. This 1960s Tradewind's interior is gross, to say the least. But with a little (well, actually lots) elbow grease and determination, it'll be an inviting and rewarding space.

a camper, you might as well ensure that it's done to your standards and avoid paying for something that's already been "restored."

Another option is a partial or abandoned restoration. However, this means putting pieces back together that someone else disassembled. It's easier to take something apart and put it back together yourself, rather than guessing.

When searching for a project, things such as a rotted subfloor and water damage are to be expected and are addressed during the restoration. And, as mentioned earlier, broken glass usually isn't an issue. The important items are a clean title, essential appliances, and original hardware.

Where to Find a Project

Locating a project camper can be a difficult task, even with the benefit of the Internet. The reality of geography and distance can quickly extinguish the hope of a perfect candidate. If you're looking nationally, the best examples are found in dry climates. First, the temperate conditions prevent deterioration, and second, drier climates have a higher camper density because of the demographic of retirees who were former vacationers settling there.

Many gems can be found in coastal and humid regions, too, but these conditions promote mold and mildew growth. This causes irreversible damage to wood and brings rust to ferrous metals. Plan to deal with these irritants when shopping in a rust-prone climate.

Trailers in cold regions experience a freeze-thaw cycle that promotes water intrusion, which, not ironically, causes the same rust and rot issues mentioned above.

National classifieds that specialize in vintage campers are a good source, but prices will be at the top of the market.

Another worthy option is to use your favorite search engine to find brand-specific classifieds. To broaden your search, you can put your manufacturers of choice into an online classified aggregator and hope for the best. Also, there are many forums for specific manufacturers, which may provide leads on available trailers within the group.

Despite the expanse of the Internet, you have plenty of other avenues to scan on your camper hunt. For example, local classifieds and bulletin boards are a good source, but finding a specific model may not be possible.

Another tip is to be aware of your immediate surroundings. Just as with the phenomenon of seeing your new car model more often after you've gained ownership or interest, you should focus on looking for campers when traveling around; you might just stumble on the perfect restoration candidate at the perfect price.

Another good source of information is couriers or postal workers. Make friends with them and ask them to let you know if they come across any old campers in their travels.

Finally, an important tip, which should be common knowledge by now when using the Internet, is to be aware that vintage campers are often targets by scam artists. Do not send money unless you are certain of the recipient and you practice basic fraud avoidance.

Transportation

Once you've located a trailer, transporting it can become a major hurdle. In most cases vintage trailers, especially those in need of restoration, are not roadworthy. It may take more than one trip to extract an old camper from its place of hibernation.

First, jack up a side to inspect the wheel, tire, hub, and brakes. If the tires are dry-rotted and need to be replaced, it could require not only changing the tire but replacing the rim as well. Old split-rims are not necessarily serviceable anymore, which many vintage campers ride on (but if you try hard enough, you might find a shop or individual that'll mount them). When reinstalling the wheels, follow the proper "star" procedure for torqueing them down. Also, stop after the first hundred or so miles and re-check the lug-nut torque. Wheel

The Internet will be your main avenue in searching for a potential camper project. When negotiating a deal, keep in mind that vintage campers are often easy targets for scam artists. Use due diligence to avoid a financial loss.

GETTING STARTED

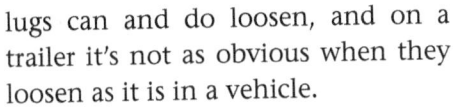

Split rims are common on vintage campers and not the best choice for safe highway travel. In many cases, you need to replace the wheel and tire combo, and often, the whole axle assembly. You can see the split part on this 1960s Boles Aero.

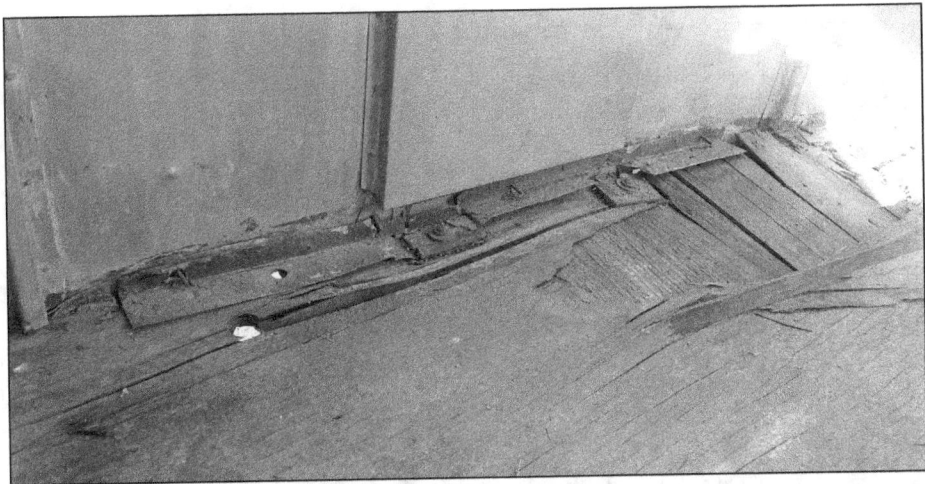

This Airstream's mounting points have actually broken free, and the body is sagging away from the chassis. This is very unsafe for transit and could lead to a catastrophic event on the road.

lugs can and do loosen, and on a trailer it's not as obvious when they loosen as it is in a vehicle.

Chances are that the running lights are no longer working (though, I've seen my share of original lights surprisingly still functioning). A quick fix is a magnetic trailer light kit; just make sure there's a ferrous bumper for attachment, as the aluminum skin won't work.

Tape, cable ties, and bailing wire are your friends when rigging up a temporary lighting solution; sometimes it's easier to route the wiring through the camper via broken windows and screens. In some cases, the body may be separating from the chassis. Be thorough with your safety inspection. If the shell or body parts are detaching, use scrap materials, grabber screws, or straps to securely attach dangerously loose components.

Similarly, make sure all windows are fastened shut. If not, wire or screw them shut. As with windows, inspect the vent covers, luggage doors, and access doors. If any of them are unfastened and capable of blowing off, remove or secure them.

In many cases the subfloor, to which the body attaches, is rotted to the point that it's unsafe for road use. Be sure to inspect the integrity of the unit you're towing to prevent any misfortune when in transit. On this Cruisette, you can see that the subfloor is rotted to the point that it's collapsed and really nonexistent. Also, you can see light coming from the outside. These are both signs that this trailer's roadworthiness is compromised.

Towing or Recovery Checklist

The following items should be on your list to check carefully.

- Grabber screws, straps, and plywood strips or scrap wood
- Airtank and compressor
- Trailer safety chains
- Trailer light kit, extra wire, connectors
- Sturdy jack and jack stands
- Breaker bar and lug wrench

CHAPTER 1

Having a climate-controlled, organized, and roomy workspace is ideal for camper restoration. There are many components to a travel trailer and, as you dismantle and acquire components, space is quickly used up.

Before departing, make sure your insurance is up-to-date and covers the items in tow.

DIY or Outsourcing

Before tackling the restoration, it will be helpful to sit down and figure out your strengths. Focusing on your strengths and outsourcing your weaknesses will help streamline the build. Here are some of the skills needed for a successful trailer restoration: painting, polishing, aluminum fabrication, steel fabrication, fiberglass work, woodworking, 110- and 12-volt electrical wiring, and plumbing.

Next, take into account what equipment you have access to, the space you will be using, the time frame for the whole project, and how much money you intend to spend on each section (i.e., chassis, body, paint, interior, floor, belly pan, electrical, etc.).

Equally important, you need to realize that a travel trailer restoration combines aspects from the automotive and housing industries, and, in the case of Airstream-style campers, aviation construction as well. For example, you may have a strong carpentry sense but lack metal fabrication skills such as welding, or lack 12-volt electrical experience but are competent in 110-volt household wiring.

You can hire a metal shop to straighten and reinforce an old chassis, including replacing axles or adding under-floor mounts for water tanks, for example. The shop can also treat the chassis with a rust-preventative coating. These things can be performed while you're focusing on other aspects, such as restoring cabinets and hardware, if that's your skillset.

Because these trailers use a riveted body, you might want to outsource panel replacement and bodywork to someone who is proficient in aluminum fabrication, often found in the airplane world.

Throughout the build, there will be plenty of large purchases. Budgeting for these will help keep the restoration on schedule and within your goal.

Once you've acquired a camper to restore, it helps to make a list of its needs, based on the discussions in various chapters in this book: chassis, floor, body, house electrical, insulation, interior skin, cabinets, appliance and hardware, propane, plumbing, windows, and polish.

You can also list what you plan to spend on each section (in both time and money). For reference,

Like cars, boats, and planes, campers are built in facilities specially designed to efficiently assemble the unit. Working in a pole barn, garage, or driveway limits your resources. Fortunately, there are clever work-arounds to make the restoration process possible. Intermountain Airstream is a factory-authorized retailer and service shop in Salt Lake City, Utah.

GETTING STARTED

this little Cruisette required nearly 400 shop hours from commission to completion.

Tools and Equipment

When manufactured, Airstreams, Spartans, Boles Aeros, etc., were constructed in a factory specially designed for camper production and assembly. Unfortunately, you probably will not have access to all the resources that a factory possesses. A handy person, however, is capable of

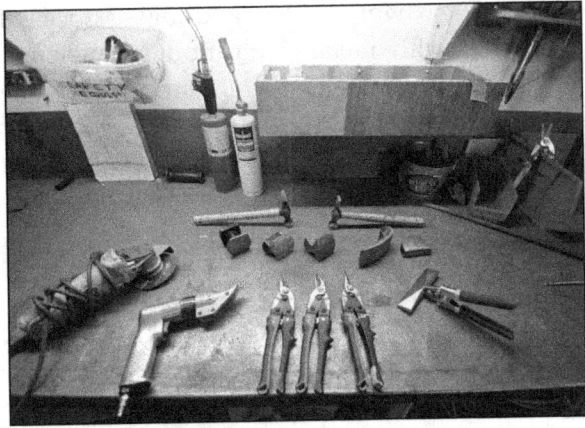

At the top you see a couple of hammers and assorted dollies used to shape sheet metal. The blue tape helps prevent marring surfaces. At the bottom (left to right) are a grinder with cut-off wheel and pneumatic shears, aviation hand shears (the handle colors coordinate with the blade: red cuts right, green left, and yellow straight), and a hand seamer. These are just a few of the metal-working tools necessary to perform restoration on a vintage aluminum camper.

Making a Brake

The bend I needed was too deep for my shop's brake with a 1½-foot throat; it required either setting up a job order from a local sheet-metal business or fabricating my own tool. I chose the latter due to the relative softness and malleability of the .032 5052 aluminum and resources on hand. If this bend had been attempted with typical .040 2024 T3 Airstream upper-body panels, there'd be little success due to the needed leverage and lack of edge-holding capabilities of this setup.

Using poplar board stock as a flat, a reinforced surface on the table, and a piece of angle iron as the clamping bar, I was able to make the 90-degree bend needed. The clamping action of both the front plate (again, more poplar stock) and clamping bar is achieved with various C-clamps.

The idea is to hold the material firmly during the bend process to avoid movement and a mis-bend or poor edge. The angle iron is set up so the bend can go beyond 90 degrees, allowing the material to spring back and settle into a perfect bend. If the angle iron was set on its flat edge, you couldn't bend beyond 90, and the piece would bow out at the bend.

A drawback to setting the angle iron on its two edges is the potential to mar the surface due to the outside edge's pressure (an actual metal break has a flat clamping surface). You could set the angle iron flat with the angled portion to the rear of the brake to create a flat edge and reduce the chance of defacing the material.

This brings up a good point: The process of restoring things is a learning experience that involves experimenting to learn what works best. ■

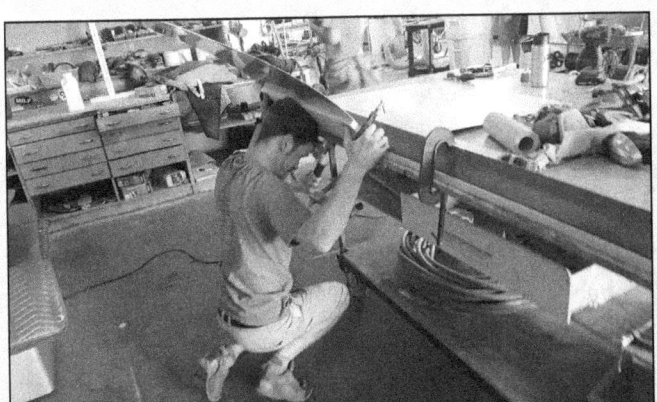

Using your head, you can work around problems such as making a deep bend on sheet metal. This requires a quickly made, yet fully functioning sheet metal brake.

With items around the shop (lumber stock, C-clamps, and angle iron), You can make a bend that would require tooling much bigger than you have available.

many things in his or her own driveway, including separating a riveted shell from its chassis.

Some important tools used for this restoration cover metal, wood, and finishing. For metal, quality hand shears, a bi-metal hacksaw, and assorted files are essential. As for powered tools, sheers (either pneumatic or electric) make quick work of cutting large sheets of aluminum; a metal chop saw is needed to cut steel frame members; and a grinder with assorted wheels (cut-off, wire, and grinding) gets a workout cleaning rust and prepping for welding.

A metal brake (used for bending sheet metal) and a pneumatic shear might be out of the budget but can be worked around by either outsourcing the job or using some creative engineering with clamps, steel straightedges, and routers (a rotating cutting tool). Also important to metal working is a variety of hammers: ball-peen, claw, and auto-body hammers and dollies. The more, the merrier.

Ideally, woodworking tools and metal tools do not replace one another. A hammer used on metal should not be used on wood, as the shavings, dust, and oils associated with metal fabrication permanently contaminate porous lumber. The same goes for saws, sanders, etc.; it's best to keep metal-working tools separate from woodworking tools. However, in some instances, it may be uneconomical to purchase two of everything. If needed, you may cross tool genres; just be mindful that the chance for frustration due to object contamination and/or tool damage exists.

In the world of woodworking, an important tool to consider is a sander. Well, let me rephrase that: sanders, plural. Not only do you get a workout using handmade sanding blocks, you will also use a random orbital sander, a belt sander, and a drum sander during this restoration. The random orbital is used heavily in prepping wood surfaces for finish; belt and drum sanders come in handy when shaping the curves that define vintage campers.

A good router is useful in many instances, including trimming laminates and tracing damaged paneling. Also using that same router mounted on a table is handy for many cabinetry and interior trim projects.

As for saws, of course, a table saw, a miter saw, and a bandsaw are the backbone of any wood shop. Equally important are a couple of good handsaws, including a flush-cut pull and a fine-finish.

General shop equipment to consider is good work lights, droplights, and flashlights. Keep in mind that you'll be working over the course of a year or more, and lighting requirements change with the seasons. Being able to effectively light your jobsite and task at hand is essential to precision and tight tolerances; it also directly affects the amount of fatigue and amount of time that goes into a camper restoration.

Finally, a well-stocked cleaning station with a quality vacuum, broom, dustpan, scrub brushes, degreasers, and detergents ensure a clean workspace. These items also help guarantee a quality finish, whether it's paint, stain, or varnish.

Fasteners

During a camper restoration, you use a variety of fasteners, from carriage bolts to grabber screws to rivets. During assembly, camper factories used particular fasteners for specific jobs. If your goal is a period-correct restoration, reusing or replacing these fasteners with the correct size and style is important for authenticity.

In 1940, about 85 percent of U.S. screw manufacturers licensed the design of the Phillips-head screw. However, during the post-war travel trailer boom, many factories still relied heavily on the slotted-screw design. The 1952 Airstream Crusette featured in this restoration used button-head slotted screws extensively, both metal and wood.

There are a few key differences between wood and metal screws. Wood screws have widely spaced,

Standard woodworking tools such as a handsaw, pull-saw, hammer, and chisel are essential to the building process. Likewise, power tools such as a jigsaw, circular saw, router, belt sander, and orbital sander, along with a pneumatic nailer, are vital to any carpentry work. Also visible here are standard wood shop equipment such as a table saw, bandsaw, drill press, joiner, and dust collector.

GETTING STARTED

medium-depth threads, whereas sheet-metal screws have sharper threads that are deeper and closer together. Although you can use a sheet-metal screw in wood (nonstructural instances, such as a light-switch plate or light mount), using a wood screw in sheet metal does not produce a secure or flush fit.

Another important screw used in vintage campers is the oval-head style. These come in both Phillips and slotted heads and were commonly used on trim and hardware; the soft dome curve gives interiors a welcoming, less industrial feel and does not snag fabric or potentially cut skin.

During disassembly, noting the sizes and styles of the screws used is paramount when it comes time to reassemble, if you wish to retain the vintage feel and construction techniques of your restoration. Even if your goal is a custom camper, paying attention to screw style and proper usage is important to building something that's special and professional.

Vintage campers used specific rivets for various reasons, such as fasteners with a helical ridge. While blind rivets were available at the time, the required additional steps to assemble and associated higher cost made them less common than buck rivets or solid rivets. This, however, changed when pneumatic blind riveters and preassembled blind rivets became the preferred fastening system in the 1970s.

Many components such as exterior and interior walls and endcaps on vintage campers were assembled using solid rivets, which require access to both sides of the piece. This often necessitates that two people perform the task. Considering the labor of two workers, it starts to make sense why riveted campers cost more than a comparable "canned ham."

At the left is an air hammer and bucking bar used to set solid rivets (the small pieces seen to the right of the bucking bar). In the center, a fan tool helps mark evenly spaced holes quickly. Above that are hand and pneumatic pop-rivet tools. Under the fan tool are some 1/8- (copper) and 5/32-inch (black) Cleco tools. Next to them are assorted pop rivets and a shaving tool for shaping Olympic rivets. On the far right is a hand setter for solid rivets.

One of the most common fasteners used in vintage campers are screws and, as expected, there are many varieties. In a Show Camper, using the correct screw for the job is the difference between an award winner and a dud. Phillips-head wood screws, wood screws, pan-head sheet-metal screws, self-tapping hex screws and oval-head screws are seen here.

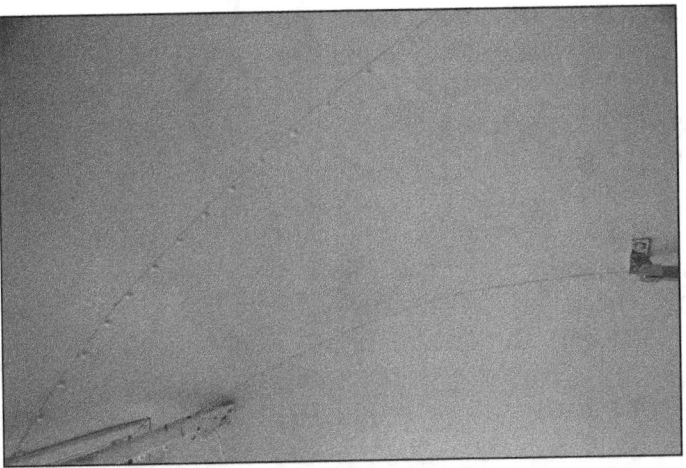

Here, you can see solid rivets on the endcap and pop rivets on the lower panel. This 1960s Airstream was built at a time when pop rivets were gaining popularity and buck rivets were on their way out (for interior skin). The endcaps were produced separately outside the camper then mounted inside, whereas pop rivets were used to apply the skin. When performing a proper restoration, retaining this detail is crucial.

CHAPTER 1

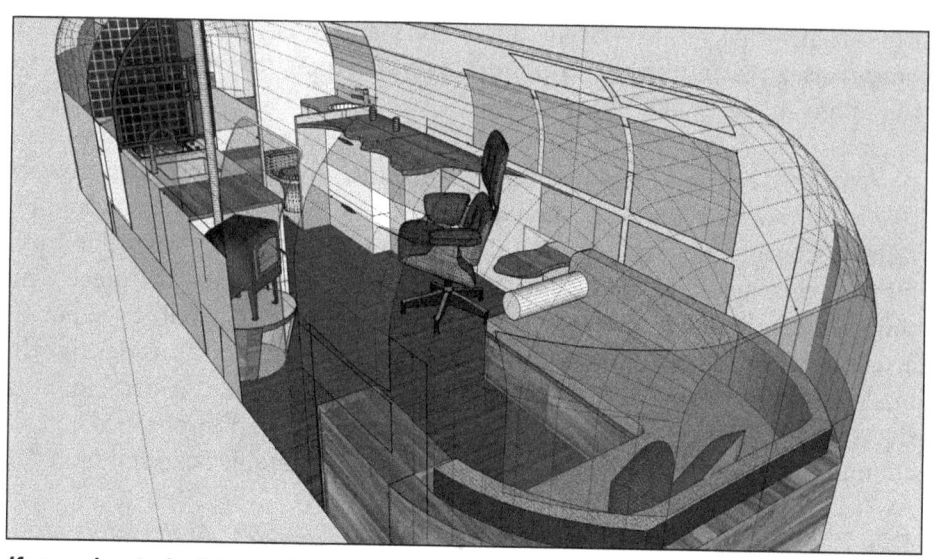

If you plan to build a custom interior, you need to carefully consider where to place heavy components such as water tanks, battery banks, and the galley to prevent listing, improper tongue weight, and trailer sway when in tow.

When disassembling a riveted camper, be sure to note where the rivets (and which style) are used and where sheet-metal screws are used (often where a bucking bar cannot be reached) because reassembly uses these same fasteners.

In some cases, you might not be able to use a solid rivet, but a blind rivet among a line of polished buck rivets sticks out like a polished spartan in a sea of canned hams. An Olympic rivet (a modified Oscar rivet) is a great alternative. Olympic rivets have a special mandrel designed to break and leave a nub that you can shave. The end result is a solid-looking head. Of course, these require a fairly expensive shaving tool. If you're only installing a few, a steady hand and dremel can be used to shave and polish the head, but the results may be less than ideal.

Design Modifications

It's likely that you may want to change a few things in your camper layout. You may be tackling a restoration that's been previously modified, or you purchased a gutted shell and there's nothing to use as a pattern. Before you start designing a new layout for your camper, keep in mind it's not as easy as modifying a floor plan for a house.

A camper is a dynamic thing, as opposed to a house that is static. Weight distribution is very important for sway control and safety when towing. An improperly weighted trailer is very dangerous and can lead to catastrophic failure.

Ideally, the trailer should have a hitch weight of about 10 to 15 percent of the trailer's weight. If you place the water tank in back, where the gray and black tanks also reside, you could easily throw off the trailer balance. If the galley is located on the curbside and you place the water tank and batteries there, too, your trailer is going to list to the curbside. Also take into consideration the weight of cabinets, water tanks, and batteries when adjusting the layout of your camper to ensure safety when in tow.

Also, in some instances, cabinetry can add structural support to the roof. If you plan to remove a cabinet for a more spacious feel, you could be compromising the load bearing of the camper's roof, which is less than ideal for traveling interstates, and even worse if you live in the snowbelt. The main components of a camper interior are the galley, beds, dinette, and bath.

Planning Your Work Space

You may have shop space, but you still need storage space. A camper restoration is like a Matryoshka, a Russian nesting doll. Once you start disassembly, the number of parts adds up quickly. The best plan of attack is to have shelving ready for components. The exterior disassembly includes large aluminum panels, windows, HVAC pieces, and the door.

Interior components include appliances such as the stove, ice chest or fridge, and sink. Also a large heater and upholstery will be pulled from the camper. Even the chassis components, such as the coupler, jacks, brakes, and wheels, take up space during the restoration. They all need to be considered when planning your restoration.

Also take into consideration the space needed for inventory when it's time to start building. You need to store sheets of plywood, metal, and countertop linoleum. And you need space for other assorted materials, such as flooring.

A good tip is to keep sawhorses handy that allow you to set up additional table space when you need to work on larger pieces. They can be set up easily and taken down quickly to keep the shop organized and efficient.

CHAPTER 2

DISASSEMBLY

The least pleasant part of camper restoration is the teardown, but it's one of the most important to document thoroughly. If you haven't used a camera recently, it's a good idea to brush up on some basics. You can find many online tutorials or community education courses to help ensure you're detailing the restoration process with quality images. You will need to reference them many times throughout the rebuild. In addition, photos can be an important asset for potential resale.

Another important tip, which should come naturally for most, is to wear proper protective gear. You'll be breaking apart components and exposing many harmful particulates that have most likely, due to toxicity, been banned since the original assembly of the camper. This includes adhesives, paints, and insulation. Be sure to use a respirator, gloves, safety glasses, and full-coverage clothing.

Safety First!

When removing old insulation and rotted members from a camper, airborne particulates travel. Be sure others nearby are not exposed to these dangers. When sanding and polishing, be sure that the dust does not scatter widely. Using drop cloths, tarps, and plastic to cover and contain debris is helpful in easing cleanup and preventing contamination.

After a full day of working on the camper, it's best to immediately remove your dirty clothing and take a shower. Dust and debris remain on clothing and can transfer to your living quarters, where it affects not only your health, but that of your co-habitants.

Animal Contamination

Scat can be, well, scratch that, *will be* present during the teardown, which is also toxic. More noteworthy, rodent smells attract other rodents.

Starting with the dinette, I worked my way clockwise around the Cruisette during demo. Here, you can see tiles that were hidden under a carpet. More noteworthy, however, is the damaged and rotted subfloor. The upper shell attaches directly to this component, and the fact that you can see light shining through is very disconcerting. Typically, rot resides by camper doors, windows, and vents.

A 1960s Airstream Bubble's belly pan served as a happy home to many animals, based on the large quantity of feces and carcasses amassed. The sedentary state of abandoned campers is a welcoming environment for them.

The walls of this 1980s Overlander served as a nest. The inside walls of old campers should be thoroughly examined for infestation. It's best to remove any animal traces right away or they will continue to attract more visitors.

If you're working in the driveway or house, it's not a bad idea to strip anything that's been marked by rodents and dispose of it quickly to prevent attracting more of their friends.

Tanks, Stove and Fridge

A good plan of attack for disassembly is to start from the inside. This allows you to work in an enclosed unit, which is nice if you're starting in inclement weather. Before the first interior screw is removed, however, ensure that there is no battery hooked up and the propane tanks are removed.

If your camper has a black water tank, it's a good idea to ensure that it is empty before beginning any work. If necessary, pull the unit to a dumping station or use a portable waste

Although the Cruisette did not have a black-water tank, this early-1950s Boles Aero Ensenada did. Before removing the tank and toilet, I pulled the camper to a dumping station and gave both the gray and black holding tanks a good flush. If you're unfamiliar with this process, plenty of tutorials are available online. Also, note the internal aluminum rib construction of this non-Airstream example.

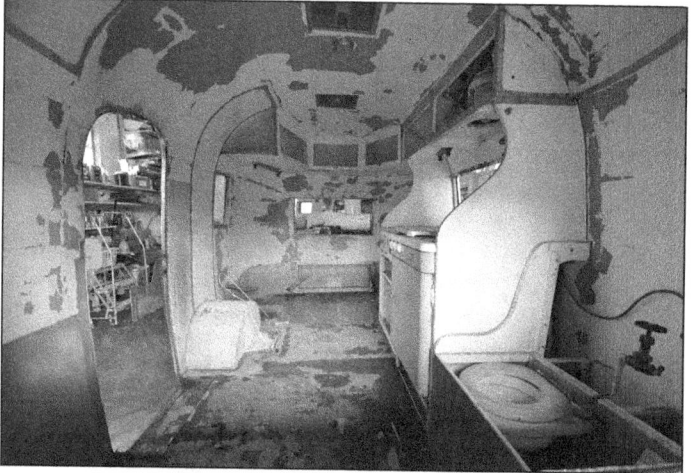

The stove/fridge/sink all-in-one unit in this galley was too big to remove through the door, so it was the last component to go when I separated the shell from the chassis. Surprisingly, this tiny Airstream had a toilet that, equally unexpected, did not drain into a black-water tank, indicating a welcome change of camping standards since the turn of the century.

DISASSEMBLY

This simple vintage Wedgewood range uses screws to mount to the galley. This one has been removed and reinstalled before, as evidenced by the modern wood-grabber screw used to fasten it. On ranges with an oven, screws are used inside the oven. These often require lifting out the grates and heat shroud to access.

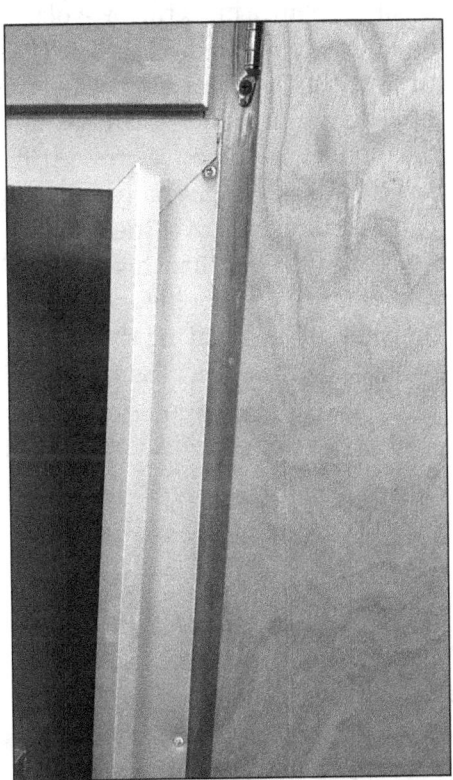

Sometimes it's easy to find the mounting points, such as this ice chest's screws that are exposed on the front. Sometimes, however, the mounting screws are hidden inside vintage fridges, or on the backside, accessible through exterior maintenance hatches and vents.

transporter to flush it out. After dealing with lead paint, insulation, and rodent scat, the last thing you want to address is human waste.

Keep in mind that the order of disassembly is the reverse order of assembly, so it's a good idea to note how things come apart. You may find that some appliances are too large to fit through the door. It's common that a large refrigerator or shower/bath could have been installed then built around. With that said, start by removing propane components such as the stove, heater, gas lamp, and water heater. If you plan to restore these, be careful not to add any damage during removal.

Stoves are usually installed in the galley with screws hidden inside. First, you need to lift the top off and disconnect the liquid propane line under the range. Ice chests and fridges are secured in a similar manner; you need to locate the mounting screws retaining these appliances to remove them.

Galley, Bed and Cabinets

Once the equipment and associated plumbing/wiring are removed, you can focus on cabinets and large components such as the galley and dinette. On the Cruisette and other early Airstreams, these were secured using large sheet-metal screws. It's important to loosen these slowly, and work your way along a line of perpendicular or parallel screws. If you release one screw all the way and leave others torqued, you could create tension and deform the camper's interior sheet-metal walls, creating more work later.

Sometime in the 1960s, aluminum extrusions were riveted to the interior skin with cabinetry walls

Like any product of industry, travel trailers constantly evolved. Early 1950s Airstreams used large sheet-metal screws to fasten cabinetry, which were later replaced with more complex aluminum extrusions and blind rivets as technology progressed, shown here inside a 1960s Tradewind closet. Also notice the (probably original) patch with slotted pan-head sheet-metal screws and the Zolatone finish.

screwed to them, which became the main fastening system. When disassembling, take note of the camper's original fastening system, as you'll be reproducing this during reassembly.

When disassembling, things can strip out and be stubborn. Before frustration sets in, avoid damage when prying, drilling, and hammering by using masking tape, sacrificial plywood, and/or cardboard to protect both metal and wood surfaces from gouges and scratches. Sometimes, screws can be hidden and difficult to access. Remember that someone put this camper together, and it does come apart. Once you've removed the galley, dinette, bed, etc., you have the start of a bare shell.

Interior Skin

Now is a good time to focus on wall preparation. As mentioned earlier, Cruisettes were known for not having interior endcaps to keep cost

CHAPTER 2

The vinyl-covered aluminum skin of 1970s and 1980s Airstreams accumulate a gross, sticky grime over decades of use. Take note here of the black mold and rotted insulation between the windows and even between the lap joints. To properly address this, discard and replace all insulation, seal interior seams, and clean and strip the panels of the grime and mold before reassembly and paint. Keep in mind that these conditions exist under most Airstream skins, and without addressing rot, mold, and grime, you're only putting a bandage over a much bigger issue.

and weight down. But like other Airstreams of this vintage, the Cruisette *does* share the Zolatone coated aluminum common of 1950s models (but it was not the more-common speckled finish). Zolatone is a two-stage paint first used on Airstreams and automobiles where durability was needed, such as the trunk.

Zolatone can be difficult to remove. It's still available today, but you need to get creative to match an original hue. You can find plenty of Internet forum talk on the process necessary to match an original finish if that's your goal. Essentially, it's going to take a certain amount of controlled chaos to achieve the splattered look. If you're unhappy with the outcome, you can always strip it and start over. Practicing on smaller sample sets helps to dial in the density and size of splatter.

Airstream did not use Zolatone for very long and ended up replacing it with a vinyl covering applied to the aluminum skin. If you're tackling a non-Airstream restoration, your camper may have aluminum or plywood/lauan interior walls. Either way, once the major interior components are removed, it's time to address the interior walls.

In some cases, it might be easier to replace panels with new aluminum then to strip and prep for paint. Before deciding what materials and products to use, visit a painting specialist for recommendations on products and techniques. Painting and prepping vinyl-coated walls (there are special vinyl paints, if the vinyl hasn't started to peel) differs greatly from prepping for a Zolatone topcoat.

In the case of the Cruisette, the owner wanted the walls stripped and repainted with a modern, low-volatile organic compound paint. With the panels in place, I began the time-consuming and hazardous task of applying automotive paint stripper to work through many layers of paint accumulated over the years.

Keep in mind that this was only a preliminary stripping and panel prep. You'll be removing the interior panels to address electrical issues and to replace the insulation, so it is not vital to perfectly strip the panels in this step.

Paint Removal

1 *The many layers of paint applied to this little Airstream were stripped with aircraft paint remover. This was a first step to prep the walls for removal. Roughing up the paint with a low-grit abrasive helps work the stripper into the paint. While a mask would have been preferred, once the stripper has dried, gassing is reduced and the open shop doors and windows provide adequate airflow.*

DISASSEMBLY

2 Letting the paint stripper penetrate for five minutes helps it lift the old paint. The many layers and durable Zolatone coating proved to be difficult to remove on this job. Laying plastic over the applied stripper helps prevent it from drying too quickly in an arid climate and allows the stripper to better do its job.

3 A plastic body filler applicator was used to scrape the peeling paint off the walls. The scrapings can be cleaned up with a dustpan or vacuum once they're dry and should be disposed of in a proper container.

Panel Removal

Once you have a good portion of the old paint removed, it's time to start removing individual panels. This vintage Airstream did not have blind rivets. While the technology existed during the camper's production, blind rivets were a relatively new technology and also required assembly, which would have slowed manufacturing. Instead, basic slotted sheet-metal screws were used. By the late 1950s and early 1960s, however, blind-rivet fastening became ubiquitous with Airstream interior assembly.

The Cruisette's wall panels terminated at the bottom, meaning the lower side panels were the last ones to go on and will be the first to come off. That might not be true for your camper, however. Some vintages and models finished skinning the campers with the topmost panel. By focusing on the lap joints, you can locate the last panel installed and remove that one first.

As with gutting the interior, you work backward from the factory assemblers. When drilling out rivets and removing screws, note what was used and where. You may find non-factory fixes throughout the disassembly, and if anything is out of the ordinary (e.g., weird fasteners, out-of-place materials, or panel damage), it should be earmarked for future attention to return to original.

You need to remove hundreds of rivets. Be careful not to let the drill bit walk and damage the panels if you plan to reuse them. To prevent the bit from walking, use a center punch and keep a stock of sharp bits and cutting fluid handy. If you need to go larger than a 1/8-inch drill bit, use a 5/32-inch, as those are easy to

Lap joints are the simplest method of assembling aluminum panels; they simply overlap one another and are fastened with rivets or screws. You can see the lapped seams of this 1960s land yacht by the door (also visible is seeping mold and dirt from water intrusion). These lap joints indicate that the lower panel was put on first and the top last. So, for disassembly (once the interior is gutted), you start removing the upper panels.

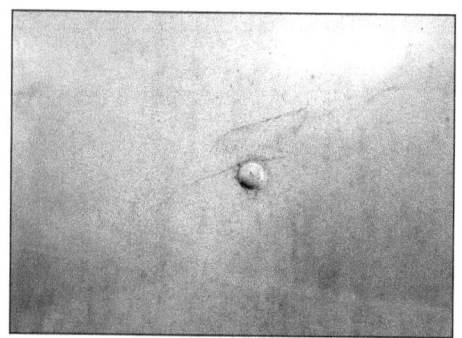 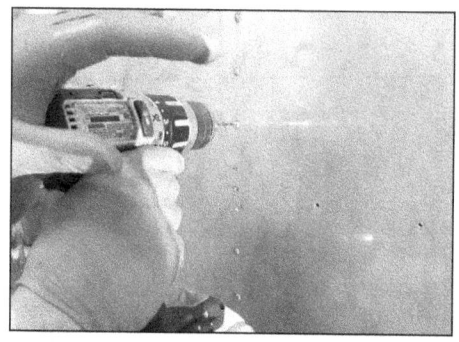 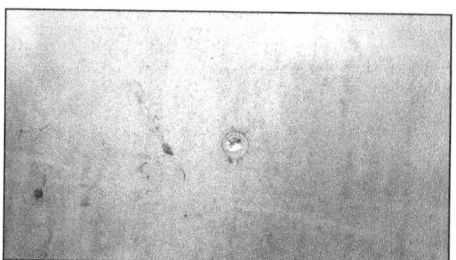

This rivet on a 1940s Spartan Manor is one of many that need to be removed to replace a damaged panel. Specific rivet removal tools are available for shaving the head. While these help prevent a drill bit from walking, they're not necessary to pop an old rivet. A center punch, appropriate bit, and a steady hand is all that's really necessary.

The rivets on this camper already have a recess in the center, so they did not need to be punched. To cleanly remove the head, you need to use a bit that's the same size as the rivet tail (usually 5/32 or 1/8 inch). If you're worried about damaging the panel being removed, masking tape can provide a protective boundary around the rivet.

Aluminum rivets are pretty soft and the drill burrows quickly into the head. Because you're using a bit that's the same size as the rivet tail, giving the drill a slight rotation helps wallow the hole, separating the head from the tail. At this point you can remove the rivet head and move on to the next hole. Before a new rivet can be installed, however, the remaining tail in the rib hole must be removed with a punch or drill bit.

find from suppliers. Cutting fluid helps lengthen the life expectancy of your bits and enhances drilling.

The Airstream endcap is a defining feature of the brand and a time-consuming, yet essential, piece. This Cruisette has a 13-panel endcap on both ends. The left and right panels are close mirrors to each other and can be easily mixed up. Masking tape or a paint marker helps to keep track of which panels go together. If your plan is to remove all the panels, which can make prep for paint or polish easier because they lay flat, you want to use a 1/8-inch bit. Be sure not to wallow out the holes too much. As rivet hole tolerances increase, you run into problems such as tenting (peaks in between rivets), a loss of roundness or proper shape, and panel wandering during reassembly.

Panel Cleaning

Once you've accumulated a pile of interior panels, the next step is to clean them. I used a degreaser, medium or stiff bristle brush, and good water pressure to remove all fiberglass insulation and many other unrecognizable substances that accumulated on the Cruisette's panels. Take your time to do a good job removing all the dirt and grime from both sides. Also, knock down any sharp edges with a file, sheers, or hammer as you encounter them.

It's easy to wash off any important markings, so be sure to keep track of (photograph) what you're doing and to go back once they've dried to remark and organize.

It can be easy to crease large panels when handling them, so make sure to have a helping hand within earshot.

Storing large pieces where they won't get damage is important. A quick option is to toss them under the shell or chassis, but they eventually get in the way. Mounting smaller panels to a chip board with screws or tacks is a good way to secure, store, and even work on them.

For wood-sided trailers, remove fasteners as necessary and save the hardware for restoration or to ease sourcing matches. A severely water-damaged panel is destined for

Washing old insulation and accumulated dust and grime from the aluminum panels is essential because you're going to be handling them to patch, re-create, and prep for final finish. I used Simple Green and a medium-bristle carwash brush with a long handle to clean the old insulation and residue from the panels.

immediate disposal, but you may want to retain pieces such as decorative curves and cabinet vents to aid making future templates. Panels that are still good can be saved for restoration. Be sure to note the order of placement and label accordingly.

Insulation

Once the interior panels are out, it's time to remove the old insulation. Depending on the manufacturer, model, and period of construction of your trailer, any number of materials can be used. From 1970s foam to 1950s fiberglass, there is a good chance that the Environmental Protection Agency (EPA) and Consumer Product Safety Commission (CPSC) do not permit these products to be sold anymore due to environmental and health hazards.

Take care when disposing of old insulation by using protective clothing, respirators, and eye protection. Once the old stuff is removed, it's time to scrub the interior walls to further remove remnants. As with an Airstream's interior panels, you want to use a spray-able, biodegradable degreaser and stiff-bristle brushes on the inside of the exterior panels to ensure insulation particulates are removed from the original aluminum.

Use water to rinse. If you live in a humid climate, a heater or fan helps dry the walls. After everything is dried, it's not a bad idea to follow up with a vacuum on the floors and walls, too, to eliminate any particulates.

Once the interior panels are removed, it's time to get rid of the fiberglass insulation, accumulated rodent nests, and mold. As with every other step in the demo/teardown process, this is another nasty step that requires proper personal protective equipment.

With the insulation gutted, you can now see some of the old surplus military aluminum (the fatigue green) that makes these early, post-war campers special. Also noteworthy is the handwriting in the upper right corner indicating that the panel was originally destined for an Airstream Bubble.

STREAMLINE ALUMINUM TRAILERS: RESTORATION AND MODIFICATION

Building a Lifting Structure

Using various long lumber stock, such as 3/4-inch plywood, 2 x 4s, and 2 x 2s or metal-bar stock, you can now work on supporting the body for removal from the chassis. Use a cross pattern where possible and support the walls where necessary. Self-tapping screws come in handy when connecting the metal ribs to the wooden (or metal) support structure.

Before separating the shell, you might want to remove the windows. Keeping the window frames installed helps the shell retain its shape and can provide a semi-weather-tight storage space. On the other hand, removing the windows allows easier restoration of the camper. For the Cruisette, I removed the windows before pulling the shell.

In some instances, you can lift at the reinforced vent holes (or fabricate a lifting point through the vent hole to a solid point) with chain falls or an electric hoist. Another option is to lift using an automotive-style post lift (if there's clearance) or a set of cable jacks like those used on truck campers. Make sure that jack points distribute the load throughout the shell structure, as aluminum folds easily with few pounds per square inch.

Next, locate the mounting hardware that attaches the shell to the chassis and floor. Typically, you'll find lag bolts and screws.

Once the shell is free, simply lift and pull the chassis out.

The plywood lattice used to support this small shell was more than sufficient, but if you're lifting a heavier model, you might want to use a thicker plywood or aluminum or steel extrusions. I also made a template of the floor print before removing the shell for the planned Marmoleum flooring.

Here you can see the support structure attached by the door and adjacent rib.

A simple template helps ensure that the floor fits snuggly.

To free the shell from the chassis, you have to remove the lower rub rails. On the Cruisette, these are attached with large pan-head sheet-metal screws. Newer models transitioned to blind rivets for attachment. You may also find rivets placed under the rub rail that helped attach the shell to the aluminum C-channel.

DISASSEMBLY

Lift the Shell

Before removing the shell from the chassis I made a template for the Marmoleum flooring. Your restoration goals and flooring medium will determine if a template is necessary or not. If it's undecided at this point, making them now could help things run smoother in the future. You can use cardboard, template paper, or scrap plywood to build the template.

Once the shell is free, there are many ways to lift it. On the Cruisette, I used a chain fall, dropped through its vents and attached to support lattice. This is a small and light trailer (four guys can easily lift the shell and move it), so lifting from the shop's steel roof structure was easy.

On the other hand, the larger Tradewind's vent holes did not line up with the ceiling's existing support beams, so I used camper jacks and 2 x 4s to lift it instead. This process proved to be successful and could be improved upon for future jobs by incorporating exterior lifting points fastened to existing structural rivet holes.

Another way to lift from a vent hole is to construct an A-frame structure over the camper shell at each vent location. This process, however, requires additional building time and materials. Used camper jacks can be found for reasonable prices and can also be rented from some industrial supply rental stores.

Now that the subfloor is fully exposed, it's time to continue dismantling. If any of the original

The Cruisette easily lifted using chain falls attached to a ceiling joist.

With 2 x 4s straddling the shell and fixed to the walls inside, this 20-foot shell was hoisted to remove the chassis.

STREAMLINE ALUMINUM TRAILERS: RESTORATION AND MODIFICATION

Jacks are placed at all four corners for this process. Visible in this non-curbside shot is panel damage to the Tradewind that will be addressed once the shell is reattached to a restored chassis so that it is stable.

Once the shell is freed from the chassis and belly pan, it can be lowered and placed on supports for minor bodywork such as vent patching and sealing exterior rivets from the inside. Any major panel replacement, such as the dent on the non-curbside, should be postponed until the shell is reattached. This prevents any tolerance issues.

plywood is in salvageable shape (i.e., not a crumbly, moldy mess), you can keep it to scribe in the replacement 3/4-inch plywood. In Chapter 10, the process of gluing separated plywood to re-create the original piece is covered. Keep in mind many parts are mirrored, which helps in re-creating gone or extremely damaged floor panels.

Underneath the subfloor there's a good chance you'll be dealing with more insulation. Use the same process mentioned earlier to remove the fiberglass and prep the belly pan panels for safe handling. As with the subfloor, left and right aluminum panels should be mirrors of each other. Label accordingly and develop a game plan on what panels will be reused and what will have to be re-created.

You can see the original subfloor and more of what lurks under a belly pan. Take note of the way the subfloor is fastened to the chassis, and the way the belly pan is attached to the subfloor when disassembling (this Cruisette used aluminum C-channels).

CHAPTER 3

CHASSIS

Before construction begins, the chassis needs plenty of work to be ready for any modifications. The most of which is typically on the suspension system.

The most common style of suspension found on vintage campers is an elliptical leaf spring, which dates back to Ford's Model T. Around the 1970s, torsion-style axles, such as Dexters, became a popular option for premium campers. If the goal is to keep a camper period-correct, you must retain the original suspension setup.

But that doesn't mean you can't replace a sagged and worn-out leaf stack with new leaves. The Cruisette stayed true to the original leaf-sprung suspension; however, the owner chose to upgrade the whole assembly (springs, shackles, axle, and hubs) for the advantage of modern electric brakes. Regardless of what manufacturer or style of suspension your trailer uses, you'll be able to find a trailer specialist to fabricate a replacement. Sometimes it's best to remove the old and take it to one for a perfect match.

Frame Members

For the Cruisette's chassis, I straightened the bent ladders. As sections of subfloor begin to rot and lose structure, the ones that remain intact end up overloaded and sagging over time. To straighten these frame members, I set them up on a flat surface then used levels, strings, and straight edges to find any variances.

From there, adjustments are made using heat and brute force. This force can be in the form of leverage from large pipe wrenches, cheater bars, and big hammers. Heat is also your friend when tweaking angle and channel iron. If your shop has solid mounting points, a come-along can be used to stretch, bend, and shrink the frame members. The best scenario for straightening a severely bent camper chassis is a chassis

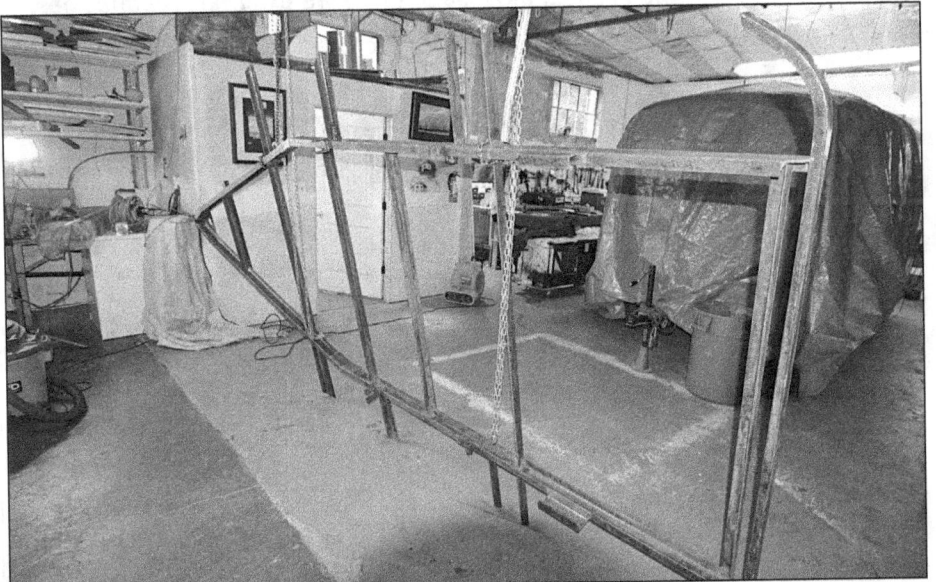

When prepping a frame, you can either use a grinder with wire and flapper wheels to remove rust or go the media-blasting route. Blasting is more expensive but less labor intensive. I used chain falls to rotate the chassis for the media blasting. Another option to maneuver the chassis is a rotisserie. Before the rust-removal and topcoat stages, the chassis is straightened, reinforced, and prepped for any suspension changes.

STREAMLINE ALUMINUM TRAILERS: RESTORATION AND MODIFICATION

alignment shop (typically they work on automobile and truck chassis) where specialty equipment makes short work of tweaking severely or mildly bent frames.

On campers with severe water damage, some of the chassis members can be completely rotted away. On these, you need to keep grinding and cutting away until you have solid mounting points for welding new stock. This is one of those unforeseeable costs that can quickly chew away at a restoration budget and time frame.

Suspension Types

During the planning of your build, it would be a good idea to find out from a local trailer suspension specialist what your options are as far as axle weight ratings and replacement parts such as shackles and springs. If your goal is modern towing performance, you may want to upgrade from a leaf-style suspension to a torsion style or go to the next level and install an independent, trailing-arm option such as from Timbren Axle-Less.

Typical trailer suspension is actually pretty archaic, and it's often overlooked when considering the dangers of highway travel at modern speeds. Upgrading to a torsion or better system helps offset towing anxiety, especially when new brakes and hubs are installed. Regardless of what suspension is used, chassis preparation is paramount to ensure structural integrity, camper squareness, and proper tracking. ■

Leaf-sprung suspension is the most basic and inexpensive option for trailers. While limited by wheel travel and clearance, unlike the other suspension options (beside airbags), leaf stacks can be modified for different weight ratings left-to-right to offset a heavy street-side galley. Over time, leaf springs collapse and flatten. This affects ride height, sometimes to the point that the belly pan sits on the axle. If there are external propane lines, they too can interfere with an axle.

Torsion axles offer independent wheel motion for a smoother ride and less shock transferred to the camper body. They also have fewer moving parts for improved reliability. A leaf-sprung frame needs some adjustments (removal of perches and/or shackle mounts and notching or reinforcement) to install a torsion design. Torsion-axle suspension systems rely on a rubberized element that deteriorates and wears over time. Manufacturer recommendations on replacement vary, but every decade seems to be a good rule of thumb.

This Timbren Axle-Less design, installed on a 1950s Traveler, provides the best clearance because there's no leaf-sprung axle or torsion spring running between the frame rails. It also has more travel than the other options, and a progressive spring rate helps to evenly support varying loads and dampen inconsistent road conditions. This design costs a little more than torsion axles and requires some additional frame fabrication to install.

CHASSIS

Damaged beyond repair, this 1950s Traveler chassis' rear ladder was chopped and removed for replacement. You can also see the original leaf-spring suspension still installed and the new independent Axle-Less design that will be installed. The Cruisette chassis wasn't as bad as this, requiring minor tweaking of the ladders using heat and leverage so that the subfloor has a flat surface for mounting.

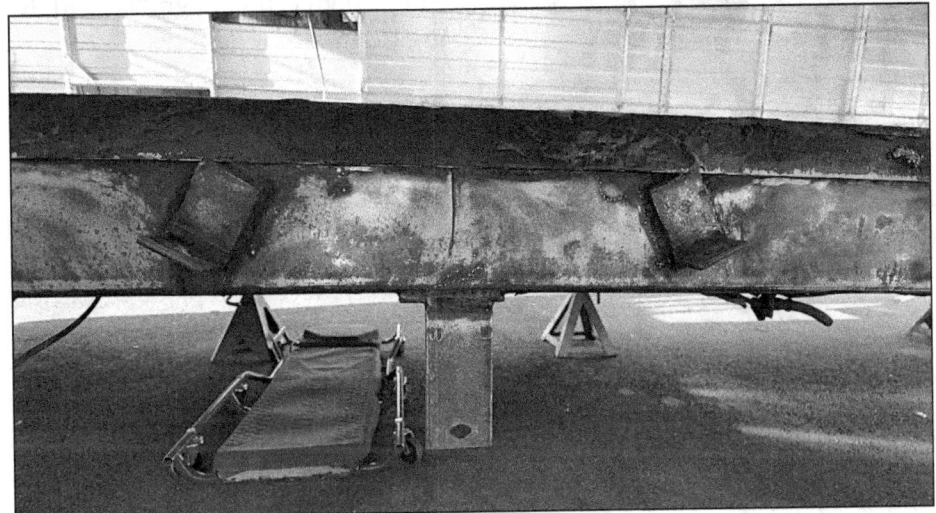

A large crack on this 1960s Boles Aero is right above the leaf-spring equalizer mount, a very important structural component. To repair this failure, the crack is welded shut and an additional plate is welded across it to distribute the suspension forces. When beginning any restoration project, it's paramount to build on a safe and sound structure.

Here, the crack is fixed and new leaf-sprung axles with brakes and wheels are installed. This setup is much safer now for highway travel, and the subfloor has a sound chassis for mounting. If this were ignored, the subfloor foundation would flex and the trailer chassis would continue to fatigue until the point of failure.

On this vintage Bell chassis, you can see that the bumper is far from original. If originality and bumper cosmetics are a concern, the whole assembly can be removed and a more svelte unit can be installed instead. Here, leaf-spring perches have been removed and the chassis C-channel is being boxed in for a trailing-arm suspension upgrade.

If metal fabrication at this level is beyond your skills, a specialist should perform the chassis work.

During this stage, I also added a structure to mount water tanks within the chassis, rather than above it. This avoids towing instability from a high center of gravity and listing from poor weight distribution.

Coupler

Make sure the coupler mechanism works properly. If the latch has been damaged or worn-out, you may need to replace the whole coupler to ensure well-being on the road. This requires cutting out the old coupler welds to remove it and welding in a new coupler rated to your trailer's weight.

Likewise, replacing old safety chains is another piece of cheap insurance. They should have a weight rating greater than the unit and should be long enough to make turns without binding or dragging on the ground.

If the hand jack is missing or damaged, you can replace it with a newer, modern model for usability (as done on the Cruisette), or you can restore the original and retain the vintage look of the camper (some jacks have deco designs).

Due to the size and space constraints of the Cruisette, I located

The tin worm did its best to weaken the Cruisette's safety-chain mount and lower coupler plate. In fact, these old safety chains would easily tear out in the event of an uncoupling. When considering towing an unrestored, well-neglected camper, there's plenty of potential for hidden danger. I often bring an extra set of safety chains and wrap them through the "A."

Instead of mounting the safety chains under the coupler, I opted to relocate them to the side. Here, all the compromised steel has been removed and the chassis is ready for media blasting to remove any oxidation and to prep the frame for a rust-preventing topcoat.

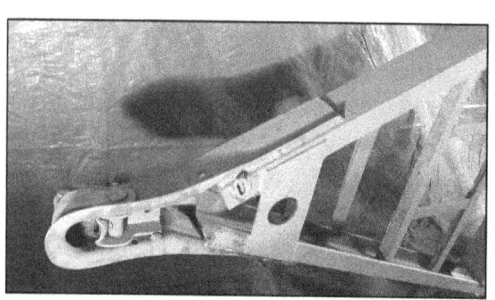

This sand-blasted coupler and chassis is ready for a final cleaning to prep for a topcoat. Many products prevent rust. When it's time to attach the safety chains, the area where the chains are attached is ground clean then covered with a topcoat once the chains are welded on.

the spare tire on the coupler (the rear compartment door prohibited mounting on the bumper). I also installed a small 10-pound horizontal propane tank.

Stabilizer Jacks and Bumper Mod

Another chassis modification to consider is leveling or stabilizer jacks. They should be mounted in a position that's free from damage when in tow and accessible to raise or lower. Likewise, a folding step should be replaced or repaired to ensure smooth operation and sturdy mounting.

While the chassis is torn down, you can also reinforce the bumper to accept a receiver hitch for accessories such as a bicycle rack or storage platform. The bumper can be a great place for a spare tire mount as well; just make sure it's not blocking the taillights.

Propane Tank and Spare Tire Mount

Because the rear luggage door would be blocked by a bumper-mounted spare, the Cruisette's owner opted to place the spare up front, along with a 10-pound propane tank. This was done instead of carrying a spare tire inside the camper (not only does it use valuable space, tire rubber gives off smelly gases) or storing it in the tow vehicle.

The original (or most recent) liquid propane (LP) setup on the Cruisette consisted of two tanks mounted on the coupler (I think the spare was originally stored in the rear luggage door, where the battery end electronics will be placed). As this modern take on a classic vintage Airstream foregoes the LP fridge for an ice chest and relies on an all-in-one Dometic heater and A/C unit, its propane requirements are greatly reduced.

The only LP needed for the Cruisette is to power a gas lamp and Modernaire stove, so the small 10-pound tank is sufficient. As with many aspects of a camper restoration, this required plenty of custom fabrication and creative thinking. The end product, although not original, looks period-correct and is a functional solution to storage problems on a small camper.

Creating a Mount for a Propane Tank and Spare Tire

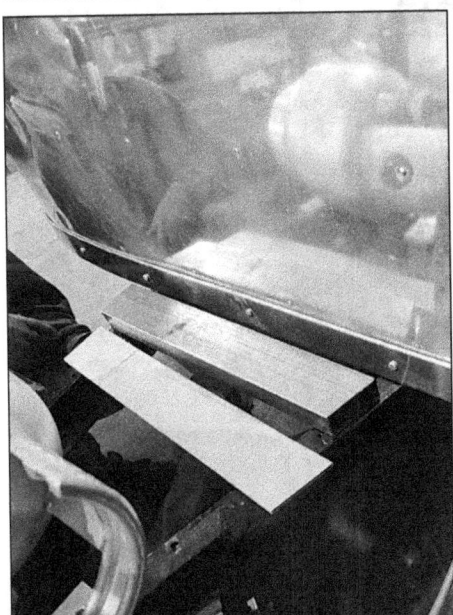

1 *Before cutting any metal, I made templates using scrap pieces of plywood and pine. Once I was sure clearance would not be an issue, the dimensions were transferred to bar stock and the pieces cut out using a metal miter saw and metal bandsaw.*

2 *Rather than fabricate another specific piece, I chose to harvest (from a generic kit) the piece that the spare tire bolts to that clamps to the camper bumpers. This piece will be welded to the support base to provide a secure mounting point for a spare tire.*

3 *When all the pieces have been welded, it's time to attach the spare tire mount to the coupler. Here you can see that the edges are clean and ready for welding. Throughout the fabrication process, the fresh welds and bare steel are coated with POR15 to match the chassis and to protect from rust.*

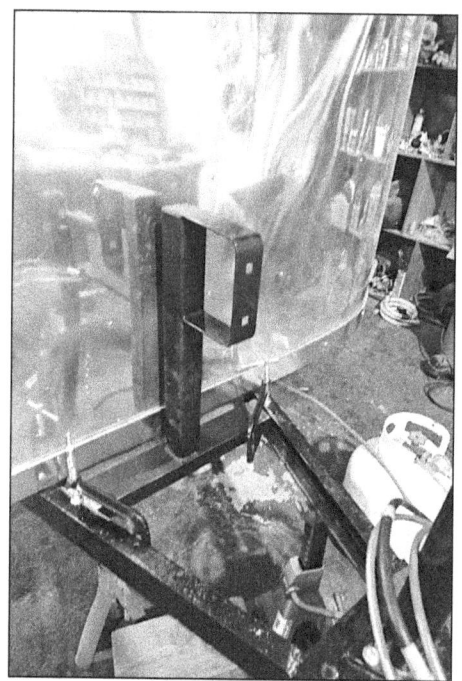

4 Here the spare tire mount is clamped in place and ready for a final weld. Before any welding, the LP tank being used to test various systems must be removed.

5 To mount the propane tank with proper clearance, it needed a custom "T" piece to lift it slightly and provide a space for the mounting hardware. Like the spare tire mount, this component is welded to the coupler. This propane tank has also been polished using a multi-step process to achieve a mirror finish similar to the Cruisette's shell and interior endcap.

6 Once the tank and spare tire is mounted, the final plumbing can be finished. For a little extra style, the spare tire is equipped with a baby moon hubcap, and the LP line will be polished for a nice contrast.

Finish Application

Once the chassis is modified and restored to your standards, it's time to consider finish. Airstream has always covered its chassis with a belly pan for optimal aerodynamics, which is nice because the metal is protected from the elements. Unfortunately, it can also trap moisture and promote rot. If you're restoring a model with exposed frame rails, protecting them from rust and exposure is very important.

Before any topcoat is applied, existing rust needs to be ground, sanded, and wire wheeled off. To save time and effort, I frequently media blast (sand blast) the chassis. This process requires not only specialty equipment and protective gear, but also a contained space to avoid making a mess. An autobody shop or steel-coating business may be a good resource to prep your chassis and save time.

Depending on your budget, chassis paint such as POR15 or powder coating (the more expensive option) are good routes to ensure longevity. The Cruisette's chassis was coated with POR15 products to keep it rust-free. Like painting any surface, prepping the surface is critical.

After media blasting the chassis, I applied a topcoat of POR-15. Another more expensive option is to have the chassis powder coated. If the budget is a concern, traditional rattle-can primer and paint also helps preserve the frame.

Once the chassis coat has cured, reassembly can begin. Before installing the new axle, I performed the floor and belly pan fabrication. You could now install the axle for maneuverability when rolling the chassis around, but access around that area would be more difficult for fitting water tanks and the belly pan.

CHAPTER 4

FLOORING

Once the chassis is a solid foundation and well protected from corrosion with a rust inhibitor, you can begin work on the subfloor and floor. These crucial structural components need to support other important interior elements such as the galley, closets, beds, etc.

Material Choices

Typically, for the base of the subfloor, I use good-quality 3/4-inch plywood that's finished with a silicone sealant on the edges and then top coated with a water-based epoxy to prevent future rot and plywood separation.

Another popular option is marine plywood, but the price is more than the cost of treating readily available plywood and your geographic location can have an impact on convenience (marine plywood is more common if you live near large bodies of water). Plywood designed for salty, nautical use holds up to the demands of a camper, but it's better matched to the demands of boating and a bit of overkill for a land yacht. Treating inexpensive plywood can save money in exchange for time.

You need to lay out the new subfloor, patterned after the old one, and then seal the edges before laying down the floor. If you have saved any sections of the original subfloor, now's the time to prep it for transferring the edge patterns to the new plywood.

Plywood Template

To use severely damaged or disintegrated subfloors for templating, cut and attach scrap pieces of wood (1/4-, 7/16-, or 3/4-inch plywood or solid) to fill any large voids. Remember, the goal is to make a template for the edge only. You don't need to reproduce the whole piece; 4- to 6-inch-wide sections should be sufficient.

The base of this Airstream Cruisette's floor is 3/4-inch plywood that has been sealed with silicone and a water-based epoxy. Camper floors need to be watertight to prevent damage from intrusion both underneath and above. A burst water line from improper winterization could ruin a camper's subfloor in very little time. Likewise, any water intrusion from towing in heavy rain or life in a humid climate promotes mold and rot. An alternative subfloor material is marine-grade plywood. But, expect to pay more per square foot.

STREAMLINE ALUMINUM TRAILERS: RESTORATION AND MODIFICATION

Cutting the Template

1 The old, rotted subfloor was extracted and used to produce this template for a late 1950s Airstream. The next step is to outline the old subfloor onto the new plywood floor.

2 Because the subfloor doesn't need to be pretty, 1/8-inch plywood was cut with a jigsaw, and then followed up with a belt sander.

3 A fresh 120- or 150-grit belt cuts through the plywood quickly. Be careful not to sand past the mark.

4 With a plywood template like this, you could perfectly match it with a flush-cut bit and router. The template is mounted under or above the stock, depending on whether the bit has a top- or bottom-mount bearing, and the router simply follows the template.

How to Salvage Damaged Wood

Start by cutting away any loose material, then trace its shape onto the scrap and cut to fit. This doesn't need to be pretty, but accuracy reduces working time.

Next, attach the new piece with lapped scrap wood and grabber screws.

There's a good chance that some old pieces of subfloor have plies that are separating. To address this, glue the separated plies back together and clamp them tight. Spring clamps come in handy for speed and ease of use. After the glue is dried, fill any cavities with body filler. Once it's cured, smooth to the original shape with a belt sander or file.

This method can be a time-consuming ordeal. If you're skilled with a scribe or flexible straightedge, you could freehand the compound curves and get close enough to the original profile to move forward quicker. Just keep in mind that precision now leads to less work later. (This technique to replicate damaged wood by rebuilding is more thoroughly detailed in Chapter 9, where I cover cabinetry.)

When the template is ready to transfer to the replacement plywood flooring, produce a marking that's visible and easy to follow (carpenter's pencil is the preferred tool here). You can screw or clamp the template directly to the working piece to keep it from moving during marking. Be sure to also mark where the template sits so you can replace it in the same spot after the unneeded portion is cut off.

After the edge marking is transferred, remove the template and use a jigsaw to make a rough-cut just outside the mark. Then reattach the template.

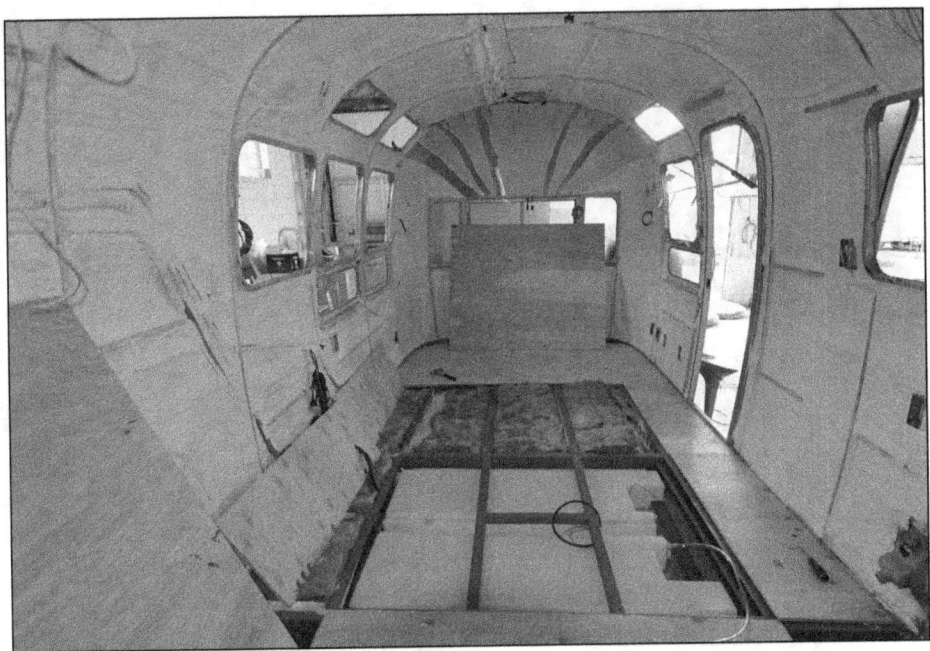

Here, I'm fitting the subfloor in a 1970s Airstream frame-on build. After all the pieces are cut to fit, they will be removed and treated with a water-based epoxy. This Airstream was insulated before the subfloor install, unlike the Cruisette, which received flooring first and insulation second. The order of operation depends on many variables.

When shaping curves in plywood or rounding sharp edges, such as this canned ham's roof profile, the belt sander is your friend. One technique to make the curved sections of an Airstream floor is to use a jigsaw and cut close (1/8 to 1/4 inch) to the markings. Then sand with an 80- or 120-grit belt sander to the mark for a clean, accurate edge.

Now, you can use a router with a flush bit that follows the template to reproduce a perfect factory curve. The other option is to run a belt sander with a coarse paper and shape the new plywood to the marking for an accurate reproduction.

For straight cuts (when trimming sheets to match your camper's width and working around the wheel wells), use a circular saw with a guide.

Subfloor Install

When you've made all the cuts and you're happy with the tolerances, it's time to fasten the subfloor to the chassis.

Here, the subfloor is installed (with 3/8-inch carriage bolts) and belly pan supports are added to the Cruisette chassis. Note the holes already cut for plumbing and the studs installed to attach both underfloor-gray and potable-water tanks. The sheet-aluminum belly-pan braces are constructed using a brake and metal shears.

Fasteners

The Cruisette originally used carriage bolts fastened through the plywood to the steel channels, which I used as well (3/8 inch). To keep them from backing out, the shank is struck with a hammer so it bends slightly at the nut, effectively locking it in place. This is the same technique used by the factory in the 1950s.

When tightening carriage bolts, be sure that the head sufficiently compresses the plywood and sits below the top surface. The 3/4-inch plywood layer is covered with another 1/4-inch plywood in the next step, so it's not crucial for a completely flush or counter-sunk bolt, but make sure they've begun to compress the plywood. This helps ensure a flat, creak-free surface. Sometimes it might be necessary to grind a slot in the top of a carriage bolt and use a flathead screwdriver to keep it from spinning.

Another good hardware choice for fastening 3/4-inch plywood to the chassis is self-tapping No. 10 or No. 12 wafer-head metal screws with a shank long enough to sufficiently grip the steel frame members. Be sure to use a proper counter-sink drill bit to achieve a flush surface. These are

Sometimes a frame-off restoration isn't a likely option. Visible here is the aluminum channel that attaches the subfloor to the body, along with a factory-bent carriage bolt dangling in the wind. Notice that the C-channels are no longer level, letting the body shift from lack of support. Replacing a subfloor here without removing the body requires finesse, using various jacking or cribbing techniques, and due care to not stress the aluminum body while fitting a new subfloor section.

Here, you can see a truck camper jack (commonly called a widow maker) and some bar stock used to lift the shell enough to add a new subfloor. These window frames are sturdy enough to support the weight, but that's not always true. It takes due diligence to find safe and secure jacking points to prevent damage or, worse, injury. To the right are new floor sections ready to install once the chassis is rebuilt and reinforced where rust had eaten away at the original frame ladders.

faster but not as secure as a properly torqued and bent carriage bolt.

The Cruisette restoration is a frame-off procedure, but you can replace the subfloor on a trailer that's on a frame by working in sections.

If the chassis is structurally sound (no obvious impact damage or significant rot), grind away the old carriage bolts, extract the old subflooring as intact as possible, and reproduce it using the method mentioned earlier in this chapter.

To extract and install the subfloor, you need to slightly lift the body. This requires common sense to avoid further damage in the form of stressed structural aluminum and exterior components (creased panels, cracked or bent ribs). You need to lift only 5/8 to 3/4 inch at most.

Ensure that the carriage bolts are removed far enough away from your working area (6 or 7 feet on each side) so the body can be lifted without binding.

Lifting a body from the chassis can be performed in many ways: using cribbing with bottle or screw jacks, truck camper jacks, block and tackle, or, of course, friends with strong backs and weak minds. Always put safety first, and consult said friends for input when in doubt.

Subfloor Covering

Remove each subfloor portion and replace with new plywood, working either front to back or back to front, as your project demands. With this method, you could run across unforeseeable circumstances such as rotted, bent, or compromised frame members.

You can also install a new floor without removing the body from the chassis.

For the Cruisette build, I installed the belly pan and body to the chassis before adding the final layer of flooring (see Chapter 5 for more details).

Once a 3/4-inch base is securely attached and sealed from possible moisture intrusion and there's no excessive movement under foot, it's time to install the subfloor covering. Drab and smelly vinyl has been a longtime camper standby when it comes to flooring and is probably what you or someone ripped out of your project quite some time ago. This restoration uses Marmoleum (natural linoleum) for the flooring. Marmoleum is easy to clean, antibacterial, eco-friendly and, due to a large palette of available styles, looks great in vintage trailers.

Marmoleum Floor

This Marmoleum floor install is for a Nissan camper van conversion, but the process is the same for any trailer or RV. You only need a few tools, most notably, a 1/16-inch square-notch trowel and 100-pound tile roller.

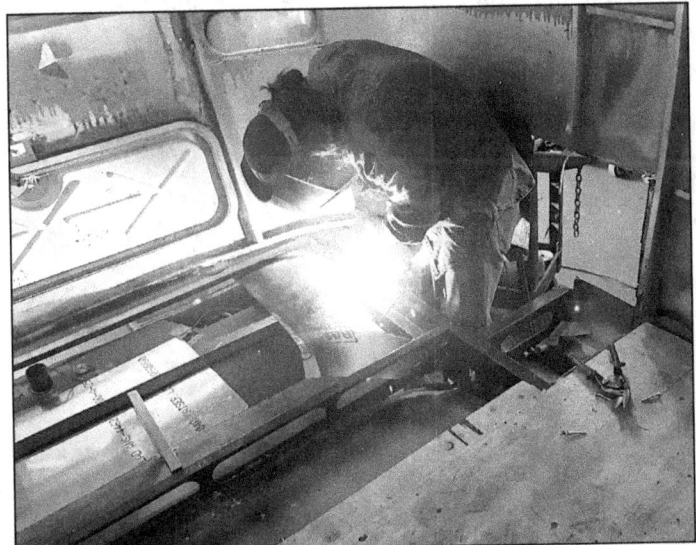

When repairing a trailer in sections, you will probably run into problems such as an unexpected rotted frame member. This Overlander needed its rear frame ladders reinforced due to rust from water damage in the bathroom area, a common issue on older campers. The rotted pieces are cut out and new angle iron is welded in place.

A good example of outsourcing work, the replacement wheelwells were reproduced by a local metal fabrication shop with proper tooling. These attach to the subfloor and need to be installed in conjunction with the belly pan. Before a final flooring layer can be fitted on an Airstream, the belly pan and body are reattached.

Flooring Options

There are many types of flooring to consider for a camper restoration, but some options are better than others. Of course, weight is an issue. So, a heavy oak floor might not be the best way to go. Bamboo, on the other hand, is relatively light and durable, making it a good choice for campers.

One word of caution comes with laminate or vinyl-lapped flooring: The extreme temperature changes a trailer experiences (freeze/thaw cycles and summer heat) results in swelling and shrinking of the panels, which causes lifting and separation. ■

While an extreme example, the floor of this 1960s land yacht shows the lifting and separation common with vinyl flooring. It also displays the plywood separation and iron oxidation expected of an early 1960s Airstream. This subfloor needs to be replaced. Using the old one as a template, you can easily re-create a subfloor.

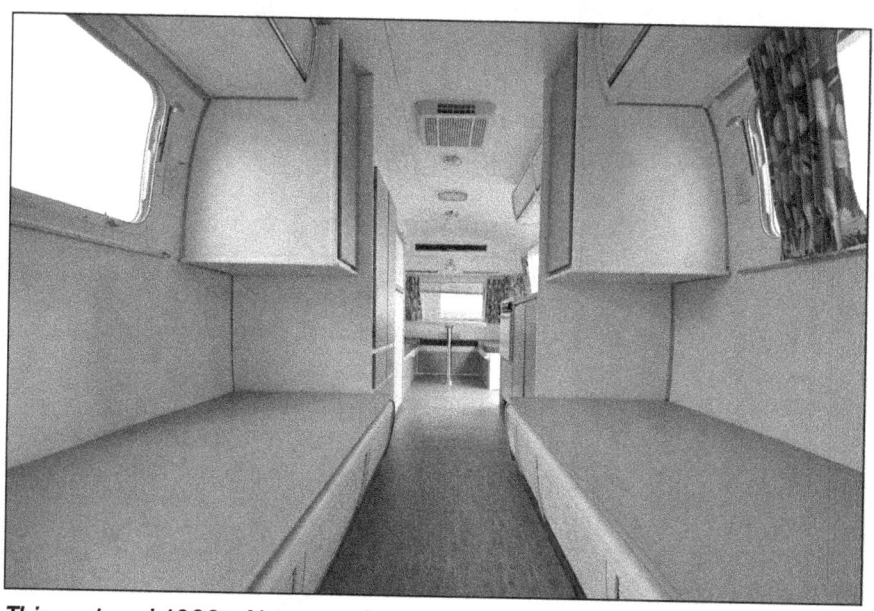

This restored 1980s Airstream features solid bamboo flooring. With a tongue-and-groove design, it's fairly easy to install, and this durable flooring option holds up well to the high traffic associated with small spaces. It's also structurally sounder than a laminate, so you can forego a second 1/4-inch plywood layer to save time or money.

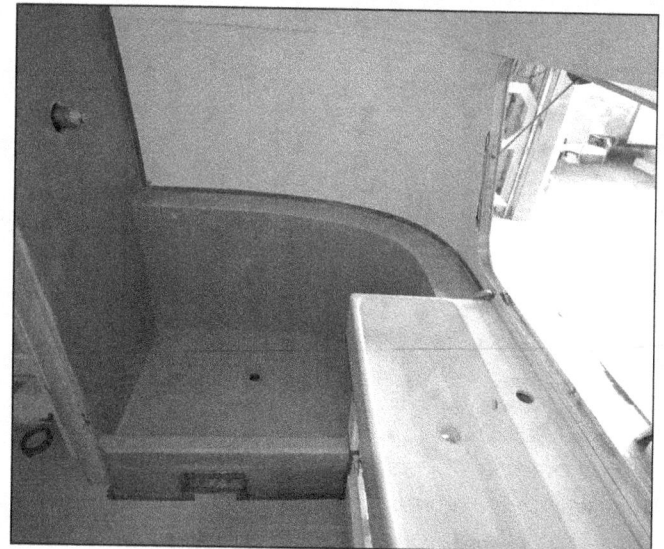
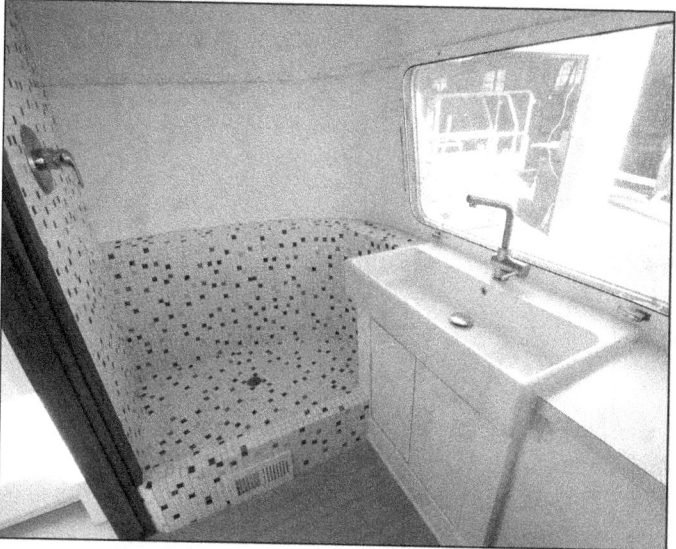

Even tile can be used for floor covering, as long as the substructure is properly prepared. Here, a 1970s Airstream Overlander's custom bathroom is finished with a colorful tile pattern.

FLOORING

Installing a Marmoleum Floor

1 Because Marmoleum comes in a roll, it retains a memory that needs to be removed. You can let it relax by unrolling it for a couple of days or massaging the curl by pulling the sheet over on itself on a diagonal plane.

2 Before the subfloor is installed, it can be used as a template. Make sure to keep the top orientation correct; confusing the top and bottom will ruin your day.

3 Use a marker to transfer the cut line to the flooring.

4 Shears make quick work of cutting Marmoleum. Relief cuts, such as the one visible here, help the shears find a precise line around a tight curve.

5 Cutting a straight line is simple. If your camper floor has holes for holding tank drains and fills, LP lines, electrical, or other items, they need to be cut out, too.

STREAMLINE ALUMINUM TRAILERS: RESTORATION AND MODIFICATION

CHAPTER 4

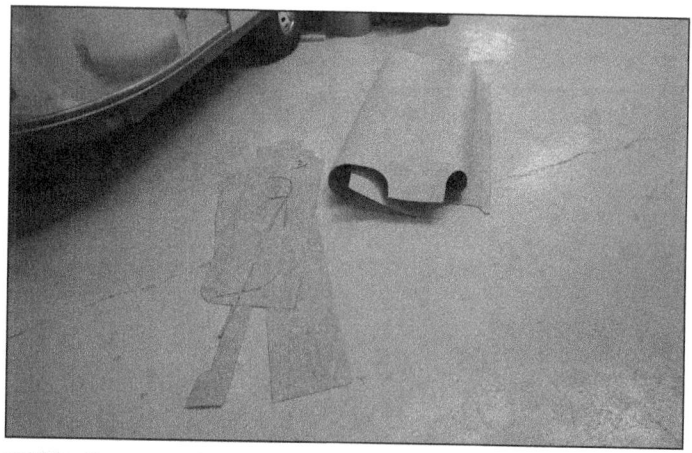

6 To move the cut floor to the camper, it needs to be rolled up again. Be careful around wheelwells and other 90-degree or abruptly ending notches, corners, and holes, as you can tear the Marmoleum. While the subfloor is being installed, you can leave it unrolled to help relax it.

7 Cleanliness becomes paramount at this point. If a small rock or other debris makes its way between the floor and subfloor, it'll be there forever. Once the subfloor is mounted and fully cleaned, it's time to install the floor.

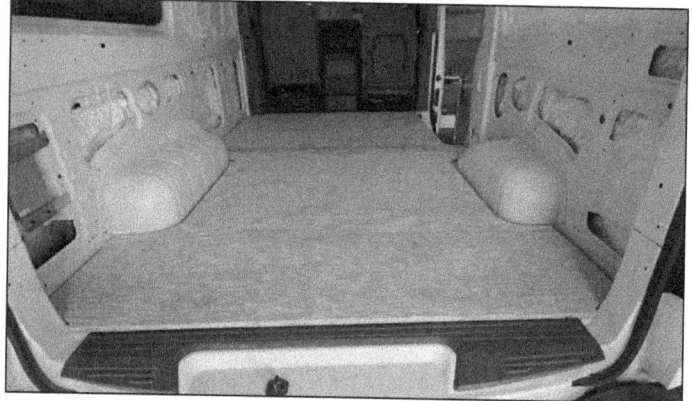

8 Before laying the floor, vacuum it as you unroll it to avoid picking up any debris. Some careful planning here makes things easier when you unroll the floor. You want two people to handle the floor to avoid damage.

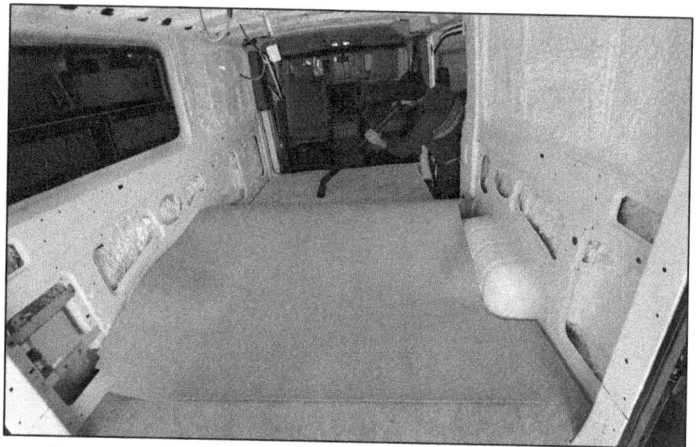

9 To avoid nicks in the surface and trapped fragments from construction in the adhesive, another pass with the vacuum is called for.

10 Once the area is thoroughly prepped, the floor is rolled back onto itself to slightly past the halfway point, and the water-based adhesive is spread with a trowel.

STREAMLINE ALUMINUM TRAILERS: RESTORATION AND MODIFICATION

FLOORING

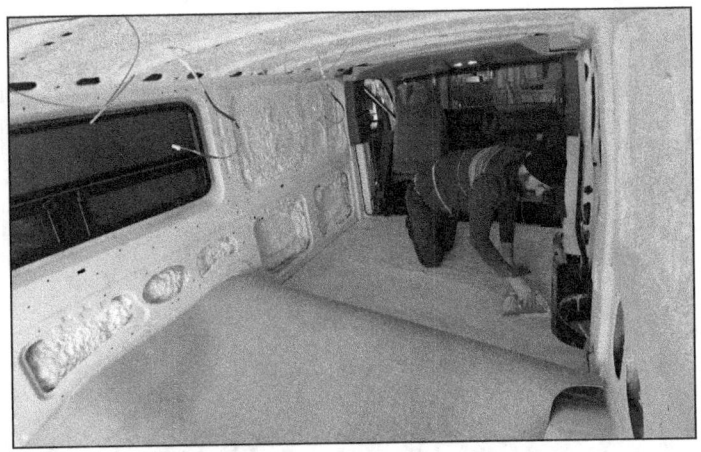

11 It helps to use two trowels, as a second one with a slightly different shape works into tighter corners or curves. A second trowel also assists in scraping off excess from the main, larger trowel.

12 Spread the adhesive in an even layer, including up to all walls and edges. You need to set the floor before the adhesive starts to dry. Always place the flooring on wet adhesive, if it's flashed. Be sure not to work yourself into a corner.

13 Marmoleum expands slightly in width and shrinks slightly in length when placed on wet adhesive. It should be rolled immediately across the width first, then across the length. Before you begin rolling, the other side needs adhesive spread.

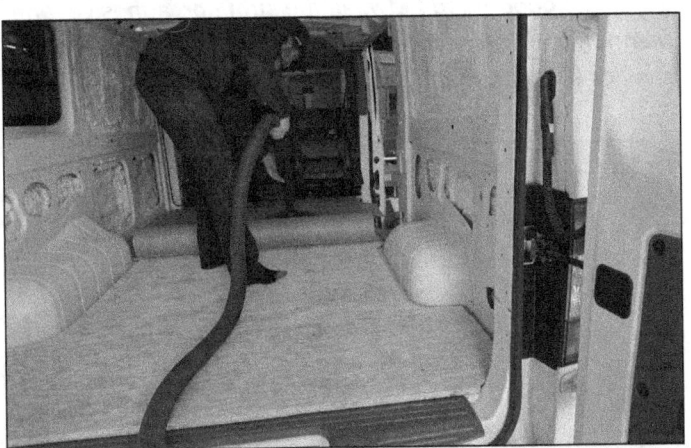

14 Use the same process with the rear as you did with the front. Vacuum, and then vacuum some more. Having more than one person here helps, as one can prep, while the other checks for proper adhesive transfer (the back of the sheet should be wet) before rolling.

15 To ensure that the roller hasn't picked up any debris from transport or storage, it needs a quick wipe down. As with any quality finish product, cleanliness is top priority.

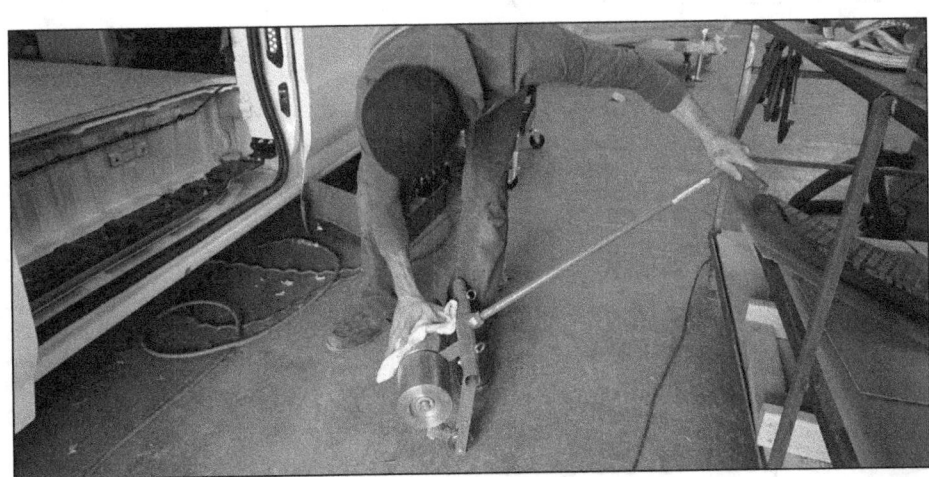

CHAPTER 4

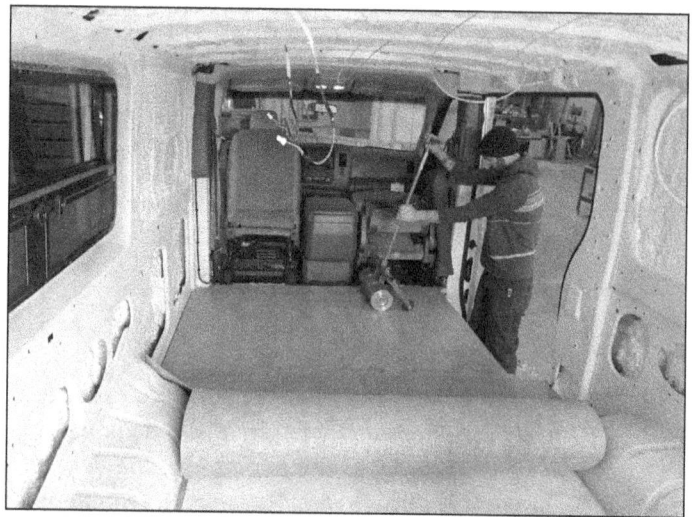

16 The bond will fail if you do not start rolling before the adhesive sets. Start by rolling widthwise to achieve a good bond between the subfloor, adhesive, and Marmoleum. The second installer starts to spread adhesive for the other half.

17 As the adhesive is spread on the opposite side, the floor is laid down. This is easier in a van, where you have access to either side via the sliding door, but the process is the same for any camper or living space.

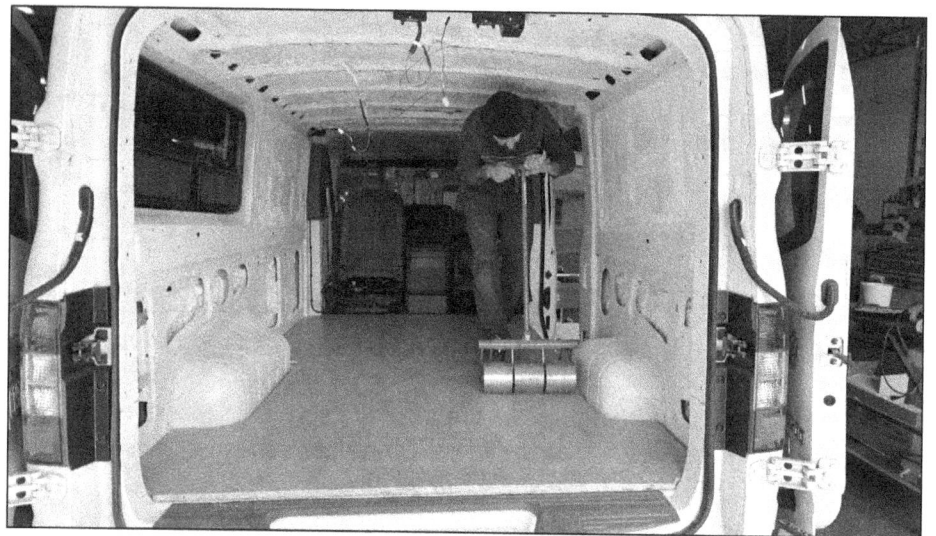

18 After the new section is rolled widthwise, the final passes are performed lengthwise. With proper installation, Marmoleum floors will last for decades, and with proper care they last even longer.

To prep the top surface for adhesion, I use another layer of 1/4-inch plywood. Marmoleum's structural properties (unlike bamboo or reclaimed-wood flooring) loosely resemble damp cardboard. It's fairly bendable but fails unsuspectingly. This second layer helps reinforce the subfloor and ensures good bonding between the two substrates.

I used a template made before disassembly (see Chapter 2) to shape the 1/4-inch plywood. It's attached with construction adhesive, such as Liquid Nails, and with nails, staples, or screws for fastening. This ensures no separation that would cause an annoyingly squishy or squeaky floor.

This layer's edge can be sealed, just as with the base plywood, with silicone to ensure longevity; however, the top is left bare to allow a good bond between the adhesive and the Marmoleum. To ensure a flat floor on the Cruisette, I used a straightedge to look for low spots. Any low spots are raised with standard body filler and once the filler is cured, a random orbital or belt sander (120 or 150 grit) is used to make the voids flush. In the same manner, any seams, cracks, and holes from screw heads are made flush with the filler. If you lay the Marmoleum over a

FLOORING

A flat, clean surface is crucial when installing Marmoleum flooring because small debris is amplified under foot. Using a straightedge, low spots and holes from hardware and manufacturing defects are marked, filled, and sanded smooth. The same goes for the seams. Before the bonding agent is evenly applied, vacuum thoroughly, including the underside of the floor. Here, you can see the cleaned backside of the rolled-up flooring, ready to unroll into position.

The red handle you see here connects to a 100-pound floor-rolling tool, available at most industrial rental stores. Using it ensures good bonding for the Marmoleum adhesive and a smooth surface free of air voids that lift the flooring and create soft spots. Likewise, the dusty keg is strategically placed to guarantee the step's edge has sufficient adhesion and doesn't peel back.

surface with imperfections, they will be visible on the floor surface.

If you do not have a floor template, the process of installing Marmoleum involves careful measurement of flooring dimensions and transferring them to the Marmoleum rolled out on a flat surface. Precut the Marmoleum to the camper's width, and cut out the wheelwell positions. Apply a strong tape that doesn't leave adhesive residue behind at the wheelwell's inside corners. This helps prevent tearing during installation (Marmoleum can tear during handling).

On campers with compound curved flooring (Airstream), it's best to make this cut outside the unit (cutting inside can result in wavy edges and folding or creasing could easily lead to repairs or irreparable damage). Once the Marmoleum is ready to install, do a dry fit to ensure that everything is in position.

To safely move Marmoleum, roll it up as delivered and secure it with tape, twine, or strapping. Be sure to properly clean and vacuum both the subfloor and underside of the Marmoleum to avoid trapping any small debris that would cause dimples and annoying imperfections.

Once the Marmoleum is ready for final install, roll it up again to expose half or more of the floor, and use a notched spreader to evenly coat the adhesive over the subfloor. Lay this portion down and proceed with the other half in the same manner, being sure to overlap the adhesive.

Next, a heavy (100-pound) floor roller (rentable from most hardware stores) is rolled over the freshly installed floor to ensure good adhesion and a flat, even surface.

Now that the floor is installed, make sure that it stays undamaged throughout the remainder of the build. Ram board makes a great protective layer; cardboard easily wears during construction. Be sure to securely attach whatever medium you chose to protect the surface. The two surfaces may be slick and could unexpectedly slide out from underneath you.

Once a floor is installed, you'll enter and exit the camper many times. Ensuring that the new flooring stays that way until the job is complete is important to avoid back tracking. I use Ram board and masking tape to protect the finished product.

CHAPTER 5

BODY

The Cruisette's aluminum shell attaches to the camper chassis by means of an aluminum channel fastened to the subfloor with carriage bolts. This channel, available through Airstream retailers or custom fabricated by a sheet-metal specialist, serves as a meeting point for the belly pan and shell. The resulting seam is concealed by the rub rail. On this project, one rub rail was salvaged, while the other needed replacement.

If your camper's rub rail needs a section replaced, many moldings and extrusions are available. The Cruisette's rub rail is a less common item and required fabrication beyond my means. While the rails were out for reproduction, I focused on buttoning up the Cruisette's under belly and remounting the shell.

Belly Pan

Building a belly pan requires cutting 5052 aluminum (available from Airstream retailers, industrial metal supply stores, or aviation specialty shops) into reproduction pieces based on templates from the originals. Using both pneumatic and hand-powered shears, you can cut the 5052 into shape, and then form the curved sections with gentle bending. To achieve this, use a Cleco tool and fasteners, and start from the camper center, working your way to the side.

The belly-pan panels are lapped and sealed using a polyurethane sealant. Skiaflex-221, an Airstream OEM sealant for vents, window frames, and sinks, is the preferred product anywhere aluminum is lapped joined. At the corners of the belly pan, a component often referred to as the "Banana" requires fabrication using gentle bending (a sand bag can help here) to form the slight curve, and by reliefs cut to allow the aluminum to shrink and bend at the edge. Be careful not to cut too far, or you could create cracks in the aluminum that would require

Before attaching the shell, I reproduced the Cruisette's belly pan. This involves aluminum shaping and fabrication and is a good place to become familiar with aluminum and its characteristics, as it's under the camper and faults are difficult to find.

starting over or patching, depending on your expectations.

To help keep the Cruisette climate controlled and to help prevent infestation, I used fiberglass insulation to fill any voids, including around the water tanks. Spray foam can also be used, but the expansion can cause deformation. Be sure to spray an adequate amount to fill the void, but not so much that it pushes the sheet metal out of form.

Belly Pan Installation

1 Here you can see the belly pan being fitted to the Cruisette. Working from the center to the side allows the flat piece to take a curved shape. The 5052 aluminum is fairly soft.

2 Before buttoning up the belly-pan sides with blind rivets (where they are covered by the rub rail) and Olympic or buck rivets (where they are visible), I stuffed the void with fiberglass insulation.

3 To temporarily hold the belly pan in place, standard Phillips-head sheet-metal screws are used. This is a good alternative to Cleco fasteners. However, if their protruding head interferes with the body during the install, they have to be replaced with rivets.

4 The corners of an Airstream belly pan are commonly referred to as bananas. This Cruisette's corner pieces, however, do not resemble the elongated and curved fruit found on the 1960s and newer models.

CHAPTER 5

5 Constructing the corners is more difficult than re-creating the curves found on the sides of the belly pan, as the aluminum has a curve in two directions. This is achieved with relief cuts in the Cruisette's banana to allow the aluminum to shrink around the edge and make the curve. Blind rivets are used through the underside to save time and money.

6 All four bananas are fabricated and the belly pan is riveted together and filled with insulation.

Aluminum Bodywork

If jumping into aluminum camper bodywork seems daunting, a good plan of attack is to start small and build your skillsets. For example, some Airstreams and Silver Streaks came with aluminum galleys, closets, or overhead lockers. The latter was true for this Cruisette, however, the lockers were covered with holes and paint from decades of modification.

Working with aluminum can be rewarding but frustrating. Aluminum can crack and fail without any warning. On the other hand, it's very malleable within its structural limit. With practice, you'll learn to work within those limits.

The belly-pan banana for this project from a late-seventies Airstream was in a condition most would deem bound for the recyclers. However, with some hammering and a few trips through the English wheel, this pockmarked and creased component was restored to a like-new condition.

The process provides the basics of aluminum bodywork and can be applied to the larger endcap panels to address dents, creases, and imperfections. Aluminum bodywork takes practice and familiarizing yourself with the fundamentals of metalworking.

Shaping the "Banana"

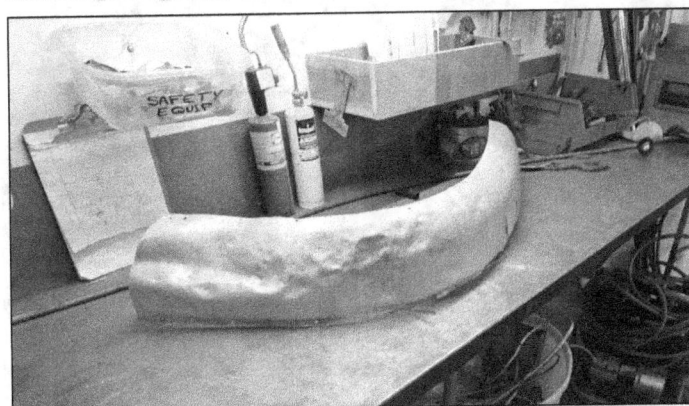

1 The valleys and peaks on this banana from road spray and other random impacts are leveled using a leather bag and various mallets. Before any work begins on this piece, it's thoroughly cleaned, deburred, and free from any remaining rivet pieces.

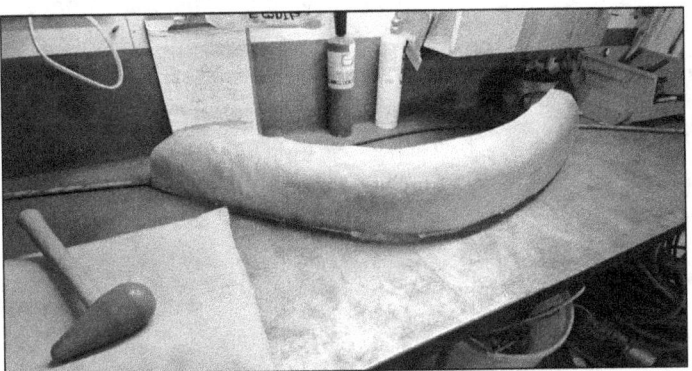

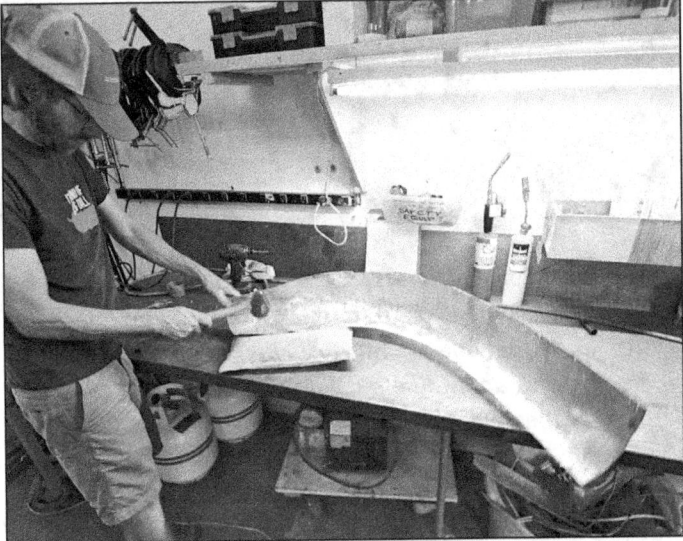

2 By forming a convex curve in the sandbag, commonly called a panel beater bag, you can pound the low spots level. Work the dents a little bit at a time, avoiding any drastic change. Annealing the aluminum helps soften it, making it easier to work. Gently heat the metal until you see black soot; however, be careful not to overheat the material.

3 Here you can see that the dents are significantly reduced and the panel is ready for a trip to the English wheel. A good tip is to start the wheel with a low pressure and make slight adjustments.

4 Using adequate pressure to flatten the high spots (too much pressure stretches the material and causes it to lose shape), you slowly work the panel through the English wheel. Guiding the piece takes some practice and it's always advised to use scrap aluminum before working your pieces through. There are various anvil wheel sizes to help match the curve you're working with. If the wheel is too flat, you risk adding creases to the panel and make additional work for yourself.

CHAPTER 5

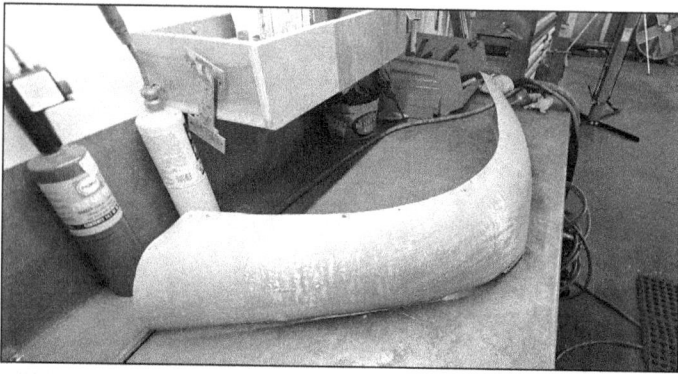

5 As the panel begins to feel smooth to the hand and imperfections are more difficult to see, you can use a file or sandpaper to help locate and highlight the high spots. It takes plenty of passes to remove these valleys and peaks.

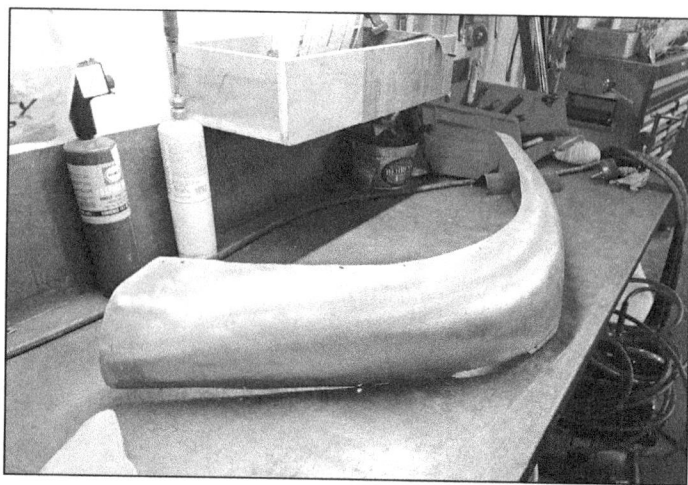

6 After about an hour of work, the once-haggard banana is now smooth and ready for installation.

7 Here, the banana is set in position with Cleco fasteners. Once it's riveted, a final polish pass completes the restoration of this corner. Note the masking tape used to protect the shell above where the rub rail will sit to avoid marring the panel during installation.

Hidden Components

If you have any undercarriage components, such as waste valves and water lines, you want to address these before the belly pan is buttoned up. One undercarriage feature of this Cruisette is venting for a Dometic trucker A/C unit mounted under the settee. I added custom-fabricated intake and exhaust venting to the belly pan.

Vents

Although far from original, other venting options include a window-mounted unit installed and vented out the rear (inefficient and requires significant alterations) and a roof-mounted unit (it would look ungainly on top of the little Cruisette). They were not chosen in favor of the Dometic trucker unit's efficiency.

These vents were constructed from 5052 aluminum using a brake and basic hand tools. They are mounted to the belly pan and allow intake and exhaust for the A/C unit mounted inside the Cruisette under the settee.

Body Reinstallation

Once the belly pan is completed, it's time to reinstall the body, which is a daunting task, but not any more

BODY

The shell and belly pan are riveted to aluminum C-channel placed on top of the subfloor. I used a couple of chain falls to hoist the lightweight body and rolled the chassis underneath.

This large panel on the Cruisette was replaced to address non-curbside damage. Instead of scrapping the large piece, I cut out good sections to use on the curbside, where street appeal counts. The door, in particular, had many holes and dents from previous latches and wind-blown slams. By using original aluminum, the polished door aluminum matches perfectly.

difficult to complete than previous procedures. Simply reversing the steps used to remove the shell (a chain fall mounted to the wooden support structure and hanger joists), I reunited the Cruisette shell with its refurbished chassis.

Once the Shell is gently placed into position, Cleco fasteners keep it in place as heavy-duty pop rivets are installed. The Cruisette's rub rail also adds structure with large No. 10 sheet-metal screws. On a contemporary Airstream, additional pop rivets attach the shell to the C-channel.

Getting to this point is a milestone. Soon your work involves prepping for insulation. But first, you must complete any additional bodywork. For example, this Airstream suffered from a large crease on the center, non-curbside panel. Rather than try to work out this imperfection, I opted to replace it with 0.32-inch 2024-T3 aluminum.

Panel Patching

If you're remodeling a riveted aluminum camper, there's a good chance you'll be removing outdated components such as a water heater, fridge, or stove that leaves a significant hole in the skin. Patching them is a great opportunity to get acquainted with riveting and Airstream construction techniques.

Replacing the large panel on the non-curbside allowed the use of good, vintage Alclad aluminum on significant areas such as the door, where visual presentation is priority. Vintage Airstream aluminum has a different shine to it; metal compositions (and suppliers) have changed over time so that the finish is never a perfect match. A trained eye can spot two different panels next to each other, but the general public doesn't notice.

For this reason, I opted to reuse old aluminum. When replacing panels, it's important to use plenty of Cleco fasteners to avoid panel walking, which is what happens when the panel shifts from buck riveting. When you compress a rivet, hole bore tolerances and the compression of the sheet cause slight variances that can add up over the length of a large panel.

By using a Cleco fastener in every other rivet hole, you can prop the heel of a bucking bar to the tip of a Cleco fastener and pivot it into the rivet mandrel as you hammer.

Creating Patch Panels

1 Cut your aluminum stock to the desired shape (this is 2024-T3 aluminum with a PCV protective coating). A fan tool (shown) speeds up setting rivet-hole locations by providing even spacing. Once the rivet holes are predrilled, you can set the panel (I'm using 5/32-inch Cleco fasteners, drill bit, and rivets here).

2 Square up the panel over the spot to be patched and drill the first hole, then install a Cleco fastener. Next, move along a couple of holes to drill and place another Cleco. The more holes you skip, the more chance for tenting (a peak forming along the seam) of the panel, so a good rule is to place a Cleco in every other hole.

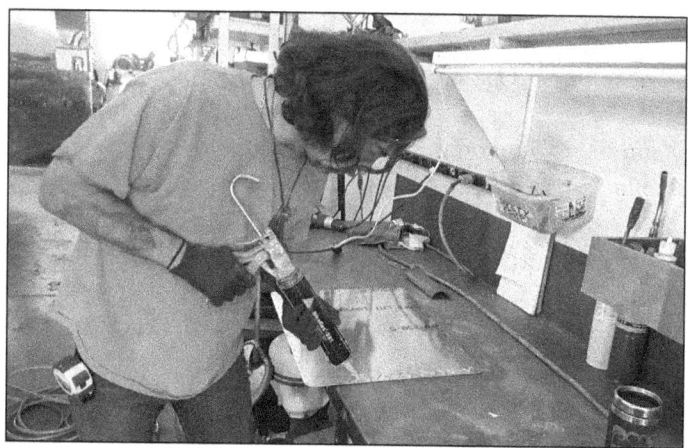

3 Once the panel is drilled, pull it and place a polyurethane sealant over the lapped portions. Cleaning both surfaces with a quick-drying solvent is recommended to remove any oil, shavings, and dirt acquired during handling.

4 Here you can see Clecos being installed to hold the panel in place for riveting. The Cleco tool compresses a spring in the fastener, which holds pressure on the expanding tip when released. This system allows quick panel placement and removal.

5 Before the first round of buck rivets, it's best to redrill the holes to clear them of any burrs and excess sealant. This helps ensure that the bucking process is hassle-free. In addition, the protective PCV (poly vinyl chloride) coating is removed from the rivet zone. You do not want to capture the coating under a set rivet or you have to drill it out. Also, if you look at the factory rivets, you see a center-left one that was hammered without sufficient bucking pressure; it has distortion in its reflection.

BODY

6 Setting buck rivets is often a two-person job that requires good communication and coordination, or you end up with a dimpled rivet (shown). The person running the hammer needs to place the rivet and make sure the bucking bar is in position before pressing the trigger. Using a piece of wood against the hammer, set the air pressure at a point where the hammer allows enough pressure to deform the rivet, but not so much that it warps the panel.

7 Here you can see the bucking bar and the tips of the Cleco fasteners. Once a rivet is placed into position and the hammer is placed against it, the "bucker" adds pressure to the rivet. Now the rivet can be compressed.

8 After the side is riveted, the remaining Cleco fasteners are removed.

9 This is a completed panel patch with the excess sealant and the PCV coating removed.

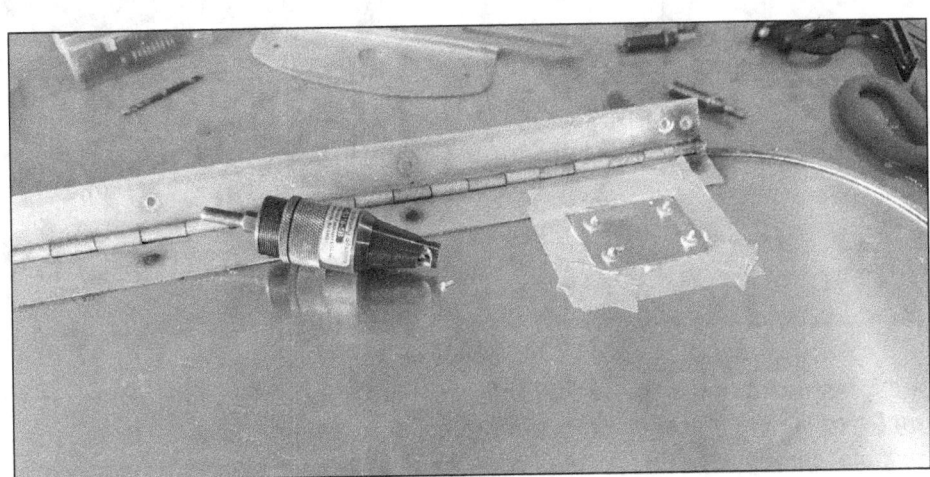

10 Sometimes it is impossible to access the back of the rivet for successful bucking. Shaveable rivets achieve the bucked-rivet look with blind-rivet convenience. The mandrel breaks off above the head of the rivet and a drill micro-stop with a profiled bit cleans the head.

11 The tape placed over the rivet head helps protect the patch from the micro-stop marring the surface. The recommended drill speed is fast, and the bit needs to be turning before it hits the mandrel to prevent walking.

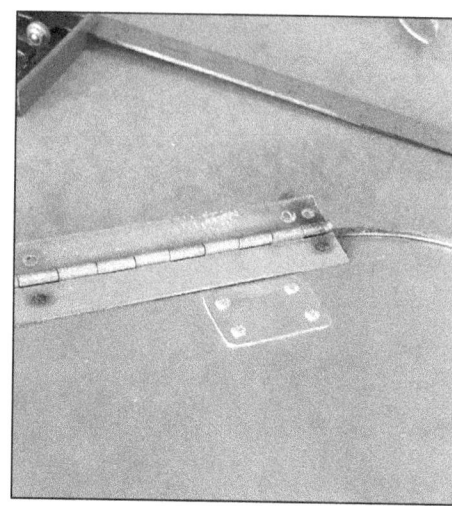

12 Here's the completed patch installed with shaveable rivets.

Panel Replacement

Often, you have to replace whole panels because damage is too great to fix. This process is similar to patching panels; you use lap joints, polyurethane sealant, and buck rivets to install new panels.

This helps prevent jumping off the head and avoids setting a rivet above the panel. Working with lap joints and polyurethane sealants can be messy. It's a good idea to keep a cleaner such as isopropyl alcohol handy and to use protective gloves. To prevent damage to existing panels, use masking tape where handling panels could cause scratches. Another good use for masking tape is to provide a clean edge. Tape off where you do not want sealant to run, and then wipe off all excess before removing the tape for a clean, straight edge.

On polished surfaces, avoid using coarse rags, as they're abrasive and leave micro scratches. Sometimes it's easier to let sealant dry before removing the excess.

In addition to replacing flat panels, an Airstream's rounded front and rear profile and the shaped panels from manufacturers such as Boles Aero and Barth are the most difficult to replicate and/or replace. In the case of Airstream panels with compound curves, the upper portions are very difficult to replicate. If your project has damaged upper panels, you should plan to replace them with factory-reproduced units.

One of the most common areas for damage is the lower front panels, where road debris and rocks are thrown up by tires. You see plenty of pockmarks on most vintage Airstreams in this area, and in extreme cases, you may find completely ruined panels from a jackknife.

Although factory replacement panels are available for direct replacement, these panels have less of a compound curve, so it is possible to replace a severely damaged one with flat stock. It takes some wrangling of the aluminum to position it around the curved top, bottom, and sides . . . and the results might not be up to

The difference between original and new aluminum is pretty obvious in this light. The new panel has a slightly yellow tint to it that is close to impossible to match to the original skin, even with extensive polishing, due to the difference in metal composition and production techniques between the 1950s and today.

BODY

Once the dents and dings from a half-century of road damage are addressed, and all holes are patched or plugged, it's time to start prepping for electrical and insulation. A final step to ensure watertightness is to seal all interior seams and rivets with a smeared bead of polyurethane sealant.

factory fit and finish, but this panel's susceptibility to more damage could warrant a less-expensive alternative.

As you work your way around the body addressing any problem areas, look for missing rivets and random holes from past fixes. Using a shop light inside the shell when there's low light outside helps locate them.

Once the body is patched and any necessary panels have been replaced, make sure that no water can get inside the walls and cause future damage. From the interior, cover all seams and rivets with a layer of polyurethane sealant. A thorough job here helps prevent subfloor rot and mold in the future.

Replacing Full Panels

1 *Boles Aero shut down its factory decades ago, and finding original replacement panels is close to impossible. However, a quality metal shop or RV repair center can use a roller and/or break to recreate long-defunct panel patterns on many campers, such as Silver Streak or Barth.*

2 *The process for replacing these panels is the same lapped construction used throughout this chapter. To get the Boles Aero's mesas and valleys to sit flush, a rivet needs to be placed in the valley and on each edge of the mesa.*

STREAMLINE ALUMINUM TRAILERS: RESTORATION AND MODIFICATION

3 The front endcap lower panels of campers always see plenty of damage from the tow vehicle kicking up debris (one reason that side-panel rock guards are a popular option on contemporary Airstreams). Large mud flaps are also good preventive maintenance to avoid damage in this area if you do not want to add side-panel rock guards. This area is also prone to damage from jackknifing.

4 Once the old panels are removed, you can see the aluminum ribs and rotted subfloor left behind. The lower panels are compound curves but less than the extreme ones found at the side and top. This means that you can use flat stock to replace these lower side panels to save substantial money over factory replacements.

5 The replacement panel is trimmed to the longer upper horizontal and front vertical lengths. The panel is placed to lap under the corresponding panels. You can then walk it around the lower horizontal line, letting the excess material hang down, and then trim it off.

6 The curve for these panels is slightly compound and is fairly easy to replace. The upper endcap panels, however, are more extreme compound curves and are harder to replicate, but new ones are available from suppliers.

BODY

Locker Restoration

To restore the lockers, I stripped the paint and sanded them using the process covered in Chapter 13. Any screw or unused rivet holes were filled with a rivet or covered using a patch fabricated from aluminum harvested from the replaced side panel. After the panels were repaired, they were polished to a mirror finish.

It's hard to believe that residing under those ugly duckling lockers were the showpieces now installed in the Cruisette. An interesting note, instead of sanding off all the paint, on one interior wall I retained some layered paint and clear coated over it to highlight the little camper's colorful history.

Overhead Locker Repair

1 The process to restore this Airstream Cruisette's overhead storage lockers mimics that of a full-scale panel restoration and is a good starting point for a novice looking to develop aluminum fabrication skills.

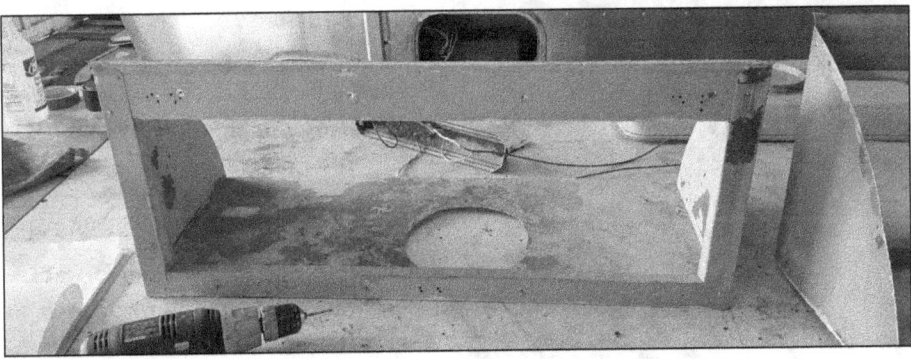

2 Begin by disassembling the lockers. Find any sheet-metal screws and rivets used to hold them together, and take note of their location for reassembly. Deburr any holes and hammer them flat. This helps save sandpaper and prevent cuts when handling the pieces.

3 Using aircraft stripper, the layers of paint begin to fall off. It's a good idea to use coarse sandpaper to scratch up the old paint and increase the surface area for the stripper to penetrate. If it's dry and hot outside, you can place plastic sheeting over the stripper to help prevent it from drying too quickly and allow it to penetrate further.

4 With the panel stripped (the inside bottom is covered with a false panel to hide wiring for the flush-mounted puck lights) and sanded to a coarse 150 grit, it's time to start patching and filling holes as necessary. Small, unused screw and rivet holes are filled with rivets, while larger holes are covered with small patches from original, vintage Airstream aluminum.

5 After the patches are installed and the holes are filled, the polishing process begins. Starting with a coarse sandpaper, and working up to a superfine paper in small increments, the lockers are prepped for polishing. Here, you can see the finished product installed on the original, restored cabinet doors. To keep some history intact, I clear coated over the sanded layers on the lockers' interior sides. Also note the false bottom installed here.

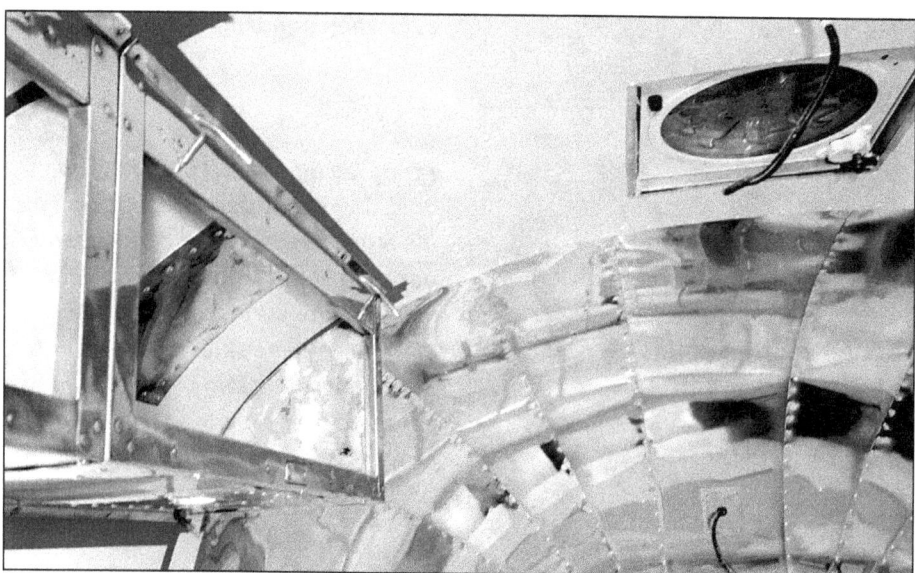

6 Here, on the finished lockers, note the large bottom patch with a flush-mounted puck light and the patch on the interior wall. This is where the old stove vented to the outside. Also worth pointing out is the polished endcap. This is the original one that was covered in paint. It went through the same process as these lockers to restore the aluminum.

CHAPTER 6

DOORS AND WINDOWS

There are many mechanical components on a vintage camper that open and close. And each of them probably needs restoration. Within each window or door are more mechanical components such as latches, levers, and locks.

The restoration of doors and windows includes dismantling them, removing old insulation, and reassembling them with new or restored components. The Cruisette had one luggage door located at the rear and, of course, the iconic Airstream has a "door in a door." Some vintage campers have two doors, a rear and a front, which can make restoration easier as you learn the mechanisms of one and apply that to the next.

Likewise, larger units can have multiple storage doors, appliance access doors, and utility doors. Typically these have similar hinges and latches. If you don't plan to use them due to an updated water heater or other reason, you can patch the exterior body (see Chapter 5) and use the old door's hardware to restore a damaged luggage door.

Main Door Disassembly

Before I address access doors or windows, the Cruisette's main door needed a full restoration. This is like a miniature riveted-camper restoration, in that it has many buck rivets and screws but smaller panels. The original door handle was long gone, so instead of sourcing an original unit, I installed a polished chrome entrance lock from Vintage Trailer Supply.

Before removing the door, take photos and note which fasteners are used and their location. When manufactured, this Cruisette's door used both 1/8-inch brazier rivets and slotted machine screws. You can see the sheet-metal screws used on the drip rail above the door, in the door, and on the hinge, where buck riveting would be impossible.

CHAPTER 6

The "door in a door" is mounted to the hinge in a fashion similar to the outer door, with rivets where a bucking bar cannot be used and slotted sheet-metal screws where there is no access to the backside. The Cruisette's original door handle was long gone, but the original dead bolt remained. Also, note the damage from a swivel-hinge hasp lock. This panel will be replaced with salvage aluminum from the non-curbside panel.

To remove a door, often a C-clip retains the hinge pin. Usually it's in the gap located under the two upper rings. This hinge did not have one installed; instead, the 1/4-inch pin is bent at the top to keep it from falling through and it can be removed by using a punch and hammer. The pins are commonly worn out (and available from many suppliers) and contribute to a sagging door. I removed the whole hinge for plating at a local shop.

After the door is removed, move it to a workstation for further disassembly. To prevent damage, place carpet or other soft material on the work surface. The original dead bolt is held in with two machine screws on the inside; the screen is held on with sheet-metal screws on the inside of the door.

Be sure to document the order of disassembly. These hinges can only go back together one way to function properly, and they need to be placed in the same locations.

The dead bolt, on the other hand, was still intact but missing its key. I removed it and took the unit to a locksmith, who was able to provide a set of keys. The shop also disassembled the mechanism and made sure the tumblers and springs were in good shape and properly lubed.

Once all the door's components, including the door-in-a-door casement latches, are removed, it's time to pull out the old screen. It is captured by slotted screws around the perimeter. If you haven't perfected your old-school screw technique, you'll have it dialed-in by the end of your work on a 1950s Airstream door.

Yes, slotted screws require quite a bit of patience and finesse if you're used to the speed and convenience of Phillips-head screws. And it can be risky business around aluminum sheet metal. The possibility for a slipped driver gouging the exterior, creating more work to fix, is real. However, using a driver with a good, proper-size head, a steady hand, and correct predrilling on assembly ensures that things go scratch-free.

With the screen removed, you can focus on removing rivets to expose the door's interior and old insulation. This job requires the proper respirator and gloves to avoid contact with fiberglass insulation.

As with the shell of the Cruisette, I plan to insulate this door with closed-cell spray foam. Conveniently, the heavily damaged panel that required replacement opened up a significant portion of the door. Also, note the way the rubber seal is attached to the door at this time. On the Cruisette, it was lapped between the interior and exterior portions of the door.

A replacement rubber seal is readily available from Vintage Trailer

DOORS AND WINDOWS

Supply along with any additional hardware such as screws and latches. To fabricate the door panel, I used the old one as a template over the salvaged stock, cut down to a manageable size.

The doorknob holes needed to be adjusted for the new unit, but the dead bolt and all fastener holes easily transferred. To create the lip on the new panel, I simply used my 6-foot brake and made a slight bend. A bead roller could also be used to create this part. As with any project, there are many ways to come to the same result. I did not have a shear at this time, so I took the old, salvaged panel to a local fabrication shop to make the cuts.

Typical with any restoration, there's often more work lurking behind closed doors. I ran into additional damage in the form of heavily oxidized aluminum and a hole in the door's exterior skin under the hinge. This could lead to a major issue if it continues to spread and could compromise the mounting of the hinge.

To keep it from spreading, I removed the oxidation with a wire brush, as this isn't a visible area. To prevent damage on the exposed exterior aluminum, I taped off the work zone and used a careful hand. I then coated the cleaned aluminum with primer and sealed the hole with a patch.

Main Door Reassembly

Reassembly begins after all door cosmetics and structural issues are addressed and it's been sufficiently

While waiting for the replacement 1/4-inch hinge pins from Airstream Supply, I had the original pieces nickel plated at a local metal-finishing shop. You can source new hinges as well if yours are too far gone. By reusing these, I've simplified mounting the door, as all the proper holes exist to line it up.

Here you can see what lies inside a vintage Airstream door: more of the same insulation as inside the wall panels. This requires a thorough cleaning to prep for spray-foam insulation.

With any restoration job, you may find surprises as pieces are removed. Here I found lots of oxidation and a hole under the lower hinge. This was fixed by removing the oxidation and placing a sealed patch under the restored hinge to preserve the original aluminum.

Once the door is insulated and reassembled using appropriate fasteners, a new piece of screen is cut to fit. Here you can see masking tape used to mark the new doorknob hole. The screen is placed under the interior door skin and held in place with sheet-metal screws. Also, you can see the new door gasket.

insulated. Because a door is smaller than full-size panels and easier to handle by one person, it is a good project to dial-in your buck riveting and Cleco fastener skills. Retaining the door's original shape is paramount, as you do not want it to deform during reassembly.

Start riveting from the top or bottom and work your way toward the other end in an even left-right pattern, with the door's natural curve supported with scrap wood covered in carpet to avoid cosmetic damage. If you run a line of rivets up one side individually, and if the door is not properly supported, you create uneven tension and the door is not the correct shape and does not fit correctly.

The process for assembling the main door is similar to that of assembling a smaller door and the endcap.

In addition to missing the main doorknob, the Cruisette was missing one of the casement latches that hold the door-in-a-door closed. Rather than source a hard-to-find original, I was able to find a suitable replacement at Restoration Hardware. It closely matched the original in both size and finish, and was not worn out from the vibrations of towing. Typically these have a gouge, which leads to failure and is why they are difficult to find in good shape. That is why remanufactured examples are as good as original replacements.

When the hinges are finished at the plater, it's time to hang the door. Because I was able to retain the original holes, squaring-up the door was pretty straightforward. However, if you do not have original holes, the process is much more difficult. It's best to take your time and have a helper. Use a 1/8-inch drill and Cleco fasteners to set the door in place, but do not drill all holes at once.

It's best to drill and fasten a couple of mounting holes, and then check the door for closing fit. If something is awry, you can make adjustments by drilling a different hole. And, when it's time to install the rivets, you can use an oversize 5/32-inch one in the holes that were off.

I ran into another issue with the door strike. Over the years, the Cruisette has had a few hardware store doorknobs hacked into it.

This left minimal material at the location for the strike. I decided to fabricate a new strike that would give the door better security and peace of mind when closed and traveling. I used a piece of 1/8-inch aluminum and marked the needed shape on some tape. Then using a drill, jigsaw, and file, I cut the piece to shape.

Creating a New Door Strike

1 Here you can see the replacement door strike in position. Unfortunately, the lower rivet has very little material to grab. Rather than retain this unsatisfactory mounting, I opted to make a piece to reinforce the door jam and give it the strength needed for decades of roadway travel.

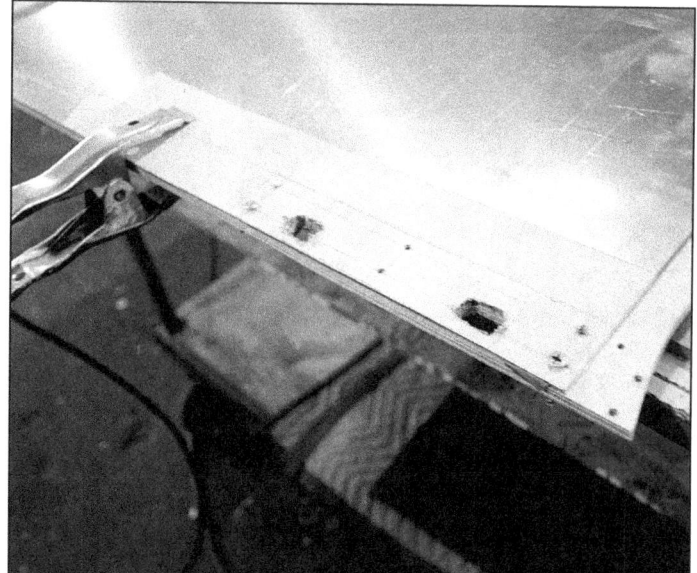

2 To fabricate a reinforcement for the door jam, I used a piece of 1/8-inch aluminum scrap and marked the shape on some masking tape. Note the piece of sacrificial plywood, held in place with grabber screws in the mounting holes. This helps reduce chatter when using a jigsaw with a metal blade.

DOORS AND WINDOWS

3 Using a hand file, the edges are cleaned up. The corners that protrude are rounded to avoid snagging loose clothing when entering or exiting. The brace extends to cover both the dead bolt and door latch to provide sufficient strength and mounting locations of the door strike plate.

4 You can see the plated hinge, restored dead bolt, replaced panel (note the three rivets filling the holes from the non-original locking latch), and new doorknob. Every trailer is slightly different, and to install this particular doorknob, I needed to add a spacer; it's the ring around the outer edge of the knob. This was fabricated using a couple of large hole saws on a drill press.

5 On the inside of the door you can see the replacement casement latches for the door in a door. These were sourced from Restoration Hardware. The first couple of latches I tried were too bulky and out of place on a vintage camper. I used period-correct screws to mount the latches, instead of the modern hardware that came with them.

6 After a final polish, the door makes this camper feel completed. As one of the highest traffic areas of your restoration, it's best to avoid any shortcuts here. This photo is from the Cruisette's maiden voyage.

Baggage Door Restoration

If a main-door restoration seems a bit ambitious, starting on a smaller door might be best. Every camper has luggage and utility doors that need restoration. The Cruisette, like most Airstreams, including contemporary ones, has a rear-access hatch. This is a good place to start disassembly and focus on the restoration practices explained throughout this book.

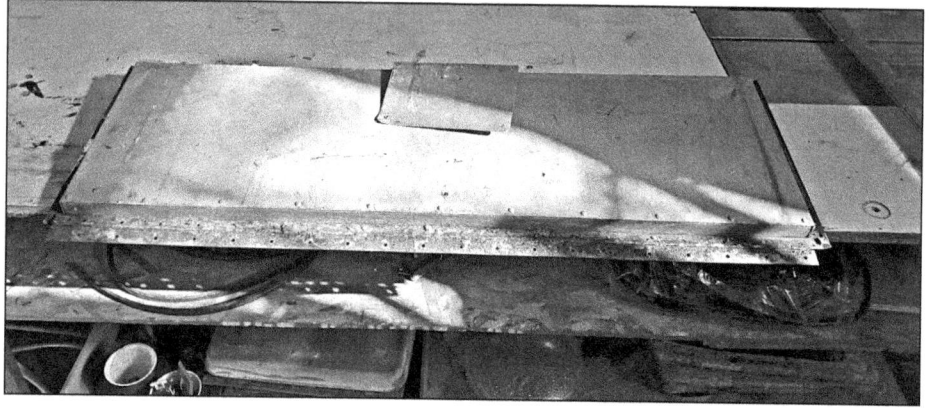

Dry-rotted seals, corroded hinge, and old insulation all need to be addressed on this luggage door. The seal, sourced from vintagecampersupply.com, is the same rivet-on gasket used on the main door.

The process to restore this baggage door mimics that of a full camper restoration; just on a smaller scale.

Restoring a Baggage Door

1 This 1970s Airstream rear hatch door was held shut with duct tape because the original telescoping locks were gutted by a previous owner for whatever reason. That same owner may have also been responsible for drilling a hole through the lower left of the baggage door. A large portion of restoration is undoing other people's quick fixes.

2 On the backside, the original vinyl-coated aluminum is covered in the usual sticky slime. The gasket (another standard 1970s Airstream door seal) is completely dry rotted and useless. Also note that someone added another location for wires to power the license-plate light.

DOORS AND WINDOWS

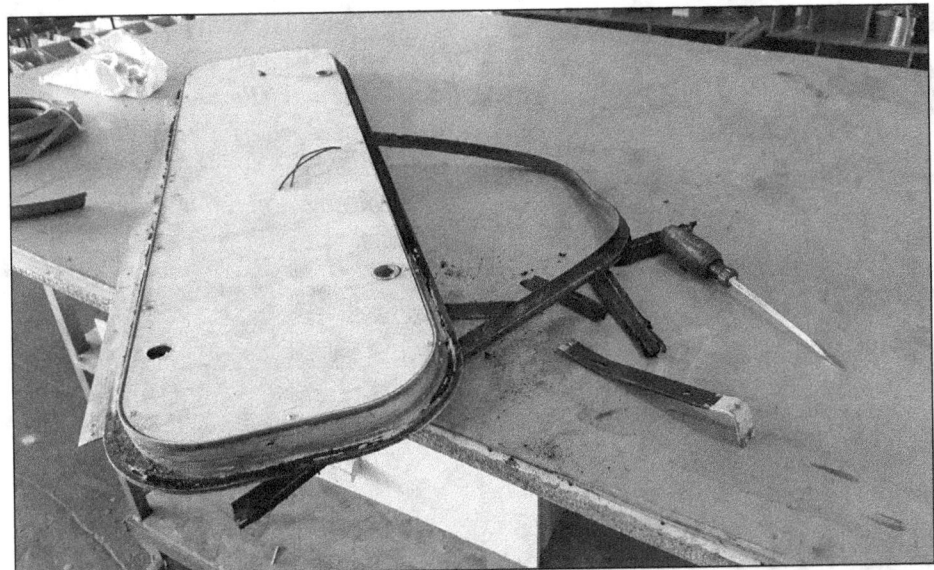

3 This restoration begins with the removal of the old door gasket. A small, sharpened pry bar and old screwdriver make quick work of the crusty rubber. Be sure to use a protective covering on your work space if you prefer not to mar any surfaces. Some clamps help hold the piece in place.

4 Using an aggressive abrasive helps remove all the remaining adhesives and rubber. I opted for a wire wheel mounted to a drill. Ensuring that the surface is properly cleaned guarantees a secure door seal when it comes time for installation.

5 To strip the tape adhesive, I used a gentle solvent and microfiber cloths to avoid damaging the clear coat.

CHAPTER 6

6 Now that most of the dirty work is done, you should clean the door. A stiff-bristle brush and degreaser such as Simple Green cuts through the sticky grime on the original vinyl and removes any solvent residue.

7 Inside of every door and panel on an old camper you often find toxins and molds. To gain access to the inside of this door, drill out the pop rivets with a 1/8-inch drill bit.

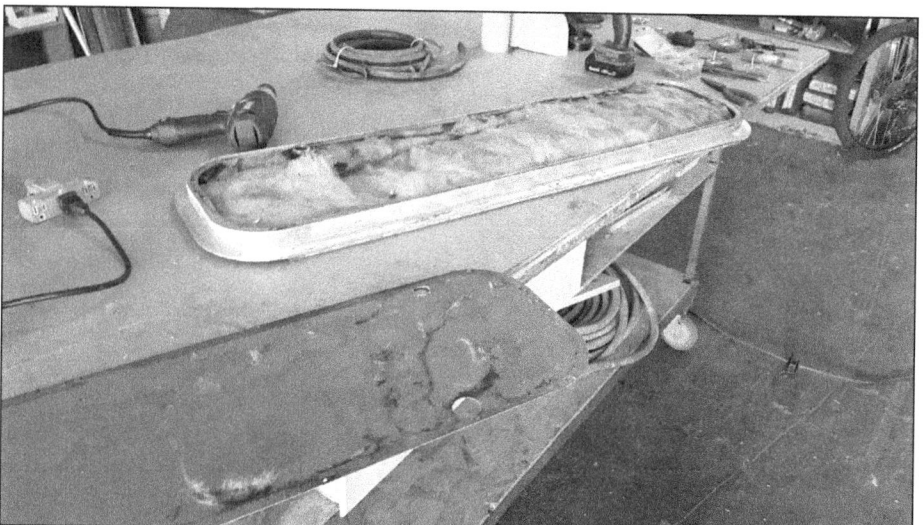

8 Once the skin is off, it's time to deal with mold and fiberglass. Dispose of the fiberglass and return the door to the washbasin for another round of scrubbing and degreasing. Here, you can see the black mold around the seam and door latches.

DOORS AND WINDOWS

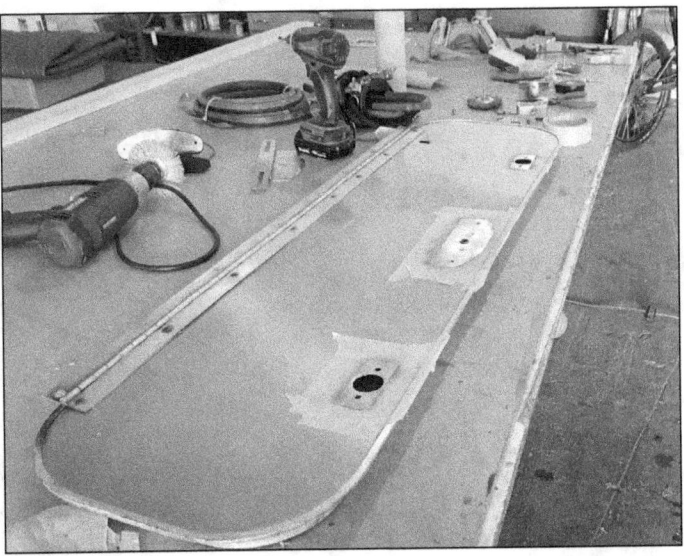

9 This baggage door is located under the bed in this particular Airstream. It's best to make sure there's no mold in such an important area. A proper restoration should include looking at any area where mold can develop and addressing any issues.

10 To prepare the latch and license-plate holder/light for installation, I taped off the surrounding area and used a less-aggressive wire wheel (note the orange color) to lightly scuff the surface and remove any old sealants. You don't want to cut through the tape but want a clean, oxidation-free surface.

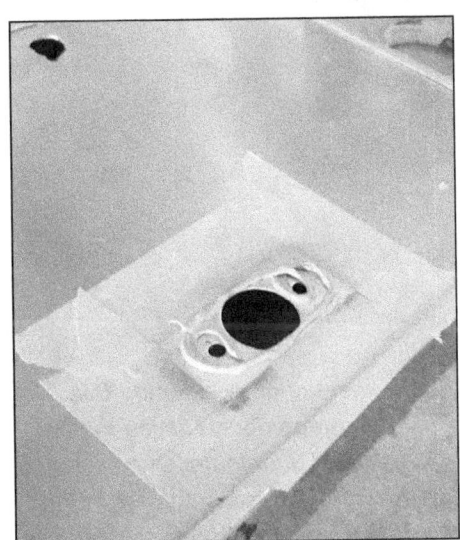

12 To cover the holes in the inner and outer skin, I cut pieces of scrap 5052 to size or plugged them with rivets. Using a combination square makes quick work of marking the patch for cutting and holes.

11 Before installing the new Airstream original-equipment telescoping latches, apply a layer of polyurethane sealant to the cleaned surface (use a fast-evaporating solvent on both the latch and skin). Leaving the tape in place helps with sealant cleanup. Once the latch is fastened and the access sealant squeezed out, pull the tape to avoid smearing the sealant.

13 With the latch and patch in place, the door is ready for insulation. Before replacing the interior skin, I insulated the door with closed-cell spray foam sourced from a local distributor.

STREAMLINE ALUMINUM TRAILERS: RESTORATION AND MODIFICATION

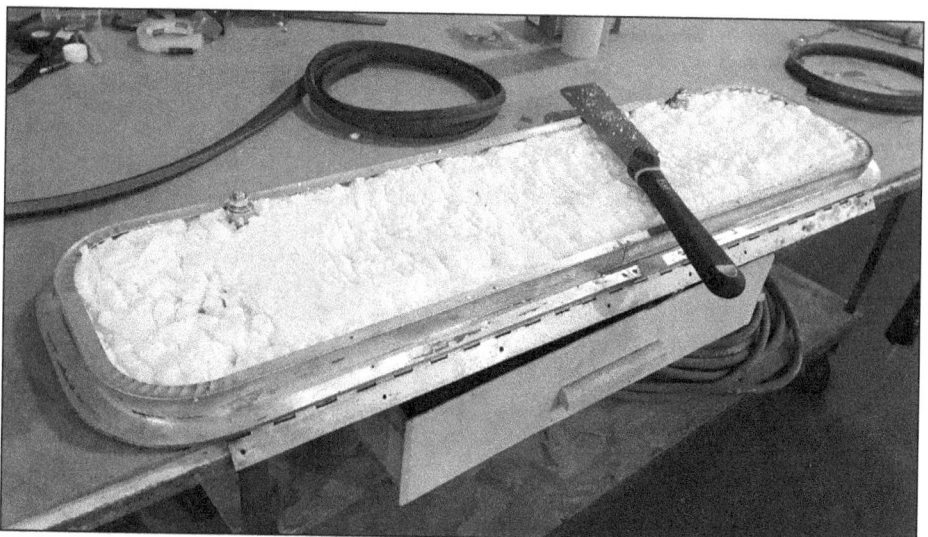

14 Once the insulation cured, a pull saw easily cut excessive insulation away. The new door seal is ready for installation. Be sure to clean the adhesive surfaces with a quick-dry solvent before taping it down. It's also good practice to compress the gasket as you install it because rubber always shrinks, and this helps prevent it from failing.

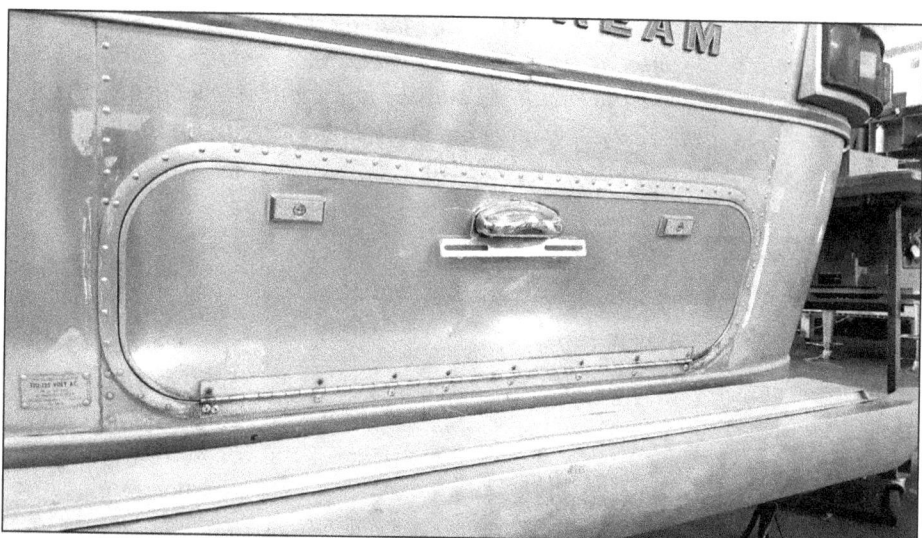

15 The completed baggage door is installed. You can still see the tape adhesive on the shell, which will be cleaned off when the clear coat is stripped and this camper is polished.

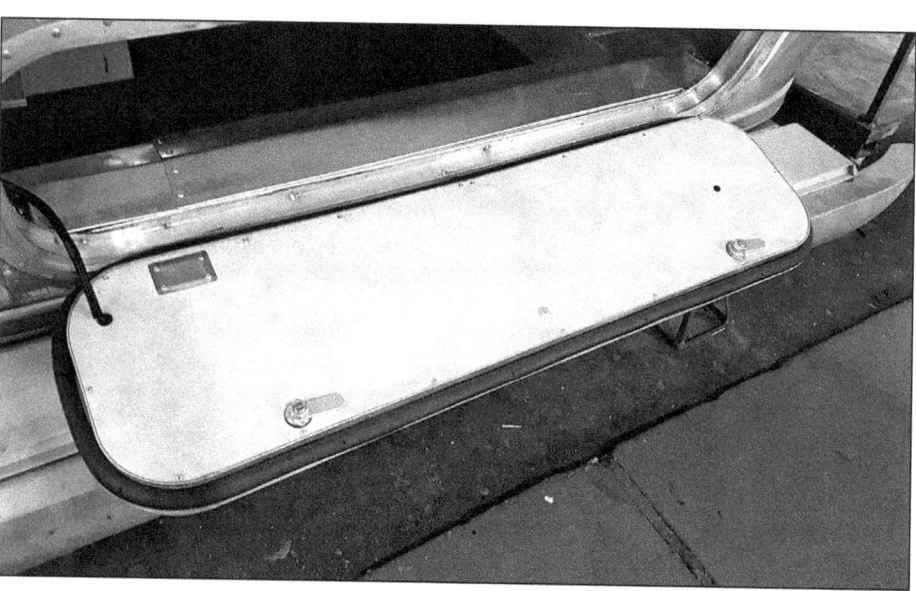

16 Instead of re-skinning this luggage door, I saved the old vinyl-coated aluminum. Once cleaned up, it was satisfactory for use in this seldom-seen area. Here, you can see the patch covering a hole for an extension cord, the new door seal, and the power wire for the license-plate light.

17 *When you insert and turn the key, the latch's handle pops out so you can to open the luggage door. This is what makes these latches "telescoping."*

Window Restoration

Another major restoration undertaking is the windows. I like to compare each window to the mechanical equivalent of a basic bicycle. Once you figure out the necessities to rebuild one window, the rest becomes fairly straightforward. By the time you've finished the last one, you'll have window mechanics dialed in.

Nearly every window has some variation of levers, slides, and gaskets to address. Hehr is the most common window manufacturer found on vintage campers. Late-model and modern Airstreams feature Airstream proprietary windows. Most parts are easily attainable for both Airstream and vintage Hehr windows.

Many vintage campers have Jalousie-style windows, which are composed of parallel glass louvers set in a frame. The louvers are joined in a sliding track that allows them to tilt open and closed in unison. The individual panes are fairly easy to replace, as is most vintage camper glass. It usually involves cutting out any adhesive or sealant, removing any retaining hardware, and gently removing the old glass.

A local glass specialist can cut any size of replacement pane and can

The Hehr windows on the Cruisette are tucked under the upper skin to help shed moisture. Once all the fastening rivets are removed, the window is gently pried and cut away from sealant holding the window in place. It's much easier to work on windows on a bench than to work on them still installed.

This Silver Streak has Jalousie windows, which use a sliding track to open and close the parallel glass panes. Restoration requires disassembly, removing and replacing old gaskets, and servicing the sliding mechanism. Each window on a vintage camper can easily take three to six hours of work, depending on your restoration goals.

CHAPTER 6

The Jalousie window on this 1950s Flying Cloud has a missing pane. Replacement glass is easy to cut with a kit available at any hardware store. The panes simply slide into the aluminum sleeves and are retained with small tabs. You can see the pane above the missing one is slightly coming out of its location. You could remove this pane to match the cuts for the bottom pane replacement.

temper it for increased strength (not a bad idea on front windows, which are susceptible to road rocks). If replacing the glass proves to be problematic, you can use an acrylic alternative, but it yellows as the camper ages.

In almost every camper restoration, you find that rubber gaskets have dried and shrunk over the years. Luckily, almost all types of rubber gaskets are being reproduced by vintage camper suppliers. If you have one that's difficult to find, you may have luck locating a distributor interested in adding your gasket to its production run.

If you've had no luck finding the correct gasket, sometimes you can find a suitable alternative. Refrigeration repair specialists can help point you to a local custom gasket manufacturer if the Internet is coming up short. They produce gaskets for thousands of purposes. And worst case, you can use a sealant such as Lexel or Sikaflex to create a gasket.

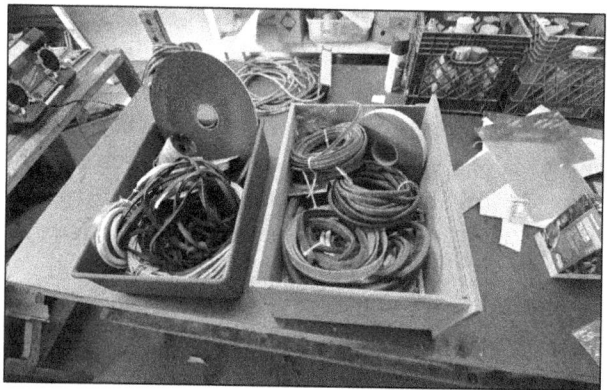

Hundreds of gaskets have been used by camper manufacturers throughout the years. Thankfully, many suppliers, such as Vintage-campersupply.com, stock many varieties of vintage Hehr and Airstream windows.

Restoring a Window

1 This 1970s Airstream window needs its poor tint job removed and its rubber seal is guaranteed to be dried out and compromised. Also its sliding mechanism needs to be cleaned and lubed for ease of use.

2 On this Airstream window, two screws on the lever mechanism hold it in place. Once these are removed, the slides fall out and you can separate the levers from the window. This involves slightly bending the window frame to clear the pins used to set the window's opening.

DOORS AND WINDOWS

3 Here you can see the screws used to hold the lever. Note the bearing at the base of the screw; it's important that you do not lose this piece, as it's crucial to the window's operation. Also visible here is the set pin used to adjust the window's openness.

4 After the screws are removed, the window needs to be lifted and released from this channel in the window frame.

5 If you lift the window above the locking point of the channel, it drops out. Take care when removing and installing to avoid deforming the locking channel. And be ready for the window to fall out, to avoid dropping it on the floor.

6 This is the channel that retains the window in the frame and allows the window to open. You can see a buck rivet lifting. This loose rivet causes binding and leaks. Once the old gasket is removed, this rivet and any other loose ones need to be reset.

7 Here, the gasket and residue from adhesives is removed, and the frame is polished before a new gasket is installed. Note the grabber screws and wood blocking used to keep the window stationary to avoid damage and assist with scraping and sanding.

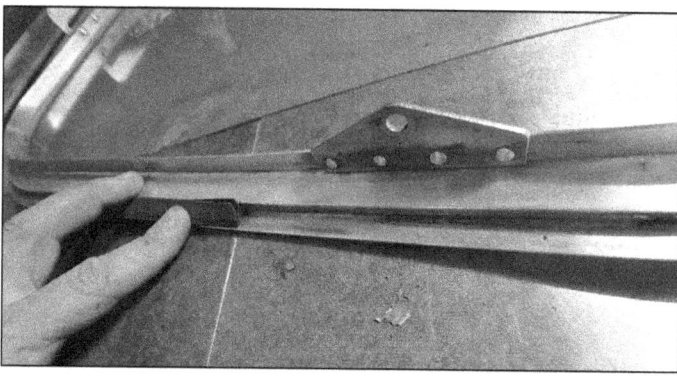

8 This style of gasket is held in place with 3M weather-strip adhesive (available at most automotive parts stores). When installing new rubber gaskets, be sure to compress the rubber and not to stretch it to avoid shrinkage as the rubber dries and ages.

9 Be sure to install the hook and channel at an angle sufficient enough to avoid binding and damage to either of these components. The underside of the hook and retaining clips prevent the window from moving fore or aft.

10 Once the lever is threaded through the window frame and the pin has found its home, you need to slide the window into its channel and install the screw at the bottom. This needs to be done on both sides. Care must be taken to not stress the windows too much, as one side is unsupported during this process.

All camper windows have to open and close, retain glass panes, and hold screens to keep bugs out. Typically a vintage camper has the same-style windows throughout, so restoration becomes easier as you work your way through the stack of windows.

The restoration process for all windows is pretty similar in concept, but each style presents its own challenges and solutions. The best course of action is to start on a non-curbside window, so any mistakes or lessons learned will be hidden on the less-visible side of the trailer.

Once you've figured out one window, the rest are much easier.

Rubber Gasket Replacement

When replacing rubber, be sure to avoid stretching it around its mounting surface. It's best to focus on slightly compressing the rubber to help avoid the inevitable shrinkage. Before any new gaskets can be installed, all surfaces must be prepped for good adhesion. Start by removing all old sealants and/or adhesives. Given the potential for past DIY fixes, you'll come across all kinds of stubborn substances used to repair windows throughout the years.

A good knife, razor blade, sanding discs, solvents, and medium wire wheels (such as those used to remove adhesives on the door gaskets) help cut through the old glues and sealants. Be sure to tape off any areas you want to avoid damaging and use some sort of soft covering such as old carpet, moving blankets, or towels on your work surface.

After the surface is cleared of any residue, be sure to clean it with a quick-drying solvent before installing new gaskets to ensure that there are no leftover oils that could affect adhesion.

Screen Replacement

Most contemporary campers use aluminum screen that's available at many hardware stores. Some vintage Hehr windows, however, use steel screens, which are a bit harder to find. This style of screen does not use a spline for installation.

Instead, it relies on a folded-over section, or crimp, of the steel screen to hold it in place. Aluminum screen can be used here, but it's much more difficult to work with and sometimes does not stay in place. You can find galvanized steel screen at vintage-trailersupply.com. When installing galvanized screens, it helps to clamp down the screw and work in the piece equally on both sides to avoid deforming the window frame. Replacing window screens takes practice to achieve good results and can be very frustrating when a simple slip-up may send you back to square one.

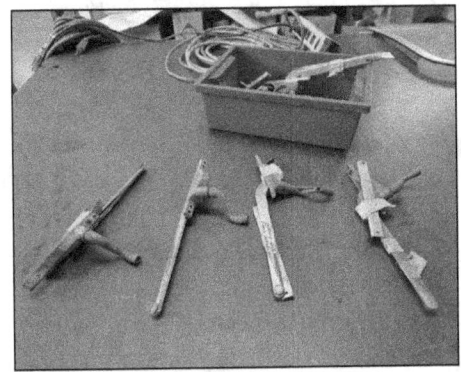

There can be many components to a window restoration. These actuation levers to a 1950s Flying Cloud each need attention to ensure smooth operation and visual appeal.

Window tools include good scrapers (with custom blades shaped and tuned on a grinder), wire wheels, and assorted abrasives. Also, screens use specialty splines (available in many diameters for various projects).

As stated earlier, many components to a camper take up space quickly. Here you can see what portion of a camper restoration is taken up by windows.

Replacing a Screen

1 The screen tools shown here are used to set a vinyl spline in a channel. One side is used to guide the spline in (concave), the other for shaping the screen. It's best to leave the screen oversized while installing it, then cutting off the excess.

Here you can see a screen's spline installed. The screen is captured inside the channel by the ribbed spline. A special tool is used to guild the spline in, then used to compress it, so that the screen is held in by friction.

2 Use clamps to hold the screen in place as you're working on it; this prevents the screen from shifting. Stabilizing the piece you're working on in a jig or clamping it onto a table helps make things go smoother. To protect polished or painted windows and doors, moving blankets or an equally soft and cushioning cloth works.

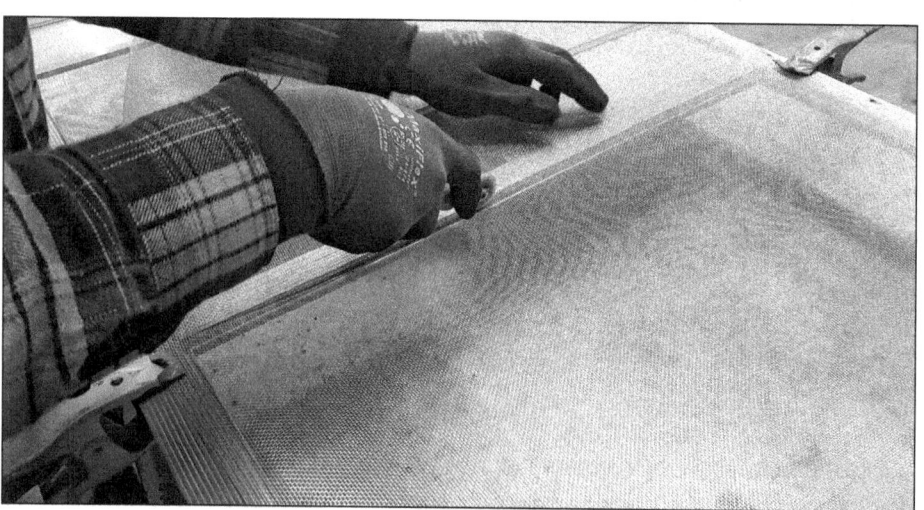

3 With the screen pulled snug, the rolling wheel with a convex side is used to form the screen to the channel. Start from one corner and, with short strokes in one direction, work the screen into the channel. Keep in mind that if the screen's tension is too tight, it will deform the window or door frame. It should be taut, but not overly stiff.

4 A good pair of gloves are recommended, particularly when cutting screen, as it produces many pinpoint ends that easily stick into skin and under fingernails. This screen's spline has been set on the straight part of the opening, as the upper portion is an arch. This anchors it and allows an even tension as the channel and spline are worked into the upper portion.

5 The vinyl spline is set in place with the concave-shaped roller. As you did with the shaping end, use short strokes in one direction. This is the part where things can go wrong: The wheel can jump off the track and ruin the screen. If that happens now, you're back at step one, cutting a new screen to size.

6 After the spline is set, the excess is cut off. At this point, the screen is nicely taut. Not moving quickly here is essential, as you do not want to make a careless mistake that will ruin the screen.

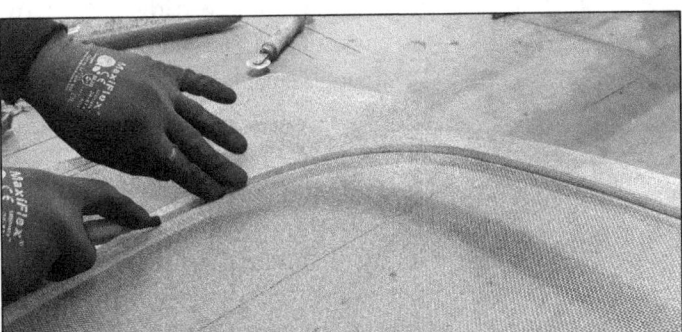
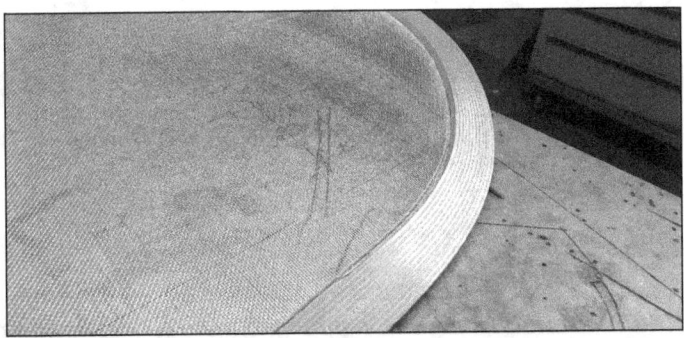

7 A quality utility knife is all that's needed to trim the extra screen. Sometimes it takes a couple of passes to cut all the mesh. It's important to be focused and use a steady hand to cut; a slip-up here could have you pulling out the screen and starting all over again.

8 Here, you can see the completed install. All the excess mesh has been cut and removed, and the screen has a nice tension throughout. A poorly installed screen has runs, waves, and excess material. This screen door is now ready to be reinstalled on a 1960s Airstream.

CHAPTER 7

ELECTRICAL SYSTEMS

The Cruisette is ready to receive the wiring for the electrical systems before the insulation is installed. In campers, there are two primary systems: house and chassis. The house system includes both 12- and 110-volt circuitry for appliances and lighting. The chassis system consists of trailer brakes and lights, including stop, turn, clearance, and sometimes a porch light.

Not surprising, the expanse of RV (and related boating) electrical concepts and practices is enough to fill a large book of its own. Before you make any major decisions about your electrical systems, it is best to do as much research as possible. Camper electrical systems are a topic well covered by many publications, including *Managing 12 Volts* by Harold Price and *RV Electrical Systems* by Bill and Jan Moeller.

Most important, operation, fitting, and maintenance of electrical systems are inherently dangerous. When in doubt, seek professional advice or services. In this chapter, I cover the electrical components installed in the Cruisette and give a general overview of batteries, charging, wiring, and vintage camper light restoration.

Volts and Circuits

The 12-volt direct-current circuits in all campers are intended for use free from shore or household power. The Cruisette's 12-volt components include lighting, stereo, fans, and TV. This build foregoes a water pump in favor of a single, aesthetically pleasing, vintage hand pump. And instead of a power-hungry fridge, the Cruisette uses a simple ice chest.

More complex 12-volt systems include a water pump, holding-tank monitors, a fridge, and much more. Most vintage campers after the mid-1950s have fairly simple 12-volt electrical systems. Prior to that, they were 6-volt-based arrangements, such as the automobiles of the time (this was pretty rare, as propane was a much easier source of heat and light). If your goal is a period-correct restoration for a late 1940s or early 1950s camper, you can restore the

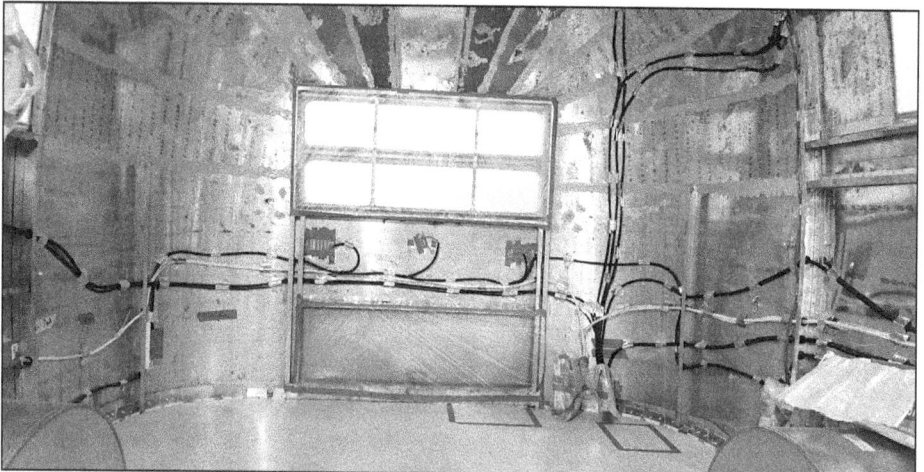

The Cruisette's wiring is run throughout the camper using plastic wire loom and foil tape to hold it in place. I plan to insulate this camper with spray foam, which helps secure the wires. Adhesive-backed plastic clips are also commonly used to guide wires on riveted campers. Here you can see two tape-outline boxes on the floor. One is for the battery location; the other is for the Progressive Dynamics distribution panel.

ELECTRICAL SYSTEMS

The box mounted on the front of this 1950s Airstream houses a battery. A common modification is to install a modern battery in another location (they're much bigger and wider) and to use the empty box as a planter.

You can tell that this is a 12-volt battery by counting the white caps. Each one is a set of lead plates in an electrolyte solution that produce one cell with about 2 volts. The Cruisette uses a modern 12-volt system that uses two 6-volt batteries wired in series.

The electrolyte solution in these cells has long since evaporated, rendering this old battery useless. All batteries require care to achieve the best performance; however, lead acid batteries such as this one necessitate the most maintenance and attention or you risk permanently damaging them.

Today, it's time to give up using these wires for anything other than scrap, as there's no telling what kind of hazards exist inside the walls. On most neglected vintage campers, it's best to update your wiring to modern standards, unless your goal is a complete period-correct restoration.

original outlets and light fixtures and rewire with reproduction cloth wiring (commonly available through classic car restoration outlets).

This Cruisette originally left the factory with one 12-volt light located in the center of the ceiling (these were often hastily wired through jagged holes cut in the exterior and interior skins without grommets). The lone light was run off the tow vehicle's battery. Pretty simple. The 110-volt shore-power system in the Cruisette powered the outlets and lighting, as was common on early 1950s campers. These were wired with Romex run through the walls between the skins.

Not-So-Safe Wiring

As hastily installed DC circuits, the AC wires were threaded through walls without due precaution, relying on the wire's sheathing to protect it from shorting. Add splices supported solely by loose insulation and you can understand why vintage camper wiring is not only dangerous, but temperamental, to say the least.

Camper manufacturers eventually started using grommets for passing wires through studs, guides to support loose wire, sealed splices, and looms to protect the wire. As technology expanded through the decades, along with the race to outdo competition, camper manufacturers continually added more electrical conveniences to the camper.

As expected, the increase in electrical devices and related circuits adds to the complexity and increases the chance for electrical gremlins in old campers. Many of these items, such as an eight-track player or built-in countertop blender, are obsolete. However, retaining such unique, period-correct items can differentiate your camper from the run-of-the-mill restoration.

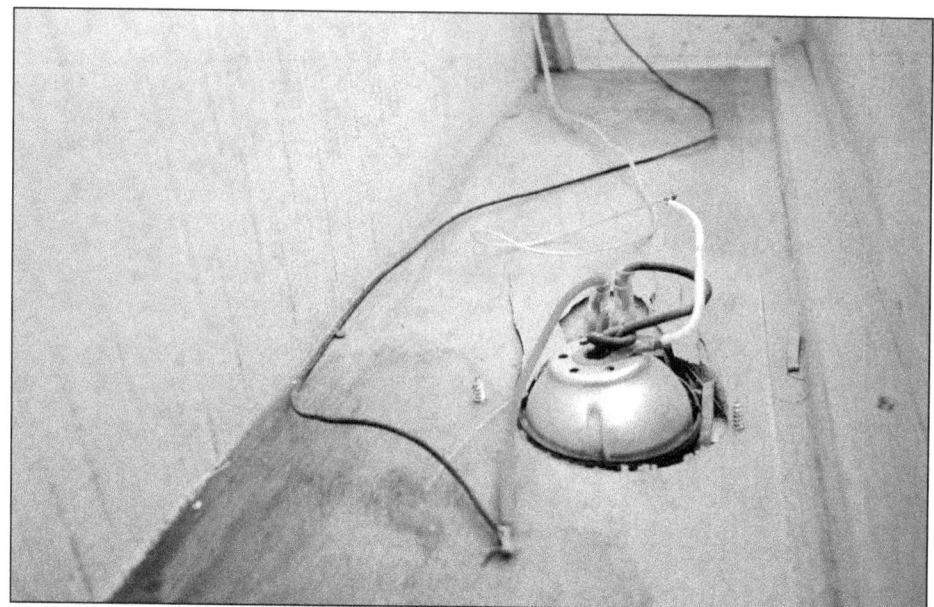

Exposed splices, loose wires, and plenty of potential to fray the sheathing by exposed screws and nails (note the nail lifting and rubbing on the power wire, a short just waiting to happen). This is a common sight for vintage campers that have had questionable, and sometimes dangerous, modifications or fixes through the years. Undoing these hasty and poor repairs is part of the restoration process.

This late-1960s power command center is a good example of vintage camper circuitry and the complexity you should expect to find. While restoring vintage electronics is possible (find an automotive dashboard restoration specialist or electrical engineer), sometimes it's best to just move forward and add modern electronic components. Here, you can see relays, 12-volt circuit breakers, and a vintage hand-printed circuit board. I wouldn't plan on too much still working reliably. The exposed wire and blue splices are just a few red flags.

ELECTRICAL SYSTEMS

A modern control center such as this one in an updated Airstream Sovereign provides electrical information such as battery charge level and solar charge information. It also contains tank level monitors, power switches for the instant water heater, and a thermostat.

Battery Choices

Many types of batteries are available to power your camper. Your choice comes down to many factors, such as storage capacity (measured by amp hours), maintenance, life expectancy, and cost. Location is another factor. If you're going to mount batteries inside, proper ventilation and battery type is essential. If you're mounting the battery outside, ventilation is less of an issue.

Lead Acid

Lead acid batteries are the most common and least expensive option. They are also dirty and maintenance intensive. Sulfuric acid can leak, and outgassing needs good ventilation or, best scenario, they should be stored outside of the camper.

These batteries are maintained by adding distilled water, which should be checked every few months. Battery acid is corrosive, so be sure to wear safety glasses and gloves, as it destroys clothing and burns skin. Maintaining a lead acid battery is not difficult or overly time-consuming but does require common knowledge and safety procedures. If you've worked with automotive batteries, an RV battery operation is very similar.

However, there is a significant difference between a deep-cycle marine or RV battery and an automotive one. A car battery is designed for a quick discharge and recharge, whereas an RV battery is intended for a longer load and extended charging. For comparison, a car battery is typically rated at 50 to 75 amp hours, with the ability to supply a high amperage for starting.

In comparison, deep-cycle batteries provide 200 to 400 amp hours of power. Lead acid batteries lose 10 percent of their capacity per month if not maintained. That can severely shorten their life expectancy, which is already half of an absorbed-glass-mat battery.

Absorbed Glass Mat

Absorbed-glass-mat (AGM) batteries, on the other hand, use a soaked fiberglass mat inside, rather than submerged lead plates to store electrical energy. These batteries require virtually no maintenance and are much longer lasting than a lead acid battery. On the minus side of the equation, these are significantly more expensive. AGM batteries do not disperse gasses when charging, so they're the best option for mounting inside a camper.

The life expectancy of an AGM battery typically falls between 8 and 10 years, and they only lose about 1 percent of capacity per month. In planning your battery choice, the initial cost of the batteries and the amount of work required are major deciding factors.

6- versus 12-Volt Batteries

There are several advantages in using two 6-volt golf-cart batteries over a typical 12-volt marine/RV for use in a camper. First, 6-volt batteries have a much longer life, as much as two times longer, than 12-volt batteries. This is a result of thicker plates that better withstand the effects of deep cycling.

Also, 6-volt batteries usually have more capacity than 12-volt batteries. Of course, there are disadvantages to using 6-volt batteries; you have to buy two batteries and connect them in series, which means they take up more space and they can weigh more.

On these two lead acid batteries, you can see the sulfuric acid weeping out of the cells, which is corrosive and dangerous if not handled properly. This style of battery is the least-expensive option, but the most maintenance intensive and has the lowest life expectancy.

On this large 1970s Airstream Overlander, electrical circuits (both AC and DC) are run through conduit to electrical boxes to protect the wires. This also allows new wire to be installed if something happens to the existing wires (a rogue screw will ruin your day if you happen to hit a wire buried in the walls or floor). To power small devices, such as local lighting or stove exhaust fans, wires are protected by loom once they leave the electrical box.

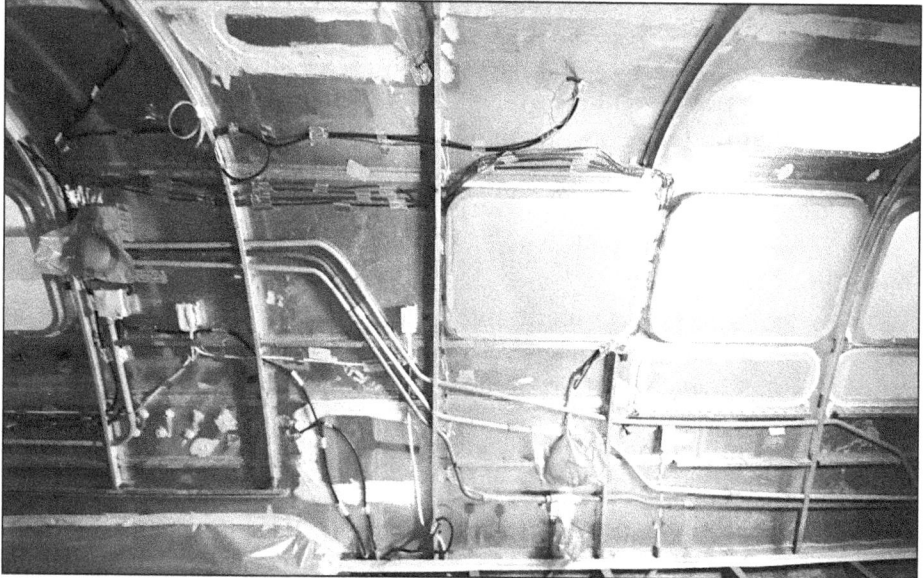

Mapping out the wiring can be a daunting task, and it often changes if you're building a custom interior. First, draft the electrical component locations and power sources in a CAD program to help lay out the wiring. Then, mark the walls with paint to indicate wire runs. You can see the variance of projected and actual location by the location of the conduit and the green and red paint. On a small restoration such as the Cruisette, this is much simpler.

Another important factor in a battery array is that if one 6-volt battery fails, the array is dead and your ability to power the camper is lost.

Because wires are often hidden from sight, upgrading to the current standards, or going beyond, is a good plan of attack for a restoration. For the Cruisette, I ran AWG (American Wire Gauge) 14- to 16-gauge wire in loom throughout the camper. Because I plan to use spray-foam insulation for the Cruisette, the wires are supported

Amp/Hour Calculations

Here is a quantification of this project's DC draw:

Component	Number	Amps	Hours	Amp/Hour
Fantastic Fans	2	3.00	4	24.00
Puck LED	6	.10	2	1.20
LED House	2	.32	2	1.28
LED Reading	2	.32	2	1.28
Stereo	1	21.00	4	84.00
DC TV	1	5.00	2	10.00
LP Detector	1	.10	24	2.40
Daily Total				124.16

ELECTRICAL SYSTEMS

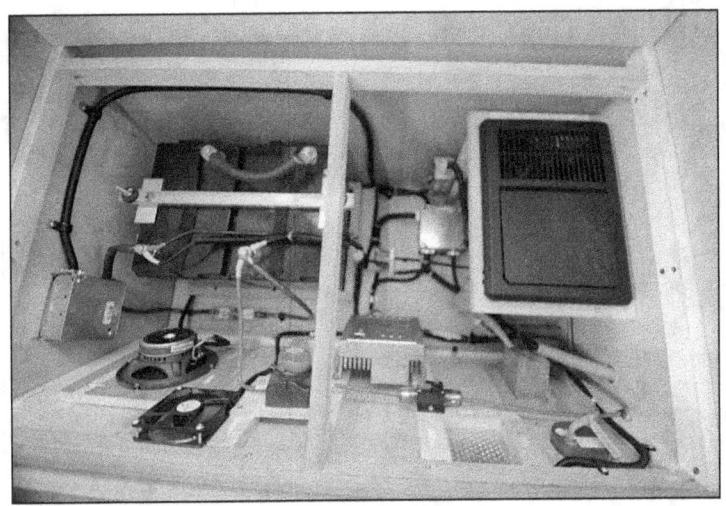

These two AGM 6-volt batteries, the same as used in the Cruisette, would provide enough power to run the Cruisette's DC electrical components for many days away from shore power. This electrical center, hidden under a dinette in a 1970s camper, also houses a Progressive Dynamics solar controller (the gray box with heat sinks) and a main power disconnect wired into a fused circuit breaker.

This settee hides a Dometic air conditioning unit designed to heat and cool truck cabs. Its relatively small size and efficiency make it a good option for travel trailers, too. The biggest selling point is that the air conditioning unit does not have to be mounted on top of the Cruisette, which would look out of place on such a small Airstream. Also visible here is the stereo and battery-level readout hidden in a cabinet.

against the interior of the exterior walls with adhesive wire clips and foil tape. The spray foam further helps secure the wires. On larger builds, I use conduit and electrical boxes to protect the wires and to enable easy replacement and upgrades.

If you take the time to calculate the total power requirements of your DC components, you can plan the necessary battery bank for your camper. For the Cruisette battery bank, I went with two 6-volt Full River batteries.

The formula for that is simple:

Number of Devices x Amps x Hours of Use = Amp Hours

Then add the amp hours for your estimated daily total.

They have a capacity of 225 amp hours each, for a total of 450 amp hours. Hypothetically, you could run the Cruisette off-grid for close to three or more days before requiring a charge.

Every camper has a different end use, and that plays a factor in designing the electrical system. The Cruisette's owners do not plan to use it for extended off-grid stays. When needed, they plan to use a small generator to top off the battery bank. The Cruisette will be plugged into shore power primarily.

The Cruisette uses six DC circuits. One powers the two fans and original overhead light (restored with a new switch and LED bulb). The second one powers the galley lights and reading lights. The third one is for the front sconce (LED house light). The fourth one powers the stereo. The fifth one powers the TV. And the sixth one runs the liquid propane/carbon monoxide (CO) detector.

110 Volts

On the 110 AC side of things, a Dometic self-contained VS7K air conditioner and galley outlets were all that was needed. Because the Cruisette will spend most of its time in a desert climate, air conditioning was a priority. While roof-mounted A/C units are the most common form of air conditioning, one of these on the tiny Cruisette would disrupt its classic lines.

Another option some people use is a standard household window-mounted air conditioner. These,

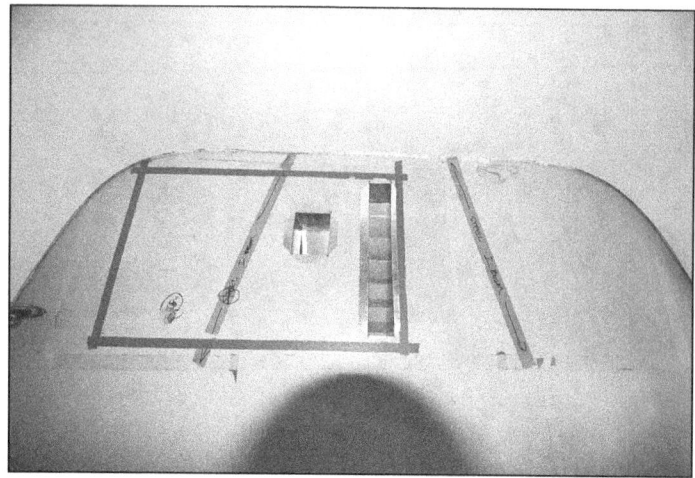

Custom fabricated vents were required for the Dometic air conditioning and heating unit. Mounting a window unit inside a camper is also common; however, they are not very efficient if improperly ventilated. The best options are either a rooftop-mounted A/C unit or a truck cab unit that's designed to be enclosed.

however, are not the best option because, similar to a roof-mounted unit, they need to protrude outside the camper to work efficiently. Without proper ventilation, the window-mounted units heat soak and are a poor source of cool air. Also, they can be very noisy.

For that reason, I went with a Dometic self-contained unit intended to cool big-rig cabs when not in motion. These run much quieter than the other two options, and although it needed special ven-

The Progressive Dynamics 4060 converter sits under the bed in this custom box and the batteries reside in the baggage compartment. You can see the red power wires running from the battery location to the Progressive Dynamics converter. Also the main power switch is located in the baggage compartment to shut the Cruisette down for long-term storage.

This empty Progressive Dynamics converter is ready for the appropriate AC circuit breakers and DC fuses. The circuit breakers and fuses are not included with the Progressive Dynamics unit but are available at any hardware store.

Here, you can see AC lines entering the electrical zone through boxes and conduit run in the floor. The Romex wires are connected to appropriate breakers inside the unit.

ELECTRICAL SYSTEMS

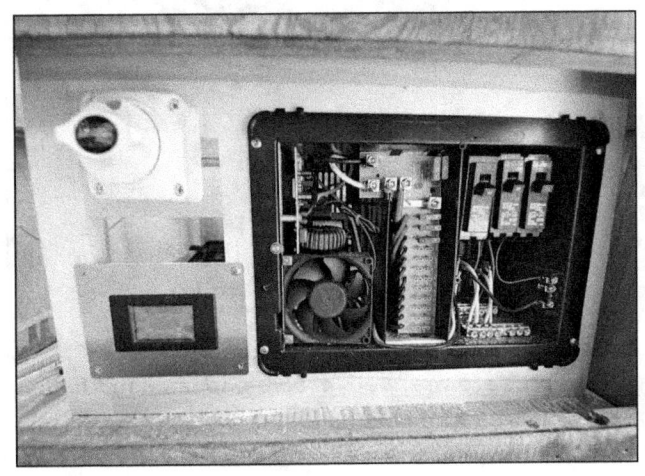

On this particular install, the Progressive Dynamics converter is wired for three AC circuits (one feeds the built-in battery charger from shore power), and three DC circuits. Having everything mounted in one tidy unit helps minimize the space and wiring needed for camper electronics.

tilation fabricated, the unit is completely hidden from sight.

To charge the battery bank and provide a fuse box and AC breaker box, I used a Progressive Dynamics 4060, which is a 60-amp converter and AC/DC distribution panel all in one unit. This saves space and wiring headaches by localizing everything.

On the AC side, three 15-amp circuit breakers protect the A/C circuit, galley outlet, and exterior outlet. A pretty simple setup compared to that for larger campers. For example, this Progressive Dynamics converter can handle 7 alternating-current circuits, and 12 direct-current circuits. It's perfect for adding plenty of electrical convenience to a camper.

Distribution Block

Sometimes it's easier to bring power to a certain location and use a fused distribution block to power devices such as a control panel, galley, or entertainment center.

The 12-volt wiring concept in a camper is the same as in boats and automobiles. Many of the products and techniques can be carried over, which leads to many possibilities. If you have experience with those vehicles, camper wiring is pretty straightforward. However, if you're not confident in your abilities, it's best to seek professional assistance.

Setting Up a Distribution Block

1 *An AWG 14-gauge wire coming from the distribution panel feeds this fused block. From there, AWG 16-gauge wire is used to power fans, lights, USB ports, etc. A power distribution block is nice to use because it reduces the amount of wire to complete a circuit away from a 12-volt power center. Rather than pull four or five wires to a location, one large wire is all that's needed.*

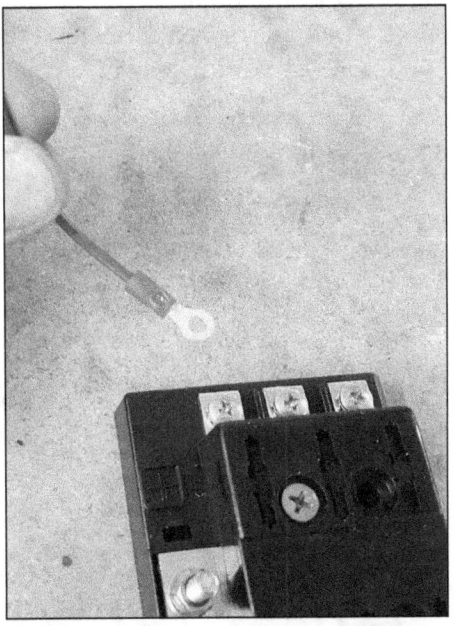

2 *Using 22-16 ring terminals and a crimper, the wire is attached to the block. This is a good crimp. It's best to tug on the wire to ensure that it can't be pulled out and has good purchase with the copper wire.*

3 *Once all the terminals are crimped and in place, heat-shrink tubing helps ensure the connections are protected from vibration and water intrusion, which causes the copper to deteriorate. Now the leads can be run and protected in loom.*

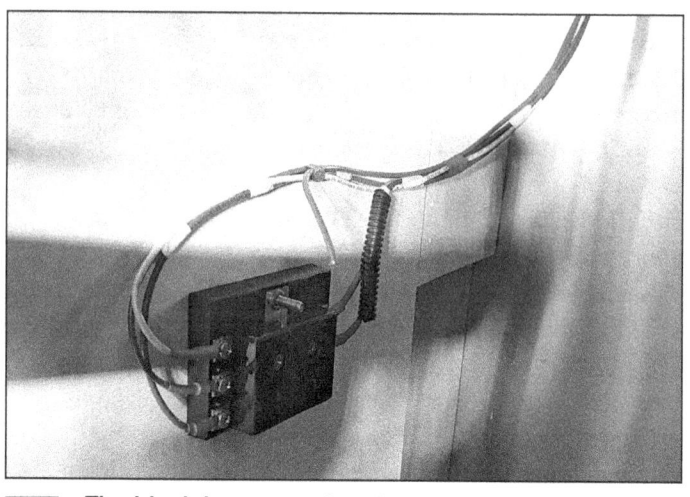

4 The block is mounted under a cabinet and the power lead is ready to be connected to the block. It's connected the same as the other wires except with a large-gauge ring terminal for the thicker wire coming in.

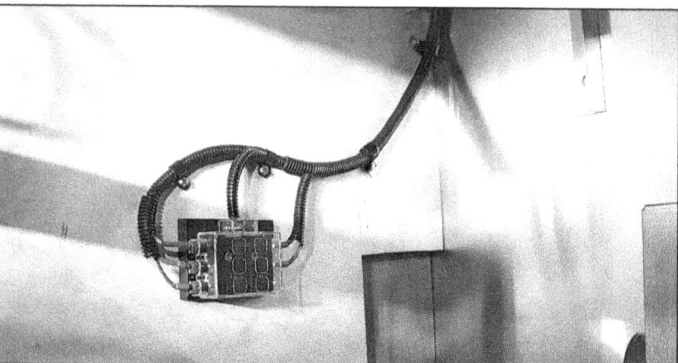

5 The wires are wrapped in loom and fastened to the cabinet wall with clamps that do not compress or deform the wires (this application called for 3/8-inch clamps, but they come in many sizes). The appropriate fuses still need to be installed once the associated components are ready for power. The ground leads from the 12-volt components are attached to grounding blocks.

Solar Panels

Ideally, you want a solar array that can replace your daily draw. A 100-watt solar panel requires nearly 15 hours to replace the Cruisette's estimated daily draw at maximum efficiency (direct sunlight, with no clouds or shade). A 200-watt array requires about 8 hours to top off the daily draw of the Cruisette.

Essentially, a good 200-watt array is just enough to float the daily energy requirements for the Cruisette's 12-volt system. (Keep in mind that peak summer sun provides much more power than winter sun, due to the angle of light rays, when planning your build). The best option would be to add another 100-watt panel, for a total of 300 watts.

These panels are about 4 x 2 feet, so a two-panel array could take up an 8 x 4 space. On a flat-roofed camper such as a Boles Aero or Barth, this is less important, but on a curved Airstream, space can become an issue.

Another consideration with the curved Airstream profile is that flat solar panels look out of place. A good alternative is flexible solar panels to achieve a flush mount to the curved roof. A drawback to this is that a good portion of the panel may not receive significant light and may be inefficient. A solar panel is most efficient when positioned correctly.

Curved, hard-mounted panels cannot move; likewise, flat panels hard-mounted without a special adjustable bracket system can leave them at less-than-optimal positions for generating electricity.

This makes the third option popular: a portable array that you can plug into the camper and place where it receives the best sunlight.

This solar array has 400 watts of potential charging. However, due to the curved roof, these flexible panels do not receive direct light over the entire panel, so they rarely achieve peak power output. In designing your solar charging system, you need to make compromises based on many variables.

ELECTRICAL SYSTEMS

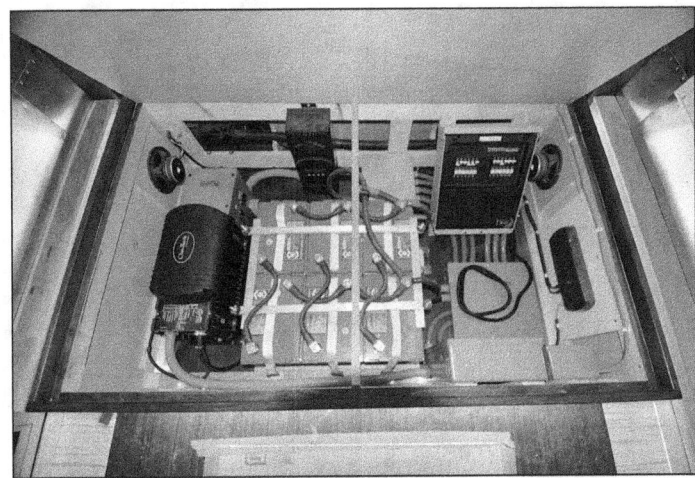

The skinny black box mounted to the back of this power center is the solar charge controller, which ensures that the battery bank is not overcharged by the panels. It works in conjunction with the information/control center to provide information on battery charge state and power usage. The higher quality the charge controller, the better performance you get from the solar panels.

Good solar power kits have a weathertight port to bring power into the camper. Because campers are driven through adverse weather that can drive moisture and contaminants onto junctions, ensuring that you have a solid port and connections is essential.

The drawback to this is the hassle of unpacking and packing the array every time you set up camp. Also, theft could be an issue. Besides the solar array, the other essential component is a charge controller. This is used to divert excess power to prevent overcharging and provides temperature compensation for summer and winter operation.

Chassis Wiring

In addition to the 110 AC and house DC circuits, vintage campers also have chassis wiring. This circuitry is attached to the tow vehicle. Various connectors, ranging from four- to seven-pin versions, allow power for lighting (running, stop, and turn) and auxiliary functions such as electric brakes, backup lights, and 12-volt power for a jack.

Choosing the best connector for your project comes down to the number of functions your camper has.

Of the many connectors available for trailers, I went with a six-way version to provide power to the running lights, brake lights, turn signals, 12-volt for charging, and brakes. The sixth pin is for the ground.

Four- and Five-Way Connectors

Four-way connectors are the most basic connection between a camper and vehicle, powering running, turn, and brake lights. Most commonly, trailers are wired green for right turn, yellow for left turn, brown for taillights and marker lights, and white for ground.

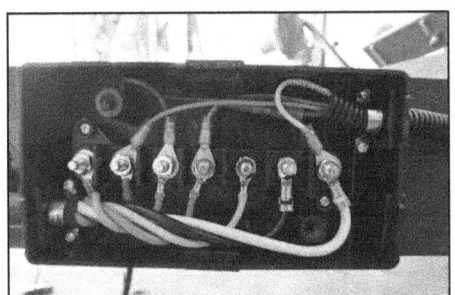

A junction box mounting the coupler allows easy replacement of a connector if it is damaged, which can happen if it becomes disconnected and is dragged on the ground while towing. Here are the green, brown, and yellow trailer lights along with the white ground. The yellow and black wires from the connector are not hooked up to anything on this particular camper but could be used for brakes or charging of the house battery.

A five-way connector provides an additional pin for either electric brake control (release hydraulic coupler for backing up, or to power electric brakes) or to power a breakaway switch.

This vintage five-pin connector was wired into the camper's lighting using butt connectors, which are on the ground behind it. It was poorly sealed with electrical tape, and a sure starting place for problems. It's best to use a junction box that's sealed from the elements and easily serviceable if you experience electrical problems.

This connector on a late-1990s Airstream is already corroded, which could affect the function of the trailer lights. To fix this, the corrosion needs to be cleaned up. You can purchase a set of picks, some small pieces of sandpaper, and electronics cleaner for the terminals from a parts store. Dielectric grease also helps to seal out moisture and prevent future corrosion on electrical connectors.

Over time, grounds can become corroded or loosen from the vibrations associated with towing and from exposure to freeze-thaw cycles. This ground is in very poor condition and causes low-power lighting, or no lights working at all.

Six- and Seven-Way Connectors

Six-way connectors add another pin for power to a breakaway kit, battery charger, or interior lights.

Seven-way connectors provide power for backup lights, which can also be used to release a hydraulic coupler.

Trailer Taillights

Trailer lights are common sources of irritation because they can be very temperamental if not properly cared for. Most commonly, issues are caused by either poor grounds or blown light bulbs. Be sure that the mounting screws are secure without overtightening and that the connector's ground is free from paint. In the world of vintage campers, many reproduction lights are available, but they are not as high quality as the originals.

Typically, reproduction lights use plastic lenses, instead of glass. For the Cruisette, I sourced original Bargman No. 2 taillights with glass lenses for the ones that were long missing. The Cruisette had at least two different taillights added to it over its life, based on all the holes left from the non-original units. To fix this, I filled the extra holes with rivets where necessary.

 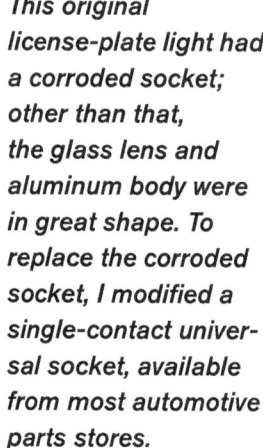 

This original license-plate light had a corroded socket; other than that, the glass lens and aluminum body were in great shape. To replace the corroded socket, I modified a single-contact universal socket, available from most automotive parts stores.

Here, the tabs of the socket are bent over to secure it in place. This is part of the ground, and if the tabs are not allowing the socket to make contact, the light works poorly or not at all. Also noteworthy are the grabber screws securing the light to the table to help keep it stable while working on it.

ELECTRICAL SYSTEMS

Once the socket is installed, it's time to bench test the light and make sure everything's working properly before final install. The glass is fragile; be careful not to overtighten the screws (the original flat heads are used here) or you'll be out a hard-to-find original piece.

On this camper, the lights are installed with butyl tape. And, like the lens screws, original flat-head sheet-metal screws are used to attach the lights to the Cruisette's shell.

Rectangle Bargman No. 2s can be difficult to source due to a short production run and limited availability. Because of this, they demand a premium over more common round Bargman taillights. Even with the availability of reproduction lights, sometimes you run into roadblocks if your trailer is less common or used a low-production light.

Renovation

This was the case for a 1960s Boles Aero that I restored, and a good example of how to rewire old trailer lights to make them shine again.

First, the lights were disassembled. This allows easy cleaning of the surround, buckets, and lenses. The wires are replaced, along with the sockets, to ensure that the lights work properly for many more years.

These fixtures feature a backup light that is tied into the vehicle through a seven-pin connector. I installed new single-filament bulbs and wires, and the tail- and turn lights receive new dual-filament bulbs, wires, and sockets, where necessary.

The lenses had some cracks in them, which were reinforced with epoxy to help them last longer, as these lenses were not currently available for replacement. When restoring obsolete items, sometimes you have to get creative. If time and the budget allow, you could have the lenses re-created. This, however, was not the case for this project, so I simply reinforced the compromised lenses.

After all the lights are installed with weathertight butt connectors and secure grounds, it's time to test for any faults. If every light turns on, you can move on to another project; if a light fails to work, you need to diagnose the issue and find out what is wrong.

The brown wire from the trailer connector powers the lower output filament in the dual-filament 1157 bulbs, which I used in both the upper and lower lights. The green wire (right turn/stop) or yellow wire (left turn/stop) powers the second filament in both lights. The center reverse light is connected to a wire feed from the tow vehicle's reverse lights.

Any additional running lights are connected to the brown wire, so they are illuminated when the vehicle's running lights are on.

Chassis wiring is pretty straightforward, but the multiple grounds at the lights can cause headaches if they do not complete the circuit.

Restoring Trailer Taillights

1 *To restore these taillights, they need to be fully disassembled. The buckets will be polished using a compound and fine steel wool to remove any corrosion so they provide an even distribution of light.*

2 *Staying organized helps keep the project moving smoothly. Here, one of the buckets is cleaned up and the remaining five await a refreshing. The corrosion on the covers will be sanded off and coated with primer and paint to prevent further damage.*

ELECTRICAL SYSTEMS

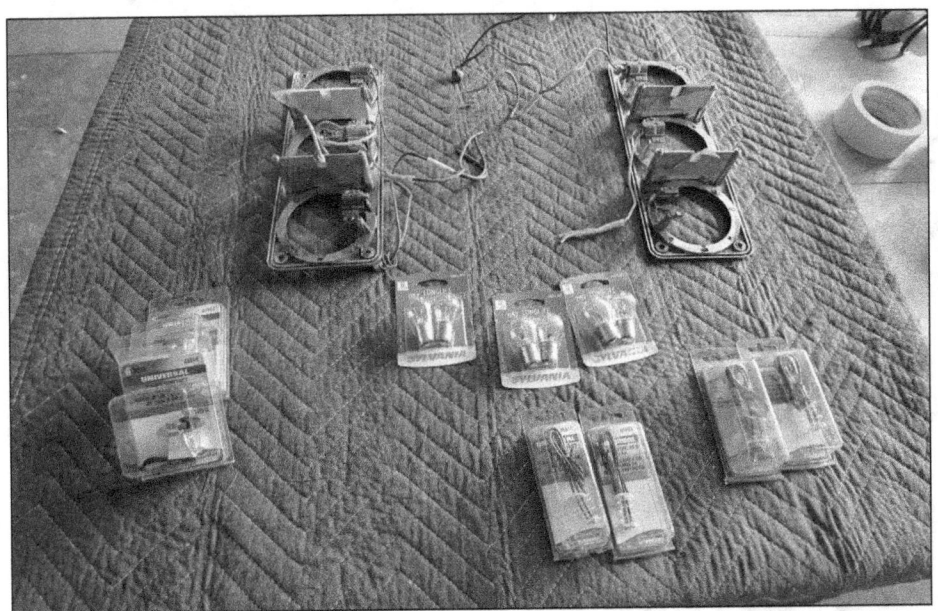

3 The bulbs and sockets used to restore these lights were sourced from a local auto parts store. The blue and yellow tape helps keep the lighting organized.

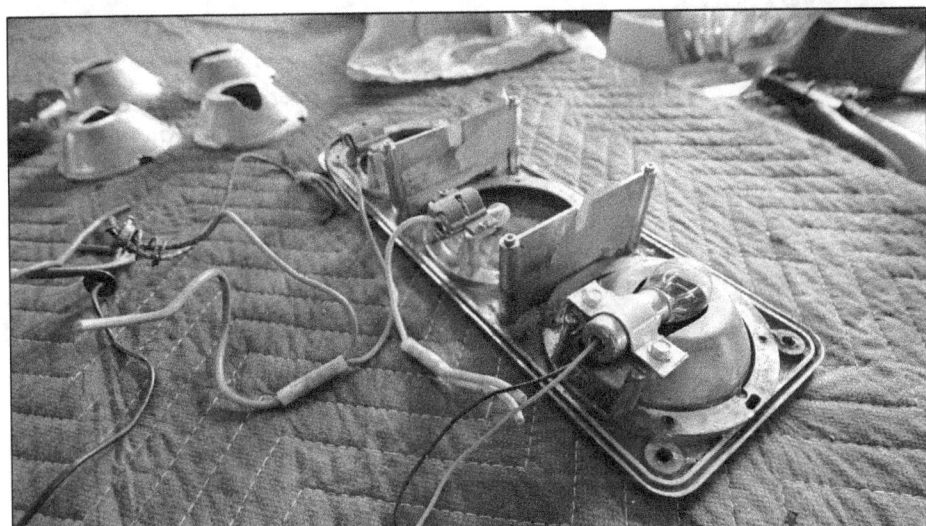

4 This light's original rivets holding the socket together had failed. To fix this, I used some scrap strapping and hex-head screws to secure it. The other sockets were in good condition, so I removed the contacts and wires from the new sockets and placed them into the existing sockets.

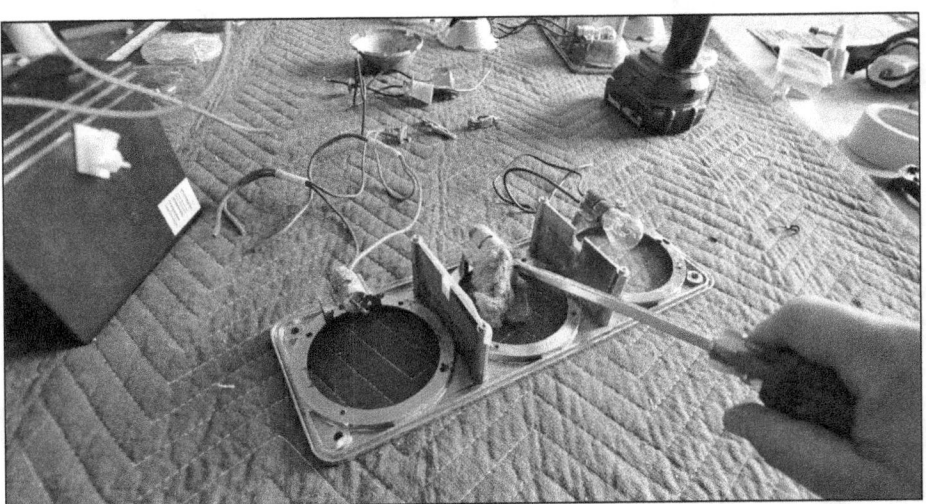

5 For the sockets that were not damaged, steel wool is used to clean them and remove corrosion. This provides a good ground for the light bulbs.

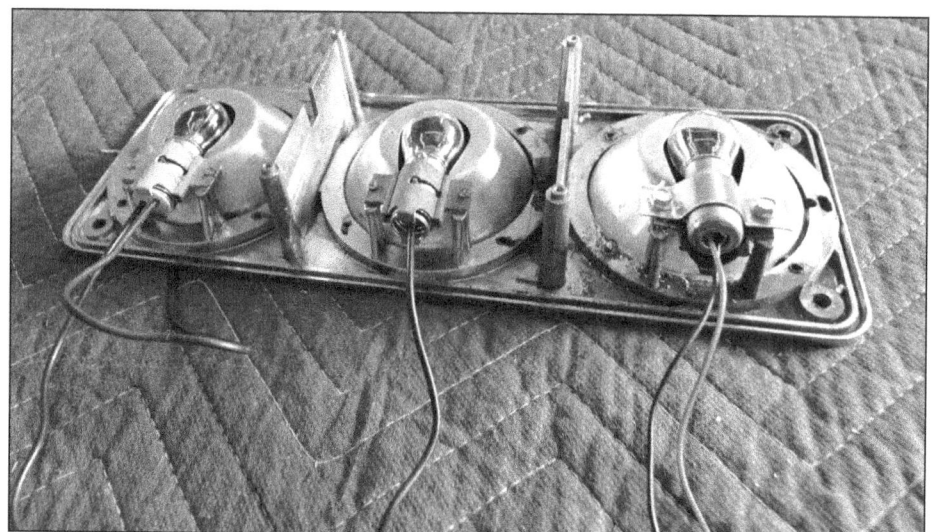

6 After the new dual- and single-bulb contacts, socket, and bulbs are installed, it's time to bench test the lights with jumper cables and a battery to make sure everything is working properly before final installation.

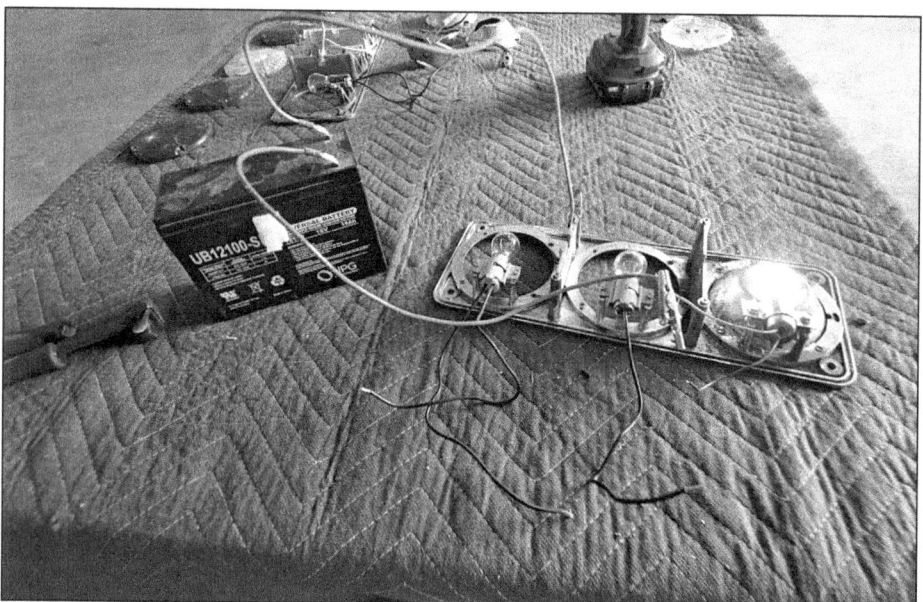

7 To test the light, simply ground the negative lead to the light housing and connect the power lead to each wire coming off the light sockets. If every circuit lights properly, it's time to place the light on the trailer and do the final wiring.

8 When the lights are tied into the camper's connector, the running lights are illuminated. Once the right turn signal or brake pedal is pushed, the secondary filament is illuminated, making the lights brighter.

CHAPTER 8

INSULATION

Many types of insulation are used in buildings, and some of them can be used in a camper, depending on the manufacturer's cost and performance goals. In this chapter, I discuss three types of insulation to consider for your restoration: fiberglass, foil-backed bubble pack, and spray foam.

Batt (precut) or blanket (continuous roll) fiberglass is the most common form of insulation used on older campers. Before fiberglass became widely available, some early campers used natural fibers, such as wool or hemp. If environmental impact and low toxicity is of concern, these are good alternatives to fiberglass, spray foam, or foil-backed bubble pack. Because insulation is hidden and does not affect the camper's originality, you can choose insulation based on cost, ease of application, life expectancy, and R-value.

Fiberglass

Fiberglass batt insulation is readily available at any hardware store. It has an R-value in the 3.1 to 4.3 range and is fairly easy to install (very little prep work and easy to cut). It is also on the lower end of the cost scale. One disadvantage to fiberglass insulation is that it's moisture and vapor permeable, so a leak could penetrate to the interior of your camper or be captured in the wall cavity, where mold and mildew start growing.

It's also an inviting place for rodents to nest, which creates a smelly and uninviting camper. The worst part of fiberglass insulation, however, is the health risk and

The Cruisette is ready for insulation. Instead of traditional fiberglass batt or contemporary bubble foil, I used closed-cell spray insulation. This product requires more preparation and specialty equipment to install, but the efficiency and moisture resistance easily outweigh these drawbacks.

STREAMLINE ALUMINUM TRAILERS: RESTORATION AND MODIFICATION

general unpleasantness of handling it. Be sure to use a respirator and wear full-coverage clothing to prevent lung damage and irritated skin. Typical batt insulation is intended for house framing (4-inch width), so it is thicker than a camper wall frame. Fortunately, it is easy to split in half to a 2-inch thickness by carefully pulling it apart.

One of the major drawbacks to fiberglass insulation, besides its ability to irritate skin and cause lung damage, is the fact that small animals can burrow and nest in it. The accumulated animal waste, along with moisture permeability (resulting in mold and mildew), contributes to the musty smell associated with original vintage campers. This is furthered by the fact that most vintage campers left the factory without a vapor barrier.

The fiberglass insulation of this late 1970s Argosy shows what happens to the batt over time. At the front left lower corner, you can see the batt bunching up and falling down. Also, black mold is present. Fiberglass insulation has an R-value around 3.5, but that deteriorates over time as moisture and gravity cause the batt to compress and loose its R-value. On a camper where aluminum walls transfer heat and cold to the interior very efficiently, this is a problem.

The width of the insulation is probably too wide in most cases as well. To cut it to shape, use good-quality scissors or a utility knife. To hold the fiberglass batt in place, use a spray adhesive such as from 3M. You spray it on the wall and to the face of the fiberglass insulation before placing the piece of insulation. Overspray here can be an issue; taping off or using a cardboard shield in areas you don't want to spend time cleaning up overspray helps.

Foil-Backed Bubble Pack

Foil-backed bubble pack (often called bubble foil) is another popular option for camper insulation, as it's fairly easy to work with and has a good R-value. Typically the value starts at R-4 and can increase, depending on manufacturer and application. This is a thin product that resembles plastic bubble wrap with aluminum foil on both sides. It also works as a vapor barrier, unlike fiberglass insulation, which allows vapor to pass through, unless an additional barrier is added.

Like fiberglass, bubble foil insulation requires only basic tools for installation. You need a tape measure, utility knife, and straightedge. Because the insulation is fiber-free, no protective garments or respirators, other than safety glasses, are required.

This style of insulation does not compress, collapse, or disintegrate over time; it also does not promote the growth of mold and mildew. Another major selling point is that it does not promote nesting for rodents and other pests. The cost of bubble foil has also decreased significantly in recent years, making it a great alternative to fiberglass in campers.

INSULATION

Cutting bubble foil insulation to shape is easy with a quality utility knife and scissors. Simply mark where you need to trim.

I used 3M Spray Adhesive to attach the bubble foil. Per the instructions, it's applied to both surfaces (cleaned beforehand) and allowed to set for a few minutes. Once it's tacky, the foil is installed.

Bubble foil seams are closed using aluminum foil tape. Here, you can see the finished insulated endcap. I removed the fiberglass batt to eliminate the need for an itchy, respirator and to help ease the process of fabricating custom endcaps.

On this 1960s Airstream, I used bubble foil for insulation. The insulation was installed in the belly pan and on a chassis that's been treated to prevent rust.

Spray Foam

The best option, and the most popular form of insulation in camper restorations, is closed-cell spray foam. It has an R-value of 6 to 8 per inch (Airstream ribs are about 1½ inches apart) and many other advantages. The few disadvantages are that it's the most costly option and requires specialty equipment and extensive preparation.

There are two types of spray foam: open-cell and closed-cell. Open-cell is lightweight foam that is flexible and an excellent air barrier, while closed-cell foam is higher-density foam and acts as a moisture barrier.

Because closed-cell foam does not allow moisture to pass through the foam, it's ideal for campers and it has a closed-cell type has a higher R-value than open-cell. Closed-cell foam is also more rigid than open-cell, so it gives the lightweight walls of a camper more structure.

When it comes to long-term investment, closed-cell foam helps keep cooling and heating costs down and it helps ensure that water does not penetrate into the camper and cause irreversible damage.

That said, before any insulation is installed, regardless of type to be used, the shell needs to be watertight.

Before any insulation can be applied, all windows, openings (vents and baggage doors), and flooring need to be covered and closed off to prevent overspray. This is a tedious task, which is well rewarded if done properly. A poor masking job can create hours of unintended work. This is the last time the original military-green aluminum will be visible for a very long time on this Airstream Cruisette.

All the seams on the Cruisette have been coated with a polyurethane sealant. Before spray foam is applied, it's a good idea to use a tape measure and photograph the wiring locations. This could help prevent damage from a rogue screw, which would set you back days or weeks if any wiring is damaged. It's also a good idea to check the continuity of the wires after the insulation is installed and look for any damage from cutting off the excess.

INSULATION

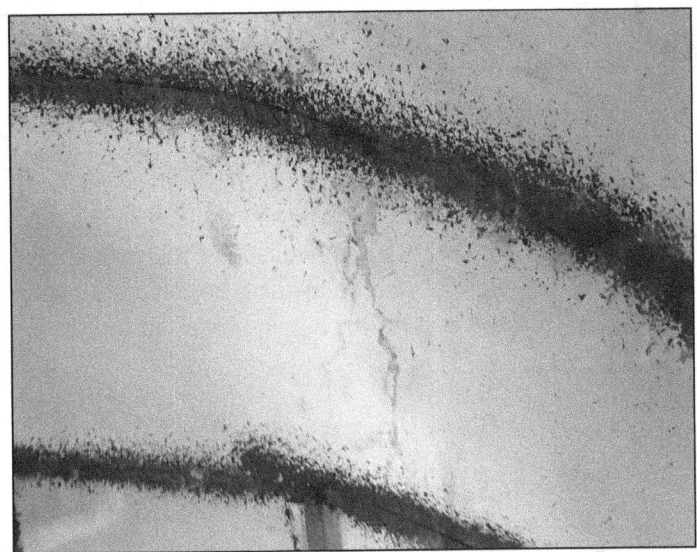

The original autobody sealant used by Airstream has failed at the seam, as the water makes evident. To fix this, the old sealant is removed and new sealant is applied.

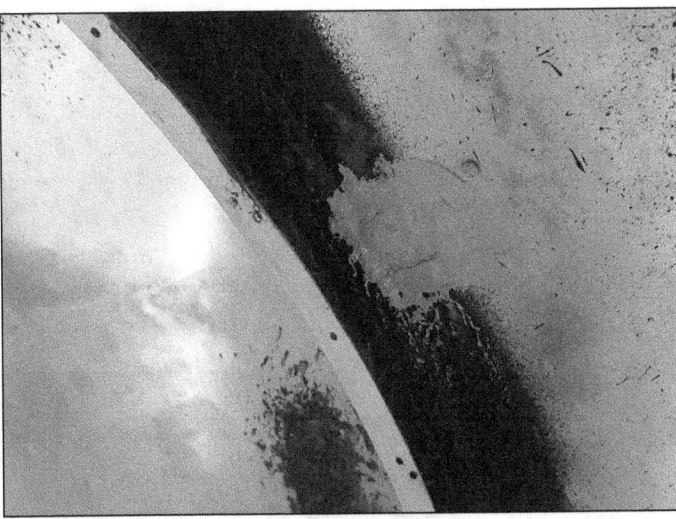

The same polyurethane sealer applied to lap joints during panel replacement or installation is used to fix any water intrusion. Here, a liberal amount has been applied after the old sealant was removed.

The automotive sealant commonly used on old aluminum campers fails over time. When gutting a camper, note where mold has developed and also look for water marks from moisture penetrating to the inside of the exterior skin. These areas need special attention before insulation is applied.

Before installing insulation, I reseal all the seams with a coating of polyurethane sealant such as Sikaflex. This is applied liberally to prevent any further water intrusion, even if I use a water-impermeable insulation. Before applying new sealant, the old sealant is scraped off in problem areas with a wire brush and roughed up along zones that seem to be watertight. Then the sealant is simply applied with a caulking gun and smeared with a gloved hand. Once the sealant has cured, I can apply the insulation.

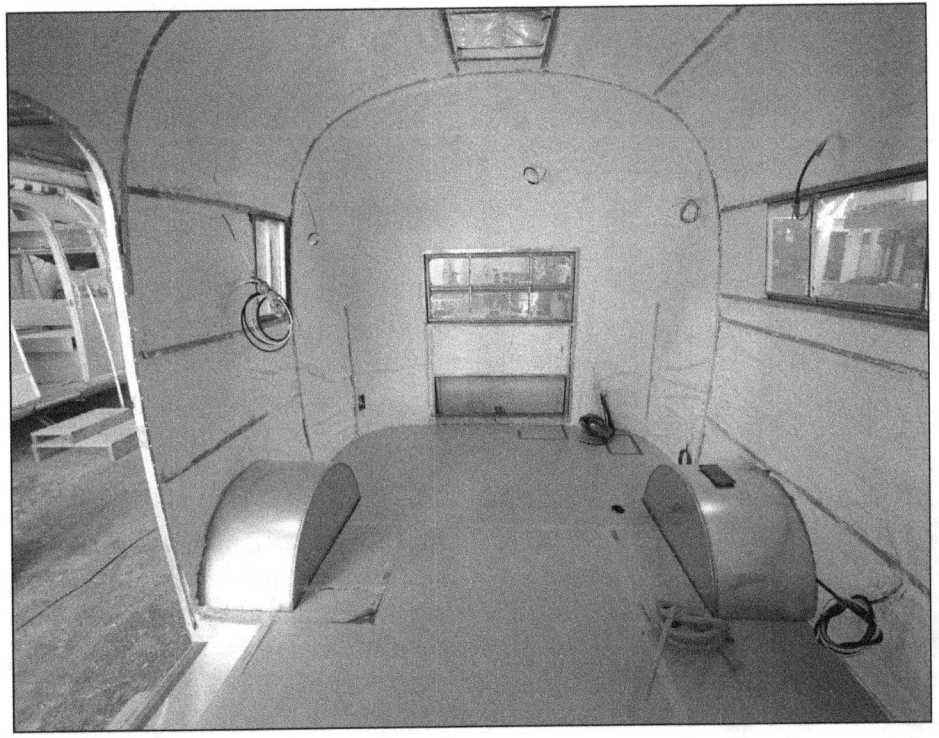

Once the spray foam is cured and the excess is removed, the masking is removed and the walls are brushed off and vacuumed to remove any loose foam and particulates to help prevent air-blown debris while the panels are worked into place. Here, the floor is marked with tape to help visualize where the cabinetry will land and to plan a lumber order for this project. Now the camper is ready for its original skin to be replaced.

STREAMLINE ALUMINUM TRAILERS: RESTORATION AND MODIFICATION

Spray-Foam Experts

Spray foam insulation requires experience and professional equipment to achieve a good result, unlike fiberglass or bubble foil, where standard tools are all that's needed.

Do-it-yourself two-part spray-foam kits are available. If you're an experienced auto painter or handy person, this could be an option. These kits have a shelf life, however, and you want to make sure you have enough to complete your project without excessive waste.

A good option is to contract the job to a specialized installer. They come to your location, prep the camper (sometimes you can save money by masking off the camper yourself), spray it, trim the excess, and clean everything up. This is a good time-saving option that gives you a professional finish.

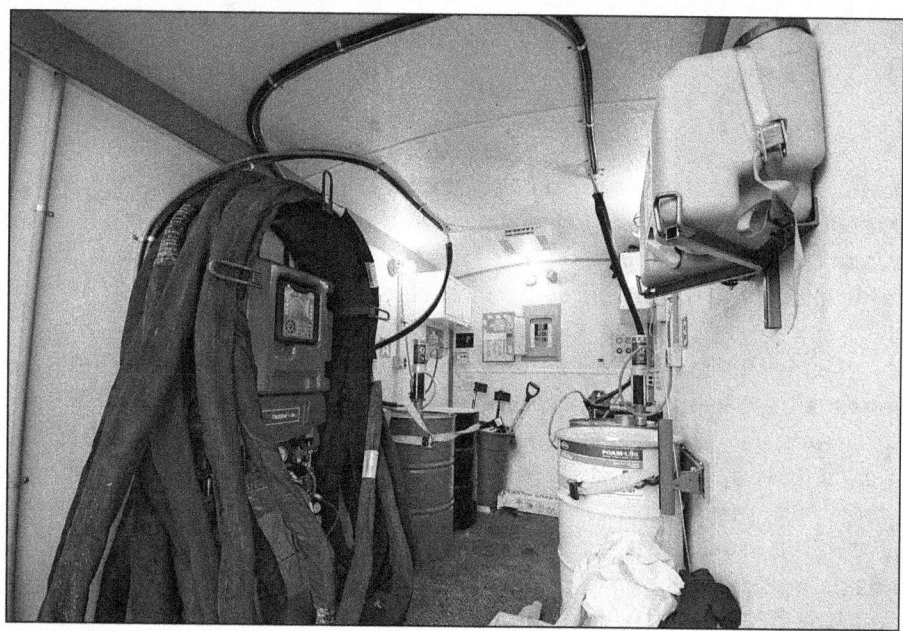

A two-part do-it-yourself closed-cell foam kit can cost nearly a grand and should be enough to complete a camper. As an alternative, professional installers use a truck or trailer with all the equipment in it.

Tape off the floor, windows, vents, and other openings to prevent overspray. Once the camper is sealed off, it's ready for the application of spray foam.

INSULATION

Two people are often needed to apply spray foam. As one sprays, the other needs to ensure that the wiring is not covered and that overspray and excess material is minimized while moving the gear around. Also, extensive personal protective equipment such as goggles, clothing, and respirators are needed during application.

After the spray foam is carefully trimmed with special serrated knives and pull saws, the masking can be removed. Before the interior walls are hung on this 1950s Boles Aero, the foam is brushed and vacuumed to remove any loose bits to reduce airborne particulates.

CHAPTER 9

INTERIOR SKIN

There are many ways to replace interior skins on campers. On some you replace the old with new; on others you restore the originals and add a new topcoat. If you're painting the panels, patches and filled holes (simply plugged with a rivet) are fairly well hidden.

If you want a raw-aluminum interior, the time it takes to strip and clean original panels easily outweighs the cost and labor to re-skin the interior with new material. Because the Cruisette uses high-quality vintage aluminum, I decided to save it.

As mentioned in Chapter 2, the Cruisette was treated to a Zolatone finish, but instead of repainting with Zolatone, the owner opted to repaint the interior walls with a modern, low-volatile organic-compound paint. Airstream did not use Zolatone for very long and ended up replacing it with a vinyl covering applied to the aluminum skin.

Campers with a vinyl coating can be cleaned and painted. In some cases, it might be easier to replace panels with new aluminum than to strip and prep them for paint. If the vinyl has started to peel, there's not much you can do to save it and achieve a good result. Some have tried to re-adhere it or cut away the delaminated portion, but the results are always noticeable.

It's best to weigh your options and pick the route that best fits your time and budget constraints. Before deciding what materials and products to use, consult a painting specialist for recommendations on products and techniques. Painting and prepping vinyl-coated walls (there are special vinyl paints) differs greatly from prepping for a Zolatone or alternative topcoat.

At the front of the Cruisette, I plan to bring the original aluminum endcap to a mirror finish to highlight and distinguish the settee area from the rest of the camper. Both endcaps were disassembled for stripping of the paint and sanding. I felt that working with the panels on a flat plane would be the best option. This, however, might not be your best course of action, depending on your restoration goals and workspace. Endcaps can be removed without disassembly and reinstalled as one piece.

This stack of interior panels is from a 1970s Airstream Overlander. Instead of restoring them or saving them, I scrapped them. It's fairly straightforward to place new panels, then cut out window, door, and vent openings. The time saved prepping and painting old skin can easily outweigh the investment in new aluminum.

INTERIOR SKIN

This panel has had the numerous layers of paint stripped off with aircraft paint remover, but some of the stubborn Zolatone finish remains. For final prep, it was sanded with 80-, 150-, and 220-grit sandpaper. At this stage, I was less focused on removing the Zolatone but wanted the panels to be smooth for the primer and topcoat. For endcap panels that will be polished, all Zolatone was removed.

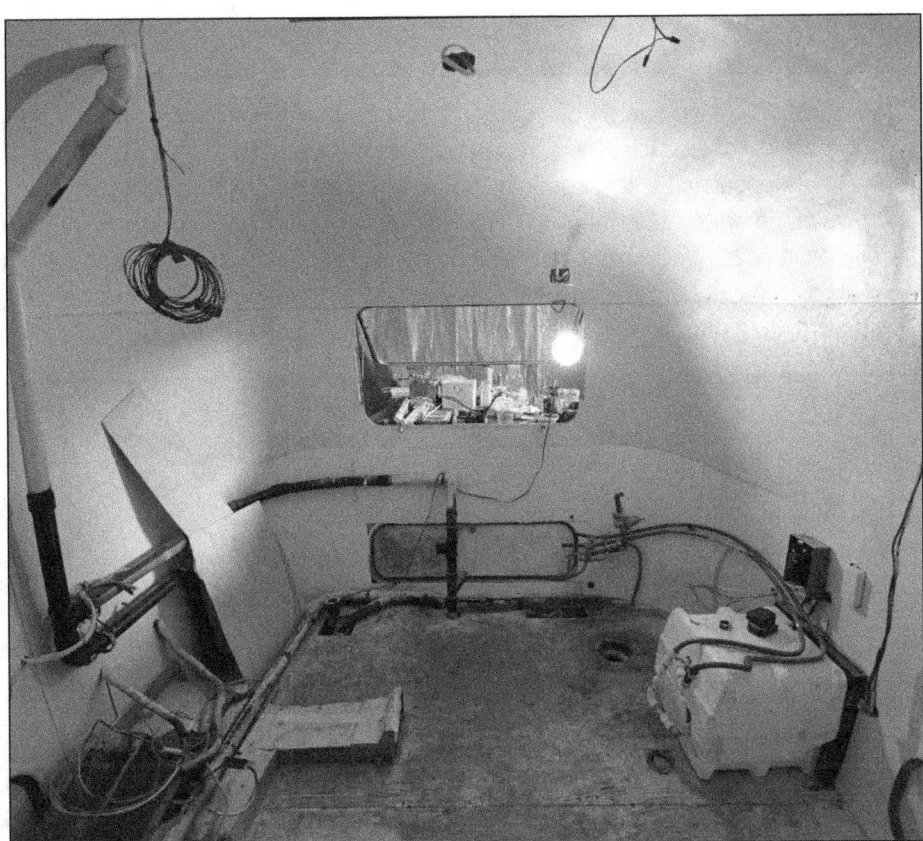

To keep this late-1970s Airstream's restoration budget reasonable, the original vinyl walls were reinstalled after the exterior skin was patched, sealed, and insulated. You can see the texture in the vinyl. This is acceptable if the vinyl has not started to peel, which can be difficult to fix with good results. The original fiberglass endcap was also reused after all the cracks and holes were filled with epoxy and sanded smooth.

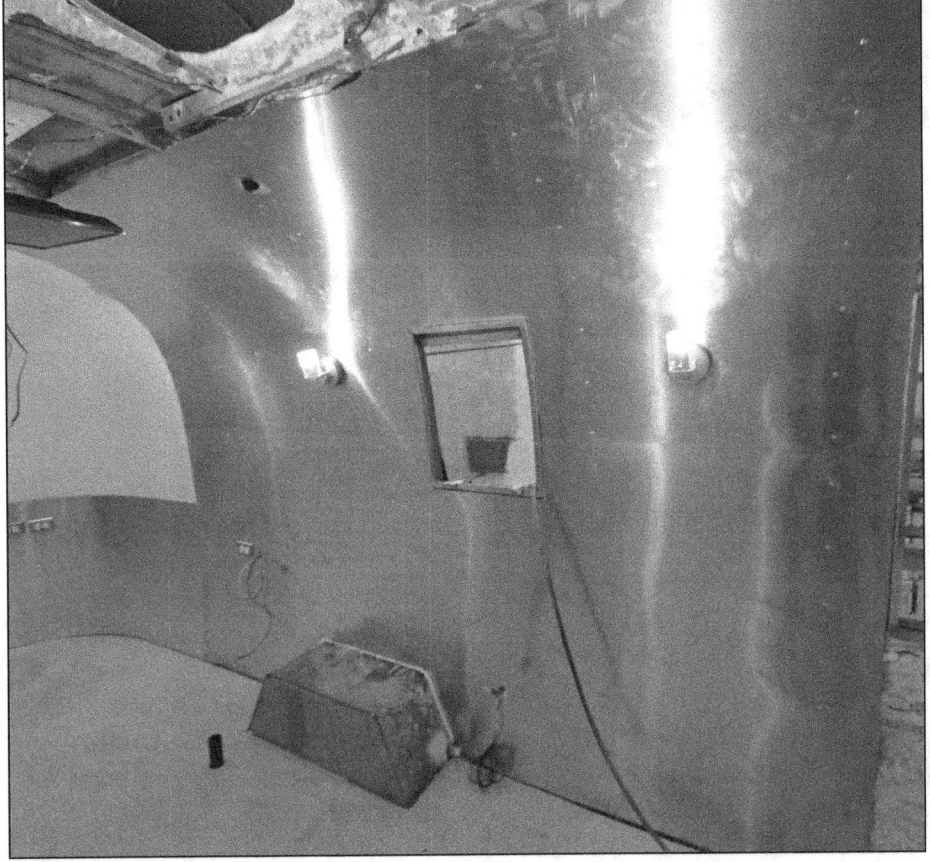

Rather than re-use heavily compromised interior panels on this Airstream restoration, I went the custom route and covered the walls with new aluminum. Depending on your goals and budget, this might be a good way to reduce time spent on sanding, filling, and patching.

STREAMLINE ALUMINUM TRAILERS: RESTORATION AND MODIFICATION

CHAPTER 9

Wood Walls

Not all vintage riveted campers use aluminum interior walls. For example, this camper's exterior was patched and insulated with closed-cell spray foam, as on the Cruisette. Completing the interior build, however, the walls are covered in finish-grade 1/4-inch plywood.

Most campers of this vintage had the wood walls treated with varnish, giving them the warmth associated with canned ham–style campers. Straying from the norm, however, this Boles Aero now has the walls painted white. Further separating this example from the run-of-the-mill restorations is a black-walnut ceiling.

Although not true to a by-the-books restoration, this interior finish is a nice break from the omnipresent varnish found at vintage camper rallies. ∎

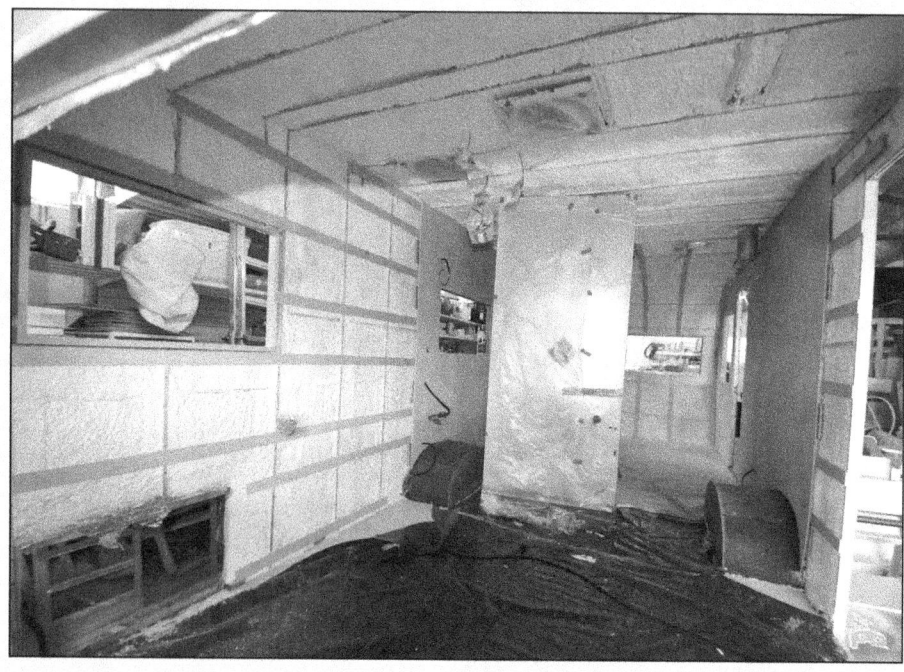

Like Airstream, Boles Aero and many other manufacturers used aluminum skin riveted to aluminum ribs. Unlike Airstream, Boles Aero used wood interior paneling. Wood strips are attached to the aluminum ribs with countersunk sheet-metal screws.

With the mounting strips in place, the plywood panels are cut to shape and attached with oval-head wood screws and finish washers, as the original walls were. The large plastic-wrapped object at the left is a bathroom shower that was too big to remove through the doors. This needed to be moved around as I worked on the restoration.

INTERIOR SKIN

Door and window openings can be cut out before fitting, but this can create an issue if measurements and cuts aren't exact. Another option is to position the panel and then cut out the door and window using a router and flush bit. This method can be faster with better results. Here, the ceiling strips are being added.

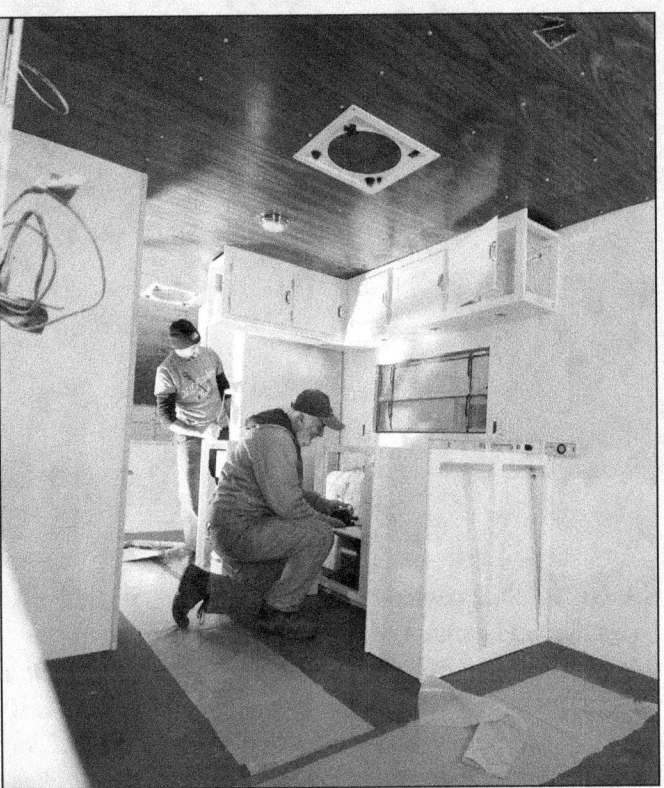

You can see the contrast a black-walnut ceiling creates with white interior paint. Most of the original cabinetry has been restored, even the art deco latches. Although this interior design is not true to what would have left the Boles Aero factory, it's a pleasant break from the norm.

The overhead lockers of the Cruisette shared the same finish and layers of paint as the walls. The paint stripper is doing its job. After this, the lockers will be sanded and then polished, as done with the front endcap.

At this point, the lockers were sanded with 220 grit, and all the original paint is gone (the interior bottoms will be covered with a panel when recessed puck lighting is installed). From here, all extra holes will be filled. And there's plenty more sanding needed, from 300 to at least 1000 grit, before the polishing process begins. These are the same steps used on the endcap over the front settee.

CHAPTER 9

For endcaps, you might find it quicker to work on the piece while it is installed, depending on your tools and technique. Some downsides to this are working over your head and the risk of burning through the finish (a flat sander on a concave piece). The advantage of working on an assembled endcap is saved time and frustration, as some use hundreds of buck rivets, and the risk of upsetting tolerances during reassembly is high.

Panel Sanding

If the panels are to be painted, they are sanded with 80- to 150- to 220-grit paper, and all unnecessary holes are patched. (Be sure not to fill holes used for mounting the panels to wall frames or each other.) They are then reinstalled in the reverse order of disassembly. The patches are square or rectangular pieces of 2024 or 5052 scrap cut to size large enough to cover any holes.

Panels are held in place with Clecos and then attached with the proper fasteners. On the Cruisette, the endcaps go in first, followed by the ceiling panel, then the rest of the panels are placed working downward.

The lapped panels are just wide enough to set a buck rivet on your own. For fastening to the aluminum ribs, where you cannot insert a bucking bar, slotted sheet-metal screws are used. In some cases, shaveable rivets

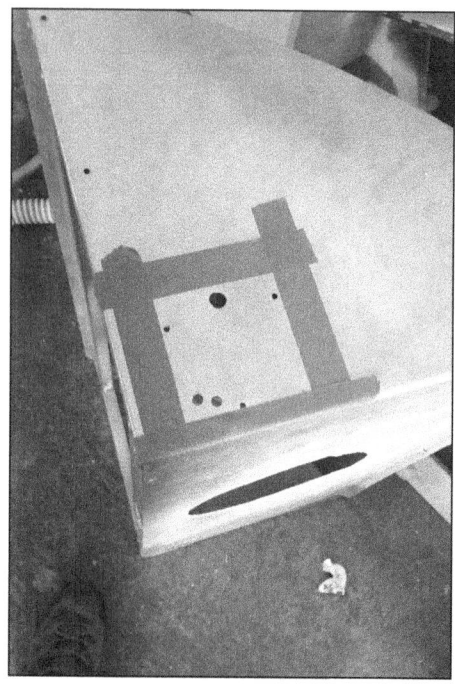

Here's a good example of Swiss cheese in one of the lockers and what you find in an original skin. Instead of filling all of these holes or covering them with a simple patch, I made a plate for the light switch that hides the holes. The tape helps size the patch and also prevents damage to the sanded surface.

This original switch worked great (before installing, the corrosion was cleaned up) and was repurposed to power puck lights mounted underneath the locker. The plate material is original Airstream aluminum harvested from a large exterior panel that was replaced. At this point, the rivets are only placed for show.

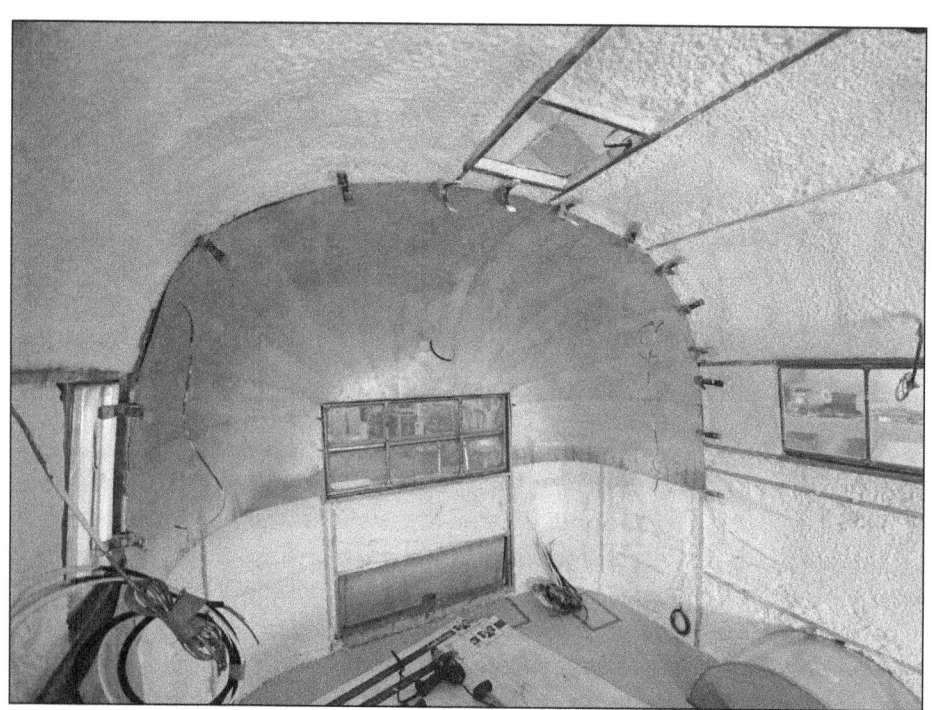

With the endcap reassembled, it is held in place for positioning with spring clamps and Clecos. If you've done everything correctly, the rivet holes should line up nicely. Once both endcaps are in place, the center ceiling panel is placed, and slotted sheet-metal screws are used to fasten it.

are a good substitute. On contemporary Airstreams and vintage ones starting around the 1960s, pop rivets are used extensively. This makes panel placement much easier and quicker.

Sometimes you can see the remaining Zolatone finish (greenish hue). This will be painted over, so it is not crucial to remove it all. It is important, however, to feather the edges so when the topcoat is laid, you don't see a hard, defining edge.

Feathering is a technique used by painters to smooth an edge. (More information on paint prep and practices can be found in *How To Paint Your Car on a Budget* by Pat Ganahl.) As the interior panels are installed, make sure that all electrical leads are pulled through and that they use rubber grommets to avoid fraying of the sheathing.

Once all panels are in place, final prep for paint needs to be completed. This entails masking everything off. Good adhesion is paramount to avoid bleed-through (when paint penetrates through the tape edge). Just as it's important to properly clean the surface to paint, removing dirt, grime, and oils (transferred from tools and hands) from the areas to be taped off is essential to a good tape job.

Endcaps

One defining feature of an Airstream, vintage or new, is the endcap. Because of the aerodynamic shape where there are curves on the x, y, and z axes, the interior skin creates a focal point. This piece was originally addressed in the same manner as the exterior skin, a series of smaller pieces riveted together to form the dome.

Through the years, Airstream tried different materials to finish the endcap, which included fiberglass. During the fiberglass era to present day, these endcaps often contain additional storage, a stereo, and readouts for camper vitals such as tank and battery levels. Endcaps can be a blank slate, and with a creative eye they can become the centerpiece of the camper.

From the factory, the top row of rivets on both sides of the ceiling panel are buck style. These are installed after the endcaps, then the lower panels are installed beneath them with buck rivets. There's just enough length to reach the back and front side of the skin to install the rivets. For the places that are impossible to reach, slotted sheet-metal screws are used, just as the factory did.

To update this late-1980s endcap, the original yellowed plastic was painted white. The original stereo was removed and a new one installed, hidden behind the rolling doors. Filling the hole left from the old stereo is a clock, thermometer, and barometer to add a touch of class.

CHAPTER 9

In later years, Airstream changed from multiple pieces of aluminum to one-piece fiberglass endcaps that housed everything from stereos to camper command centers. This 1960s fiberglass endcap had its various holes filled with fiberglass resin, then filled with body filler and sanded smooth to take care of years of use and modifications.

With a fresh coat of paint and a modern stereo added to the original endcap, this vintage camper's interior has a distinctive atmosphere.

Endcap Rebuild

1 *As found in the custom automotive world, panels begin as paper templates, then are transferred to metal, and in this case, to .30-inch 5052 aluminum. The endcap begins with the keystone and spreads outward. Find the center of the camper and mark it on both the template and rib.*

INTERIOR SKIN

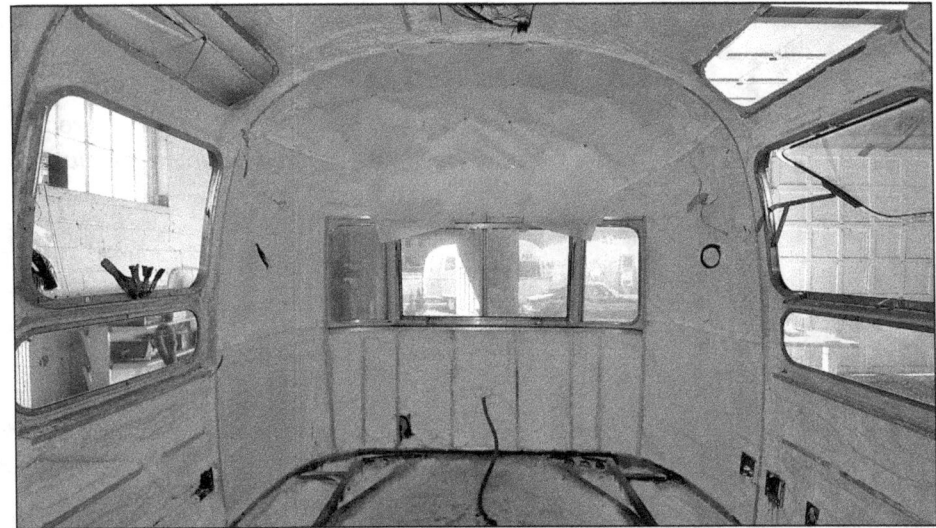

2 Rectangular pieces of paper are laid over the corner stone (the lapped edge is straight, but appears to curve). These are held in place with masking tape and, in this case, grabber screws (with washers to avoid tearing the paper) jammed into the spray foam. Also noteworthy is the foam board cut to width that's buried in the spray foam. This was used to ensure a constant depth.

3 As the paper templates are laid out, you can begin to see the endcap taking shape. Keep track of the width at the wide and tapered ends, marking the measurement on the paper for future reference. The access material will be trimmed away. Now, you can start marking the edge where the lap falls.

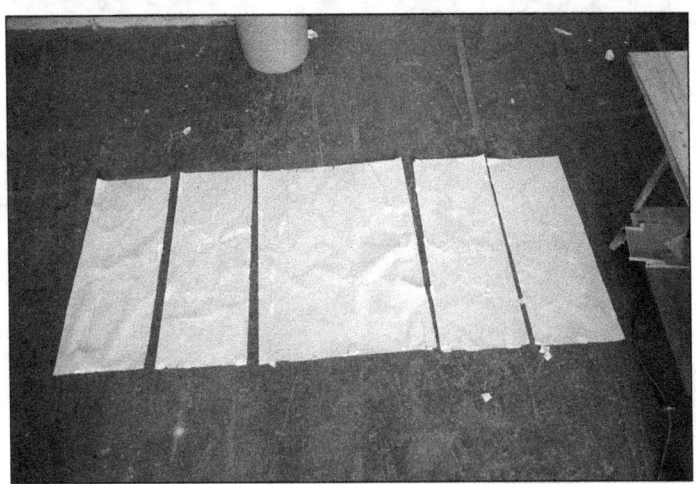

4 Once you've marked the edge on all the templates, they can be pulled. The curved shape is laid flat. Rather then peel the masking tape off, these were simply cut with a utility knife.

5 Because the endcap should be symmetrical, you can layer opposite sides over each other and find a middle ground to transfer to the aluminum. In the case of the keystone, simply fold it in half. Here is a variance of about 1 inch between the two lines.

CHAPTER 9

6 After you've created a symmetrical curve based on the original layout, extend it 3 to 4 inches for the lap joint. After that, secure the template to the aluminum and cut it out using shears.

7 Once a panel is cut to shape, rivet holes need to be pre-drilled. A fan tool evenly spaces the fastening tools. Also notice that the straight edge is the external lapped edge, not the curved side. This is misleading, as the curved end is cut to provide clearance for the curved shape. Because the panels are mirror images, you can save time by drilling holes when overlapped.

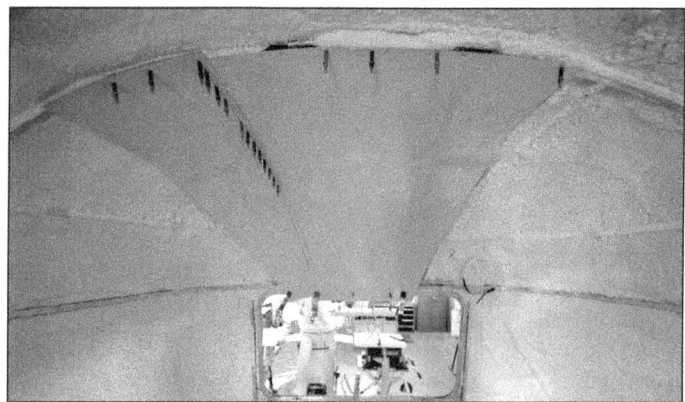

8 With the keystone panel centered and fastened with Clecos, you can see the curve formed from the straight edge that was pre-drilled for rivets. Spring clamps were used on the lower end to hold it in place. As you work, the panel can shift, so keep an eye on its alignment. The reason for using a spring clamp and not a Cleco is to allow the panel to stretch and avoid tenting at the seam.

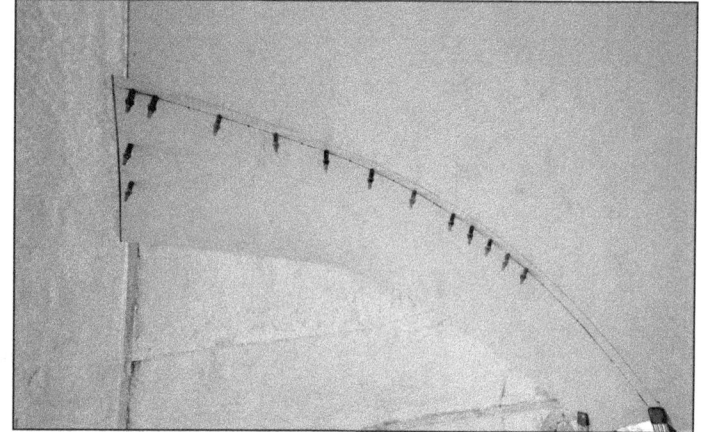

9 The Clecos are now spread out, alternating every other hole until they are close to where the drilling for holes is occurring. Once the hole is drilled at the front of the five Clecos in a row, one Cleco (the second one in the row of five) is moved forward to the new hole to help keep the panel lap flat.

INTERIOR SKIN

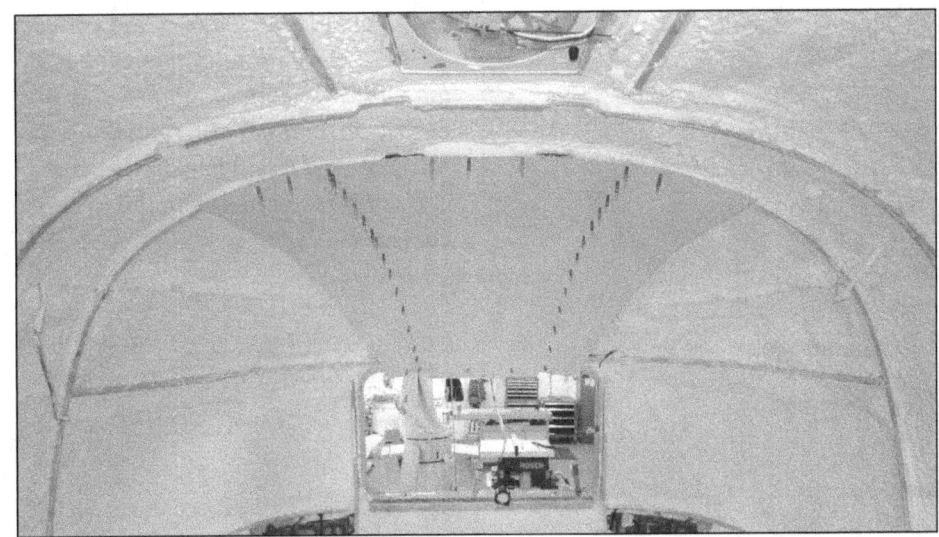

10 When both panels are temporarily held in place, you can start buck riveting the empty holes. Work your way down both sides. To avoid capturing the PCV protective coating, peel it away as you work down the row.

11 To reach behind the endcap, you need to remove Clecos to access the bucking side of the rivet. Be gentle here to avoid creasing the keystone and other panels as you work.

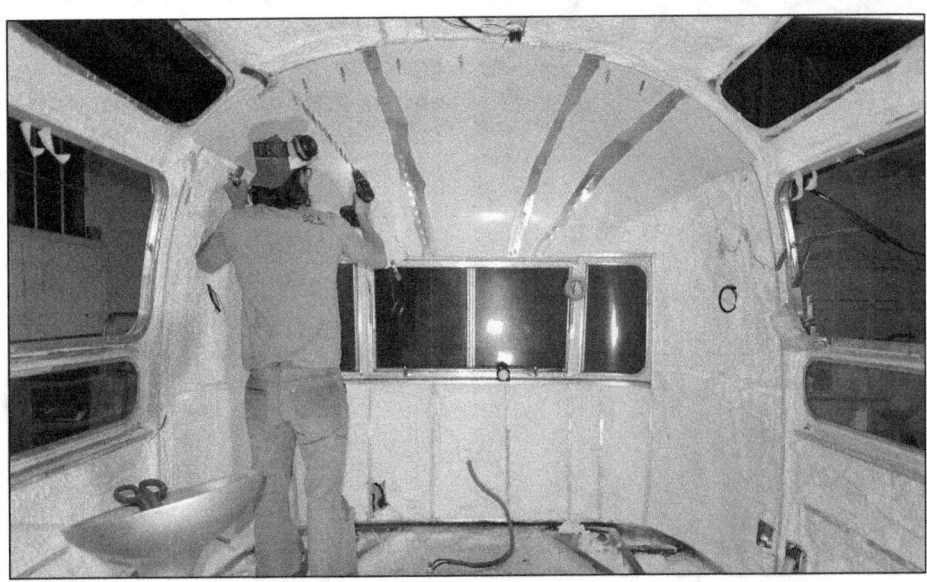

12 The process is repeated side to side until the endcap is completed. The Clecos are lined up; about 10 of them hold the panel flat. As the holes are drilled, you can remove every other one from the upper end and place them in the next freshly drilled hole.

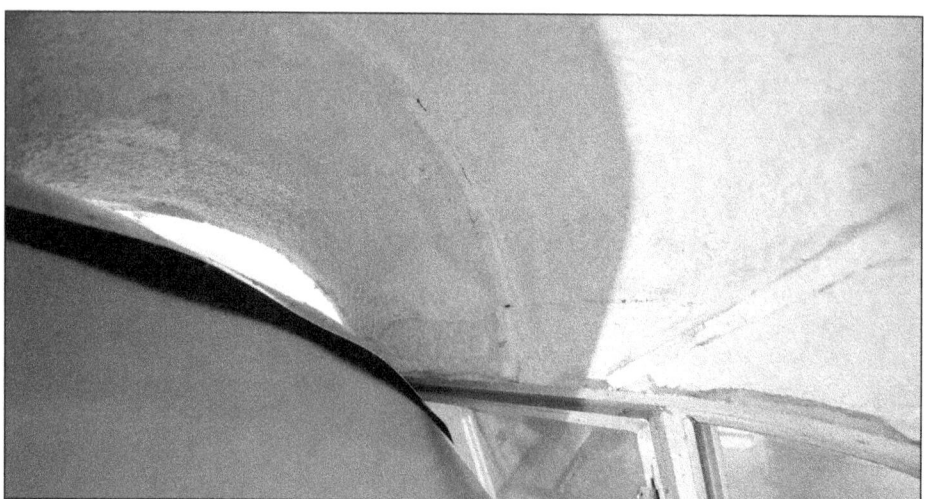

13 On the backside of the endcap, tenting (or lifting) is caused by the curve. Be sure to monitor this and use rivets long enough to capture the rear panel. If lifting is extreme, you can cut slits in the aluminum to relieve compression.

14 When the panels reach the window, notches need to be cut. This is an approximation and will be trimmed flush now that the panel is in place.

15 The finished endcap features back-mounted woofers to complete the custom look. Now the endcap transforms the interior from the original fiberglass version by harkening back to the hand-fabricated endcaps of the early Airstreams with a dash of modern hi-fi audio.

INTERIOR SKIN

Here you can see the rear endcap installed. All panels were sanded with 80- to 150- to 220-grit paper while laid flat on a worktable and then reassembled using buck rivets. This is a time-consuming process but retains the camper's history, rather than replacing it with new aluminum. Also visible is the masking used to prevent overspray on the windows and wiring.

Panel Painting

Early Airstream interior endcaps, like the outside panels, used more pieces to create the dome shape. As years passed, panel count decreased to ease production and material costs, until one-piece fiberglass units became the norm. These fiberglass endcaps housed everything from stereos to camper command centers and are fairly brittle. Years of use causes stress cracks, and often they've been modified into automotive parcel shelves, for example, with large, jagged speaker holes.

Sometimes an endcap has gone missing, or it's so far damaged that it is best to scrap it and start fresh. If that's the case, you can create an endcap in aluminum. An alternative is to create a wood endcap in the same manner.

If paint were to bleed through on the polished endcap or the masking failed on a restored window, you would lose days of work to a rushed masking job. A good-quality

An HVLP (high-volume low-pressure) spray gun was used to apply the low-volatile organic compound paint to the Cruisette's walls. This provides a smooth, even finish compared to rolling or brushing paint on the walls.

The polished endcap is covered to prevent overspray. Also, the patch panel (covering a stove exhaust vent) in the upper left corner is masked off. It's a piece of the original exterior skin, and I thought it'd be neat to leave it polished. This patch will be hidden inside the overhead lockers that will be mounted above the galley and is a nice reminder of this Airstream's history.

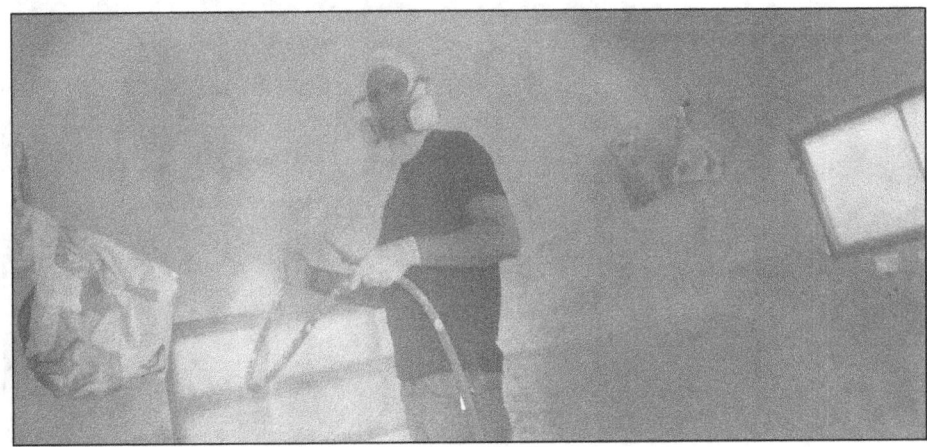

CHAPTER 9

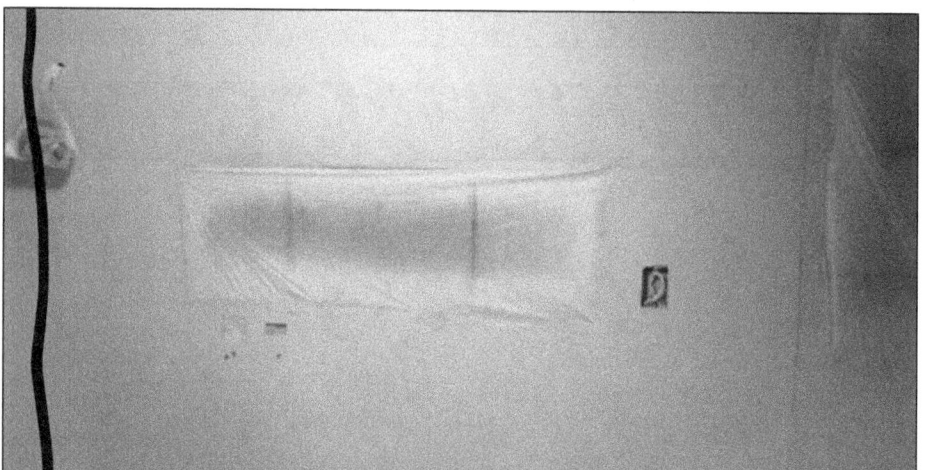

Depending on the type of paint, drying times vary. It's essential for the paint to fully harden before beginning the next step. The soft white for the walls provides some contrast to the new black-walnut cabinetry. Here, you can see some of the patches and how they look when painted over.

Between coats of paint, the walls are lightly sanded with 320-grit paper on a soft sanding sponge. It's important to sand close to the rivets, but it is easy to sand through the paint on them, as they are high points. It's best to go light around the rivets and avoid going over the top.

masking tape is also important; do not use old tape or one that's inexpensive. When choosing the paint products you plan to use, also choose compatible cleaning solutions.

When the masking is done, including covering the floor, the trailer walls are fully vacuumed with a soft-bristle attachment to eliminate any remaining dust. Before the first coat of primer can be applied, the Cruisette's walls are wiped down with a tack cloth. For a smooth, even finish, I used a spray gun to coat the walls. This might not be for everyone; you could hire the job out or apply paint with a brush, roller, or other means.

Interior Panel Repair

Sometimes, you do not need to remove all the panels to update a trailer, but you may need to patch some panels. On this 1990s Airstream Bambi, the closet where the fridge was located must be removed. The new fridge is a smaller modern unit and will better fit in the galley. This Airstream also received some damage to the interior panel, which necessitated replacing it.

Many finishes can be used on the interior of vintage campers. This Airstream from the early 1990s uses a mouse fur or haul-liner fabric. These can become dirty and will sag over the years as the adhesive loosens.

INTERIOR SKIN

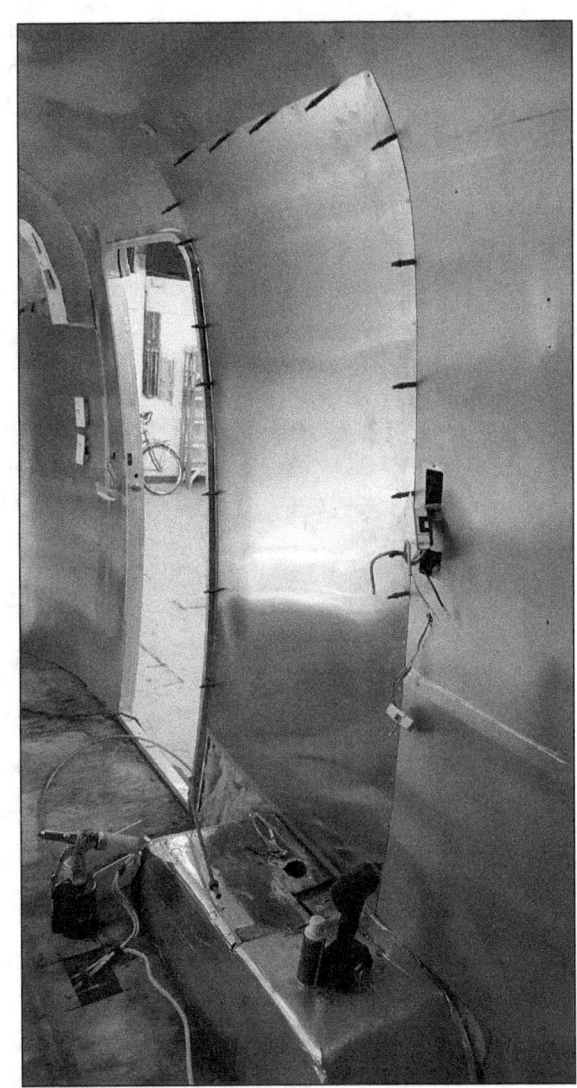

The damaged portion of the skin is simply cut out using shears. Here, you can see the original holes left behind from the fridge. These will be patched on the exterior, and the interior will receive one large aluminum panel to cover them.

The new panel is held in place with Clecos in every other hole. Because this interior will be painted, the panel will be sanded just like the rest of the walls.

Because this contemporary Airstream uses blind rivets, fastening the replacement panel is much quicker and more foolproof than in vintage Airstreams. Here, a pneumatic riveter is used to ease installation.

STREAMLINE ALUMINUM TRAILERS: RESTORATION AND MODIFICATION

CHAPTER 9

Once the damaged portion is removed, a replacement panel is cut to shape. The door curve at the top is cut out using a scribe to mark the curve. I plan to retain the original 12-volt and 110-volt wiring. This interior will be prepped for painting after all the holes are patched and filled.

Originally, the Bambi interior was covered in a mouse-fur fabric. Instead, the owner has opted for a painted surface. The old fabric is held on with an adhesive and it needs to be removed from the walls, requiring a combination of strippers and sanding.

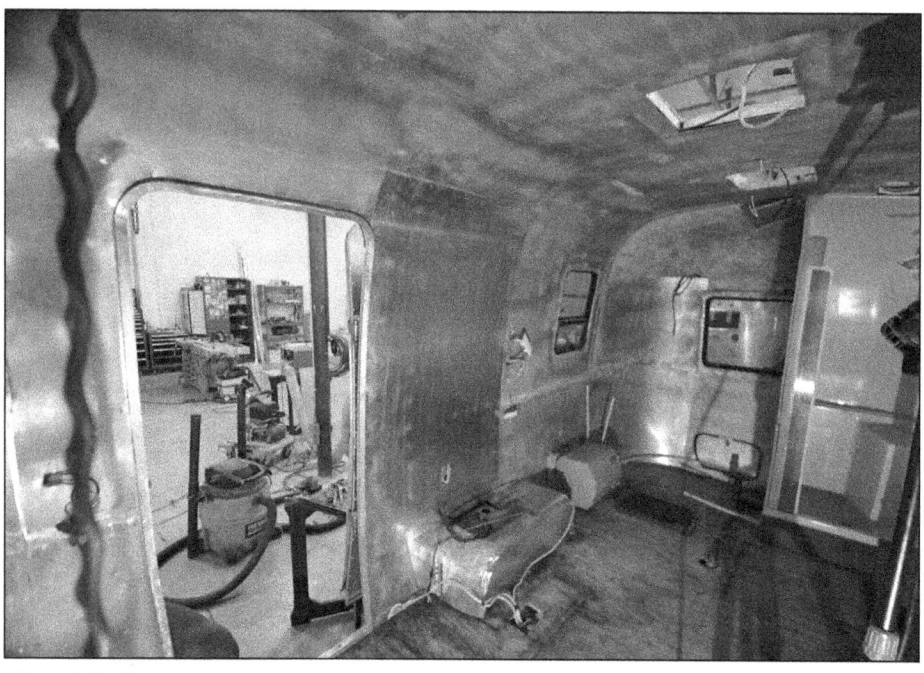

Now that the patch is installed and the wires are sorted, the panel is sanded. At this point, the interior is almost ready for a topcoat, then the custom cabinetry can be installed.

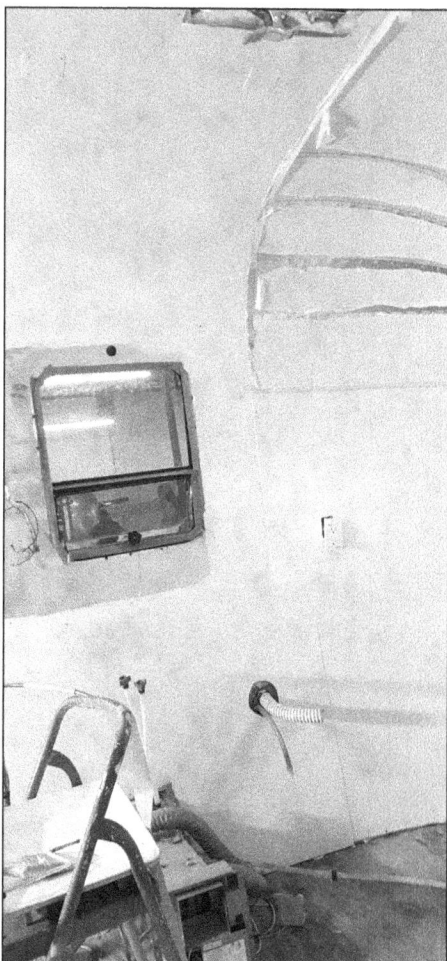

After sanding with 150- and 220-grit paper, the windows and components not intended for paint are masked. After a proper cleaning, the walls are primed and painted with a quality brush and roller.

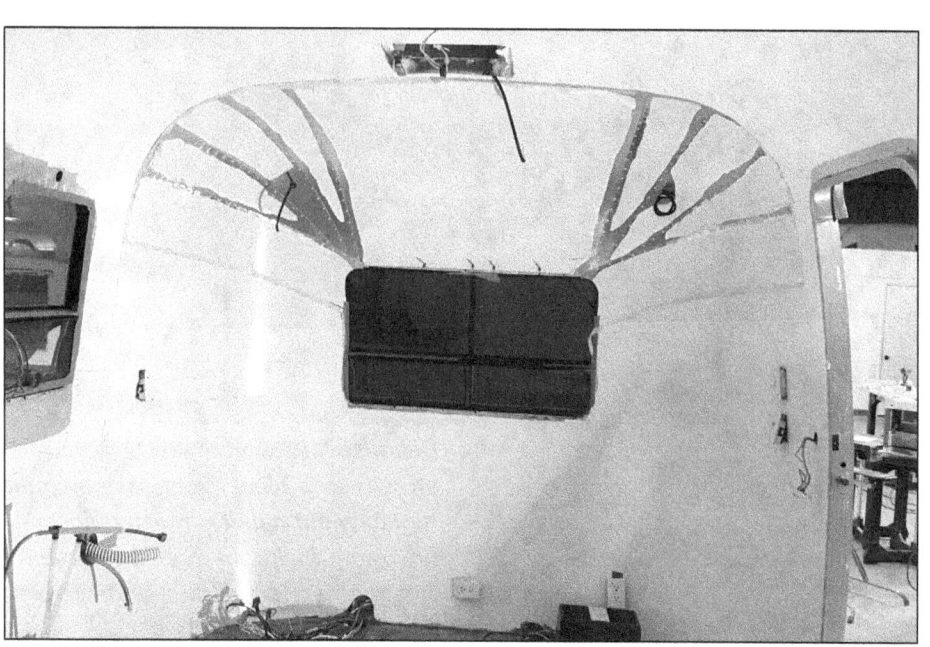

The painted walls (the unpainted portion will be covered with a backsplash) are now ready for interior cabinetry. Also visible is the custom aluminum endcap (with protective plastic coating still applied). It was left bare similar to the one in the Cruisette.

114   STREAMLINE ALUMINUM TRAILERS: RESTORATION AND MODIFICATION

CHAPTER 10

INTERIOR CABINETS

The topic of woodworking contains enough material to fill its own book, and there are plenty of them readily available to study and perfect the craft. In this condensed look at the woodworking involved with camper restoration, I cover the processes and techniques to replace damaged wood, refinish existing wood, and build new wood components.

The Cruisette's owner wanted a restoration that respects the original but has some new features that suits it. One was a larger bed and elimination of the dinette at the front in favor of a settee. This required a custom galley (using period-correct appliances), moving the closet forward, and constructing a custom settee that houses a Dometic A/C unit for truck cabs.

To start a custom build, rough drawings ensure that the new layout works. I used SketchUp modeling software to render layouts such as the Cruisette's new interior. On larger builds, textures and color help design the interior.

To save time, original closet and overhead components are usually retained for reference. But because this interior build changed significantly, they are not useful. Instead, new templates are made and used to guide the construction of the new cabinetry. Before templates are made, however, the interior layout is marked with masking tape.

Laser levels come in handy here, but be sure that the floor is level before marking cabinet positions on the walls and floor. A trailer on unlevel ground or sitting unequally on jack stands results in crooked cabinetry.

After the locations are laid out and checked for level based on window and floor locations (marking the camper center makes another good reference point), construction of the templates begins. There are many mediums and methods to construct templates.

For the Cruisette, the builder opted for hot glue and thin plywood scraps. Other options are MDF (medium-density fiberboard),

Woodworking takes experience and knowledge. Vintage camper manufacturers used a variety of techniques to join and finish various woods. The way you tackle your interior restoration comes down to your build's construction techniques, the carpenter's ability, and the tools and materials available.

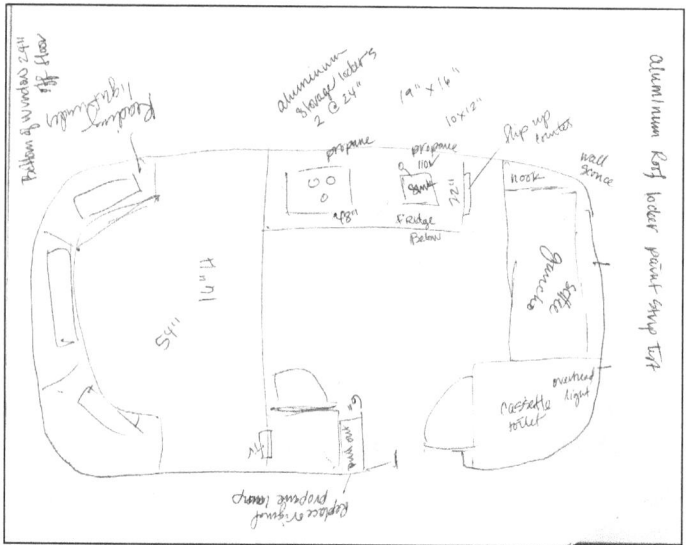

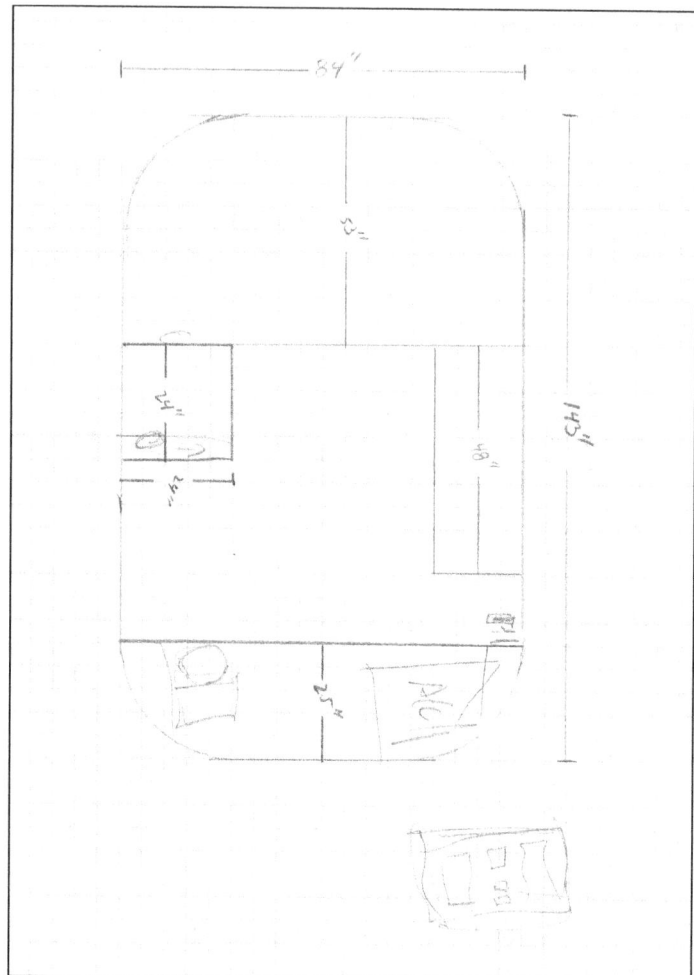

Any changes to a camper begin with rough drawings. This quick sketch on the back of some scrap paper is the beginning of the Cruisette's new layout. In this version, the front settee shares a cabinet that houses a toilet.

A refined sketch, done to scale using graph paper, is the next step to changing a layout. In this drawing, the bathroom closet has been eliminated and the toilet is a low-profile self-contained cassette-style unit.

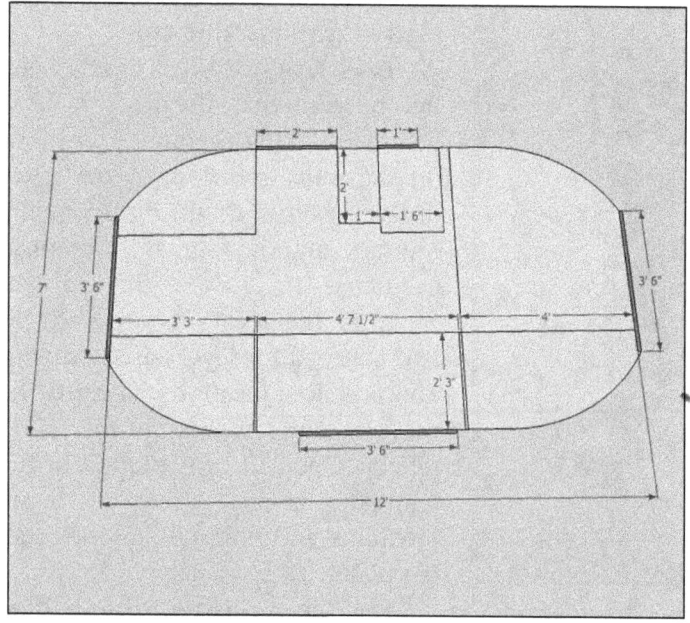

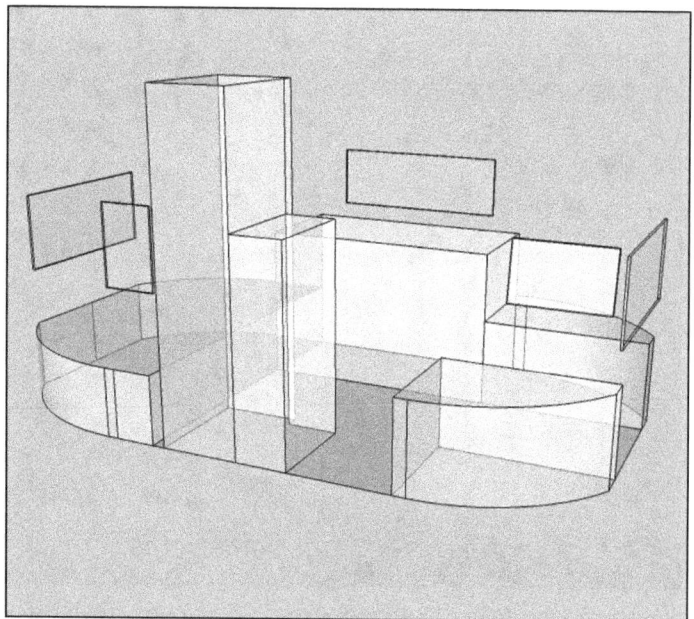

These 3D modeling software renderings are of the original interior dimensions. They plot where the windows fall and help in planning the new interior. Using layers, the original window location is retained, while the new floor plan and cabinetry is designed.

INTERIOR CABINETS

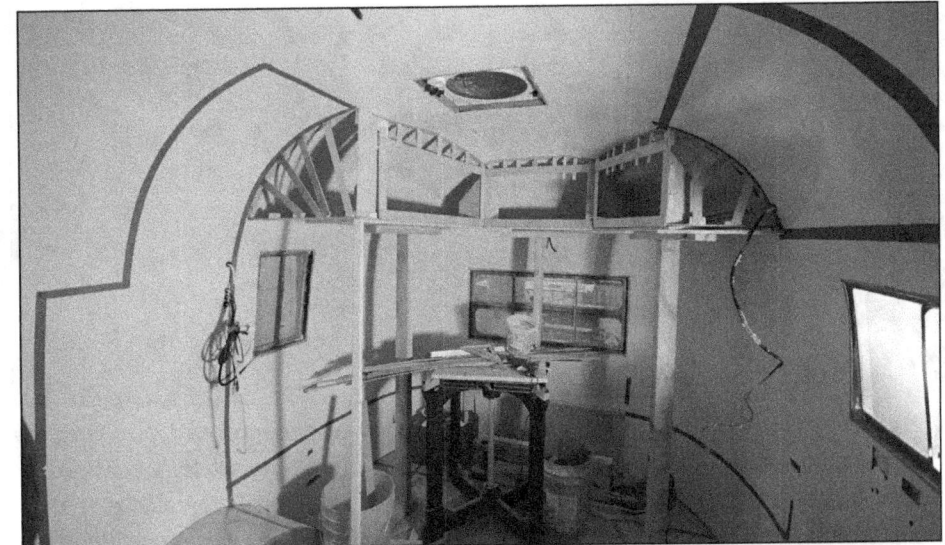

To start the cabinet build, masking tape, squares, and levels (both laser and traditional) are used to map out cabinet locations. These overhead cabinet templates are constructed out of hot glue and thin scrap plywood and positioned with framing.

The template is ready to be removed and transferred to the actual wood to be used to build the cabinet. There are many curves here, and it can be time-consuming to produce a good template. Patience and attention to detail are important here.

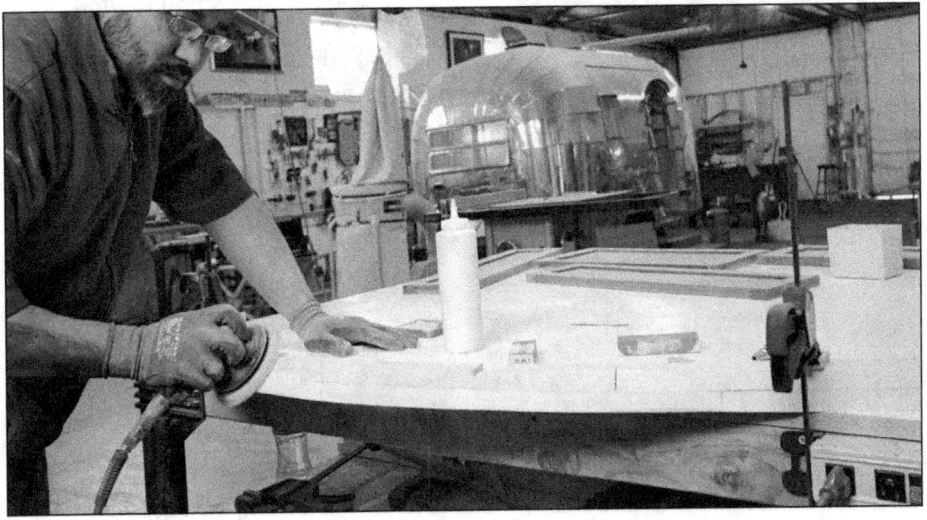

The back support for the overhead cabinets is finely adjusted with a random orbital sander. It attaches to the wall using large sheet-metal screws. This process requires constant checking to ensure a flush gap.

CHAPTER 10

This 1950s galley has seen better days, in particular and not visible here, the 1/4-inch plywood at the galley sides suffered from rot and water damage. The solid wood framing is salvageable but requires plenty of sanding and reinforcement in the form of glue and hidden screws.

The rotted and damaged plywood is replaced here, and the glue is left to set. To remove the old wood, take care not to damage the cabinet framing. These are typically fastened with nails, staples, and screws. A good carpenter hides any modern fasteners and joints to preserve the original character.

cardboard, or template paper. An experienced carpenter can also scribe in the wood components, but this can be detrimental if too much material is removed at a time, rendering a piece useless, and the need to start over.

Once the templates are produced, it's time to transfer them to the new wood. One method, if a template is thick enough, is to use a router with a flush bit to perfectly match the curves.

Wood Finishes

Traditionally most vintage campers used varnish to preserve their wood, of which many types were used. From pine to oak to fir, manufacturers used whatever provided the best cost-to-performance ratio and whatever was available in their region. Wood, particularly plywood, has changed significantly from what was available from the mills in the 1950s and 1960s.

Finding a perfect grain and finish to match a destroyed vintage camper interior is difficult. I use what's available locally at the various lumberyards and typically finish the

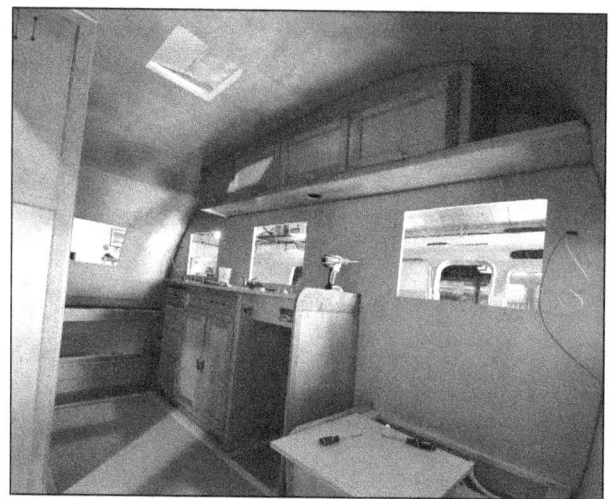

Here, you can clearly see the difference between original wood and the pieces that have been replaced with modern plywood. The newer, golden plywood (birch) yellows slightly with time, but for now it's a significant shade different from the original. What's important is that the rot is gone and this old camper has a new lease on life.

Of the ways to join wood, dowels and related biscuits or dominoes are preferred because it allows the wood to expand and contract naturally. Dowels are also helpful to fill blown-out holes, much like toothpicks used in stripped screw holes in wood. The can, seen here, is used for water, which is used to help clean up excess glue once pieces are clamped together.

INTERIOR CABINETS

When gluing large pieces, grace under pressure is essential. As the glue sets, you can get into trouble if it dries before the pieces are assembled. Another issue with the "glue panic" is drips. Smearing the glue on both surfaces helps provide an even coat. But if drips dry on surfaces intended for finish, it can create problems with how well the finish comes out.

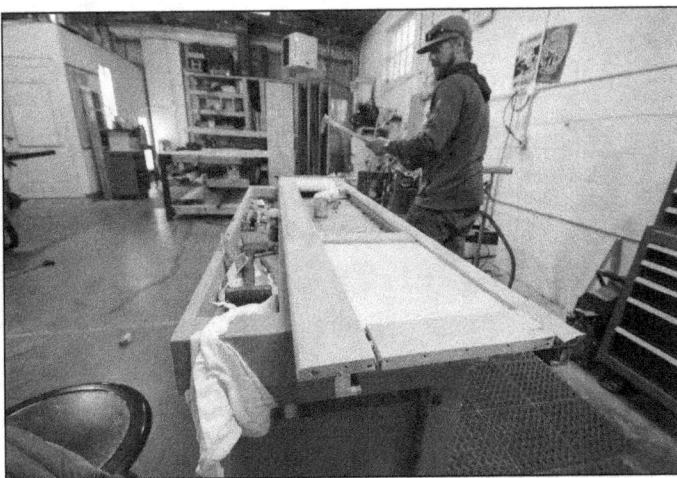

Any major glue drips can be wiped up with a wet rag, or allowed to dry and cut away with a razor blade if not on a finished surface. Before the pieces are glued, pre-select your clamps and practice the clamping routine so things go smoothly. This piece is a large cabinet front.

wood with a water-based wipe-on poly to restore original cabinetry. This is because of budget and time constraints.

If your goal is a perfect match, you can experiment with stains and finishes, such as an oil-based product instead of water, or use traditional varnishes. Finished wood yellows and changes over time, but how much and how quick is difficult to predict. Unfortunately it is a tedious process and often difficult to justify the time spent matching wood finishes.

To help achieve a good match, you can take a sample piece to a local finish specialist. A professional at Sherwin Williams or other retailer can guide you through the multitude of wood-finish products.

Repairing a Cabinet Drawer and Door

1 This drawer front suffered from separation of the plies. To fix it, glue is applied liberally and forced into the crack with light air pressure and splinters, then it is clamped and allowed to dry fully.

2 Here, the drawer front is drying. Note the pieces of wood to prevent marks from the clamps. While this drawer front dries, similar issues on the other drawers are addressed.

3 This cabinet door had its hinge screws break during disassembly. Instead of making new doors, I extracted the screws and filled the holes.

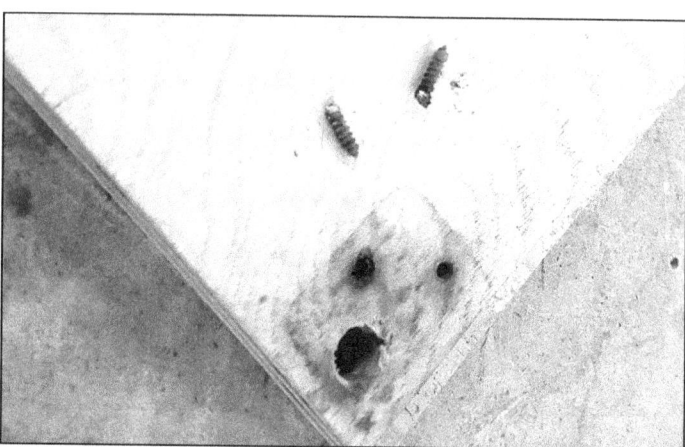

4 The broken screws are drilled and removed with a needle-nose pliers. This is a delicate procedure; you do not want the hole to enlarge more than the dowels used to fill the void.

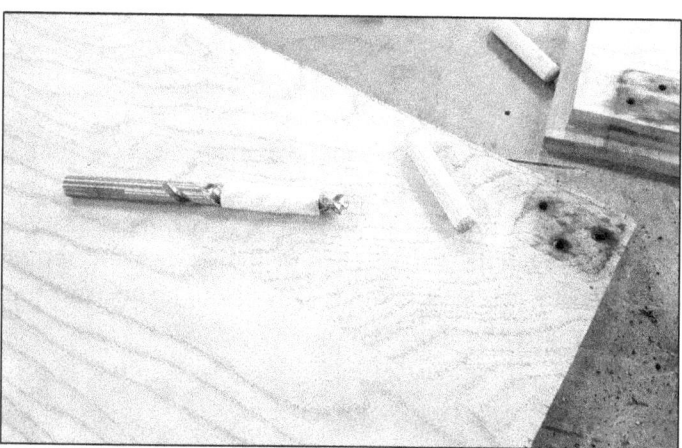

5 Tape is used to prevent drilling through the face of the door. The dowel and drill bit are 3/8 inch in diameter.

6 Once the holes are drilled and dowels glued in place, the protruding ends are removed with a flush-cut pull-saw. Also, these vintage cabinet doors had suffered from rot and plywood separation at the base. They were too far gone to save by gluing the plies.

7 The rotted portion was cut away and a piece of poplar was joined to the bottom with dowels. A dowel jig is used to line up the two pieces.

8 A table saw makes the relief cut in the door by matching the height and depth. Another method to make the recess cut is to use a router table. The choice comes down to what's available and your preferred woodworking technique.

INTERIOR CABINETS

One of the easier and less toxic ways to finish wood is to use a water-based polyurethane. You do not achieve the pure golden, shiny finish that's traditionally found with varnish. These vintage cabinet doors are freshly sanded with 220-grit and receiving their first coat of a wipe-on polyurethane.

Woodworking Procedures

As I mentioned at the beginning of this chapter, there's so much to woodworking as diverse as camper restoration that can't be covered in a book. But I touch on some of the major processes of a typical restoration.

Wood Finishing

There are many ways to finish wood. Some are easy and some are difficult. Your choice is based on many factors.

This walnut has just received some stain and will be sealed with a polyurethane after the stain has sufficiently dried. To prevent damage, the stain and topcoat are applied in a paint booth. No matter the product, application, or drying time, cleanliness is essential.

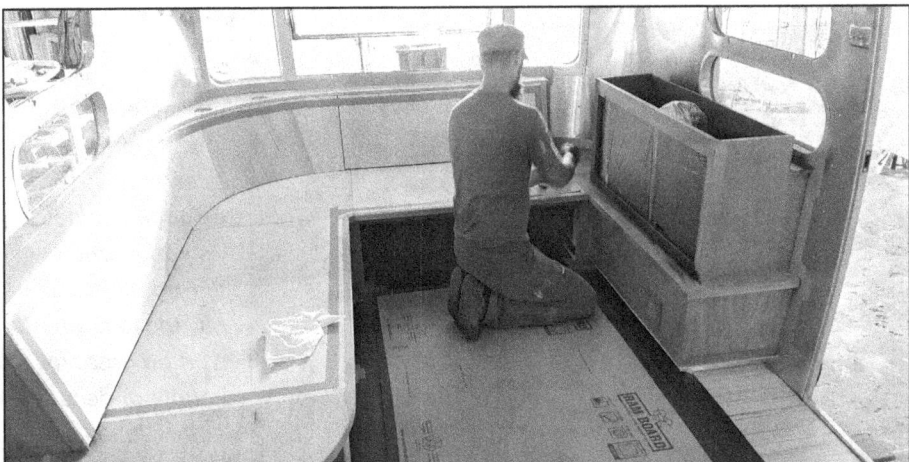

Wood can be finished in place as well. Proper masking and cleaning are essential to a quality finish.

Here, you can see that the stain darkens the walnut. After the stain dries for three days, the topcoat is applied. Typically three coats are used, but it depends on the product. It's easy to see how finish carpentry can use up a large portion of a restoration budget, if professional results are what you're after.

CHAPTER 10

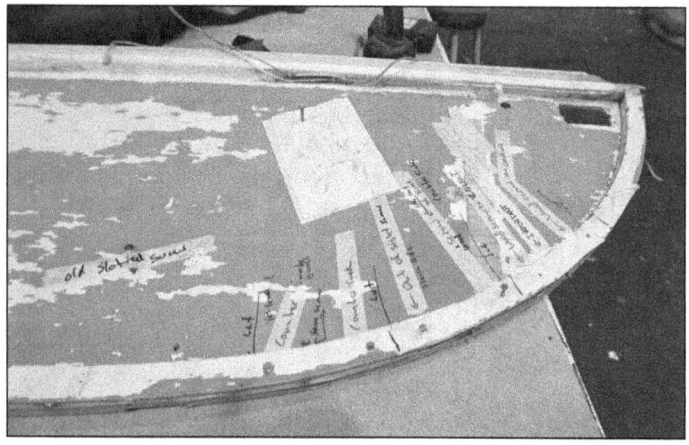

This is the Cruisette's original closet wall. You can see the old, slotted sheet-metal screws used to attach the closet wall to the Airstream's interior sheet aluminum. The hole bore in the wood needs to be slightly larger than the screw. This prevents the screw from binding and pulls the cabinet wall flush to the interior skin.

The Cruisette's cabinetry features black-walnut faces. The framing is constructed from cabinet-grade plywood. First, the galley is laid out based on drawings. To make sure everything fits, the ice chest frame (the ice chest is disassembled for restoration) is placed into the galley.

Cabinet Attachment

You can transfer the template with a pencil or marker. With the marks laid out, a jig- or bandsaw is used to make the cut. To prevent blowout (splintering, or separation of the wood grain), use a fresh blade and tape over the cut line. It's good practice to cut about 1/8 inch from the mark and to use a sander to finish the edge.

This helps prevent blow out and can provide a nice, tight tolerance. Airstream and other manufacturers used a couple of ways to attach cabinetry to walls.

During the 1950s, when the Cruisette was produced, Airstream used large, 1¼- to 1½-inch sheet-metal screws to attach the wood to the walls. On contemporary Airstreams the cabinetry is screwed to aluminum rails attached to the camper walls. Paying attention to disassembly pays off here, as you'll be reproducing the factory work.

A good tip when attaching cabinetry to curved walls is to start at either the top or bottom and work your

This is the beginning of custom cabinetry for a 1990s Bambi that replaces the factory chipboard construction. Here, you can use a square to ensure correct tolerances throughout the build. This cabinet will sit over a wheelwell.

Typically, vintage campers used nails and screws, followed by staples in later years, to join wood in cabinetry. As you learned during disassembly, these methods worked great for a couple of decades before loosening and coming apart.

Nontraditional pocket-hole joinery (shown) has come a long way in terms of efficiency and accuracy and is a good way to reinforce old cabinetry.

INTERIOR CABINETS

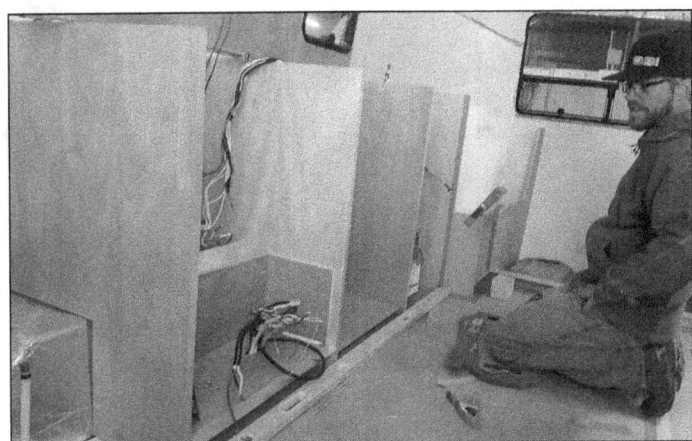

When connecting the components of cabinetry, using a level ensures that the individual cabinets are perfectly lined up. This is checked on the toe kick and on top. On this build, the Progressive Dynamics panel sits in front of the wheelwell.

To help square up doors and drawers, a simple block like this can come in handy.

way along, tightening the screws a little at a time to avoid binding and tenting of the skin (much like tensioning a spoked wheel). On campers that use a mounting rail, this is less important. You want to focus on a good scribed edge to the wall.

I needed to design the Cruisette galley around the new appliances: a vintage Modernaire range, vintage ice chest, and sink with correct vintage hand pump. The range and ice chest were sourced by the owner from various antique camper parts suppliers and dealers. I had a hand pump and sink left over from other camper restorations.

Once the walnut faces are milled to size, they are joined with pocket screws and glue. The Cruisette's framing for the galley was built using cabinet-grade plywood and poplar. Both are joined with pocket screws and glue. Poplar was used instead of pine because it holds its shape better in these dimensions and, for a hardwood, is easy to work with.

As a hydroscopic material, wood changes shape as it exchanges moisture with its surroundings. This instability can cause drawers and doors to bind and jam; it can also result in separated joints and split wood. Some woods are more vulnerable to warping and splitting than others.

Countertop Installation

A restoration must use the materials and hardware available to the builder that most closely match the original. Countertops are a perfect example. The GE Textolite laminate countertop found in most vintage late-1950s and 1960s campers is no longer available. Because of this, the owner chose a countertop from a local supplier.

Because the Cruisette countertop is custom and not original, an MDF template was first produced to help locate the sink, pump, and stove. Once the placement was confirmed, it was transferred to a 3/4-inch piece of plywood.

The countertop is cut to shape using a hole, jig-, pull, and circular saw. From the factory, the sink's cutout edges are always in rough shape because the sink will cover the edges. Here, you can see the hole saw used to create the opening for the sink.

The plywood sides are also covered with aluminum trim, but preventing blowout and chipped edges is more important here than around the sink. Once the holes are cut, a jigsaw makes quick work of the 3/4-inch plywood.

While the adhesive is setting, a roller, weights, and clamps are used for a solid connection. While rolling the top, be mindful of the edges. If you roll over one, you could crack the linoleum and be back to step one. This router has seen better days but still gets the job done. Make sure there's no debris trapped between the router plate that could scratch the new countertop while using the router.

The laminate countertop receives adhesive, then after it has dried, is trimmed to shape with a flush-mount router. Follow the manufacturer's directions for applying adhesive. In most cases, it is applied to both the countertop and linoleum, allowed to tack up, and then sandwiched together.

Aluminum Trim

If your vintage countertops are in good condition, they can be restored by polishing or careful use of filler and paint. Most often, an original countertop is too far gone to save.

The aluminum trim used in a galley is often worth saving and fairly easy to restore. Vintage aluminum trim, like vintage aluminum exteriors of riveted style campers, can be polished to a mirror-like finish due to the metal matrix composition of these early alloys. In fact, wood

The galley trim extrusions did not come with holes pre-drilled. This allows you to set them at even places based on how the cut pieces fall. The tape helps protect the piece while handling and provides a clear marking for hole placement. The screw holes are countersunk so that the oval-head slotted screws sit flush. Countertop trim, and any trim for that matter, is a touch point, and sharp edges should be avoided.

Clamps help position the trim and prevent it from walking during installation. You want the upper lip to be flush with the countertop. The center punch is used here to create a concave hole in the plywood before a pilot hole is drilled. This guides the bit between the plies so the trim does not lift if a hole is too high.

Clean, mitered cuts can be a difficult task. A miter saw with a standard wood blade easily cuts aluminum; or a handheld metal saw can be used. Blocks of wood with a 45-degree miter help with positioning and support during cutting. They also help ensure that you're cutting the correct miter and not the mirror image.

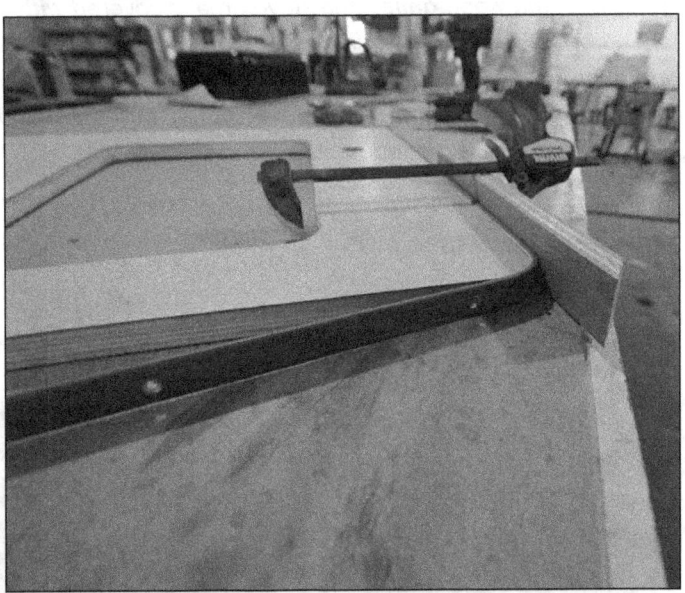

Making bends with aluminum trim is fairly simple if you use the countertop as a buck. Tight radiuses like this corner are more difficult because the inner lip may crease due to compression.

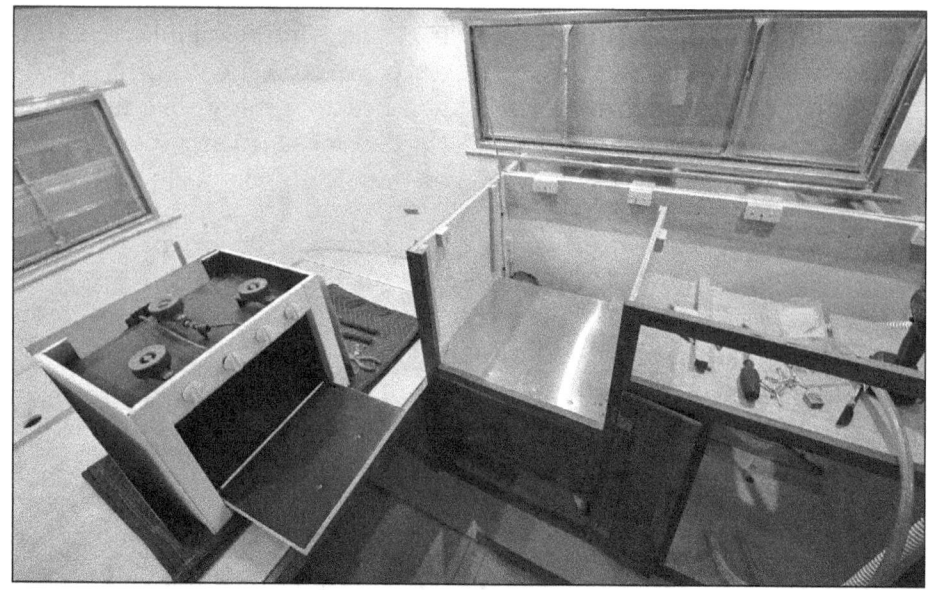

The galley is almost finished, but before the stove and countertop can be installed, a heat shield must be fabricated.

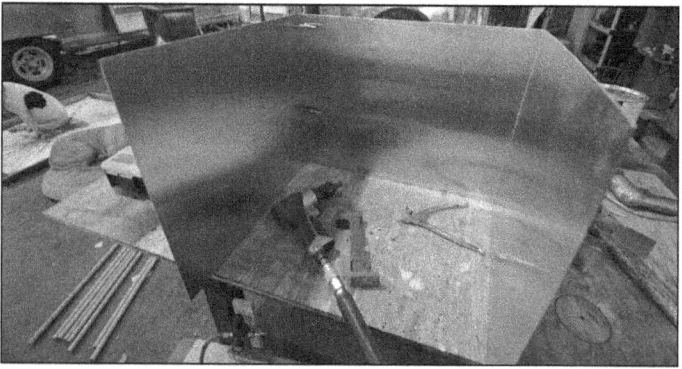

To protect the wood galley, the stove area is covered with sheet metal. A couple of quick bends on the metal brake are all that's needed. Also, you can see the cleats used to mount the countertop, the copper LP tubing, and drain and water line for the sink and hand pump.

I used some aluminum to fabricate the heat shield, but thin-steel sheet metal can be used, too.

Now the stove can be installed (a couple of screws on the oven and under the range cover). After that, the sink and hand pump are fastened and plumbed.

INTERIOR CABINETS

components in a camper are most likely to deteriorate first, as the metal parts are more resilient.

Sometimes, interior trim can be damaged beyond repair due to a rough life. Luckily, replacement aluminum trim is available from many online suppliers, such as Vintagetrailersupply.com. However, these extrusions do not always match up to the originals.

Typically they're close enough, but sometimes, you need to just replace all the old trim with new trim so it matches, especially if your countertop and galley trim is missing or heavily damaged. In the case of the Cruisette, I used all new trim for the custom galley.

The trim that I sourced from Vintagetrailersupply.com came with an anodized finish, which is fine for durability. This finish, however, is more modern than the traditional polished trim associated with vintage campers. To compensate, I stripped the coating with abrasives, and then proceeded to polish the trim using the techniques described in Chapter 14.

The hand pump and back splash (constructed out of the salvaged exterior skin) were polished also. Sometimes trim comes packaged with screws; however, they are not always the correct hardware (contemporary versus vintage). On the same note, trim with pre-drilled holes does not mean it's ready to install.

The trim on countertops are points that your hands touch and are cleaned with towels and sponges, so they should be free from protruding screw heads that may scratch or snag. The proper screw type is an oval-head (slightly domed and smooth), and the hole should be correctly countersunk so that the screw sits flush in the trim.

The countertop construction, 3/4-inch plywood with a laminate top and aluminum trim, is produced using the same construction methods used on tabletops in vintage campers. Because the Cruisette now has a settee instead of dinette, it does not have a tabletop.

However, if your project has one, the reproduction/restoration process mimics that of a countertop. Manufacturers used many methods to store and assist with lifting tabletops that are part of a dinette/bed combination.

Tables and Bed Lifts

Sometimes table parts are in reusable condition, but often they can be damaged and/or worn out. Finding individual parts at a hardware store, such as screws and nuts, is possible; however, levers and pivots may be more difficult to find. Vintagetrailersupply.com offers suitable replacements.

One nice upgrade to a vintage camper is bed lifts; these can be purchased at many RV and boat supply retailers. It's best to hold off on final placement until the bed top is finished and the mattress is installed. This ensures the shock placement and pressure rating is sufficient to lift the bed.

Overhead Lights and Lockers

The original overhead lockers were tossed and replaced with new ones, constructed out of black walnut like the rest of the cabinetry. The Cruisette came with aluminum lockers over the galley, and they were most likely original to the camper. Many early Airstreams and other riveted campers, including

The owner wanted to be able to store airplane luggage underneath the queen-size bed. For that reason, there is no lower crossmember. Here, you can see the start of the power center installation, too. It's best to have systems buttoned up before the final carpentry is finished to prevent damage to the wood. Also note the ball joints for the gas shocks.

Before installation and final finish, the overhead cabinets were wired for lighting. I used LED puck lights for house lighting (incorporated with puck lights in the aluminum lockers) and swivel units with LED bulbs for reading lights. The wires in all cabinets are hidden with a false bottom.

Inside the overhead cabinet are hidden speakers custom made with scrap walnut. They are powered by an amp under the bed and a small Bluetooth receiver hidden in the settee for wireless sound. The polished-aluminum band hides the mounting screws for the cabinet.

Silver Streaks, used aluminum interior components rather than wood.

I saved the original overhead wood cabinet doors and restored them. This process included sanding and fixing separated plies with wood glue and clamps. After a couple of coats of primer, they were painted. The hardware, hinges, screws, and clasps were restored from original by polishing (see Chapter 14 for details).

Metal Plating

Sometimes hardware can be so far gone that simple polishing cannot bring back its original luster. For these cases, plating might be a good solution. I often source large batches of plating for various components (light shrouds, faucets, door hinges, etc.) when polishing and cleaning won't save the finish.

There were just enough hinges and hardware from the original

These vintage camper hardware components are headed to a local plating company for a fresh coat of metal. Sometimes, the cost to simply replace these hinges and latches is less than the plating. However, the quality and shape of reproduction hinges and latches isn't always the same as the original. They are often fairly cheaply made and have a more delicate feel than true vintage hardware.

INTERIOR CABINETS

camper to cover the needs of the galley build and closet on the curbside. The hinges used on the settee and under the bed were modern, soft-close units. Rather than use reproduction hinges that had a similar but not perfect match, the owner opted for hidden hinges.

Upholstery

The Cruisette needed only the front settee covered and was a simple

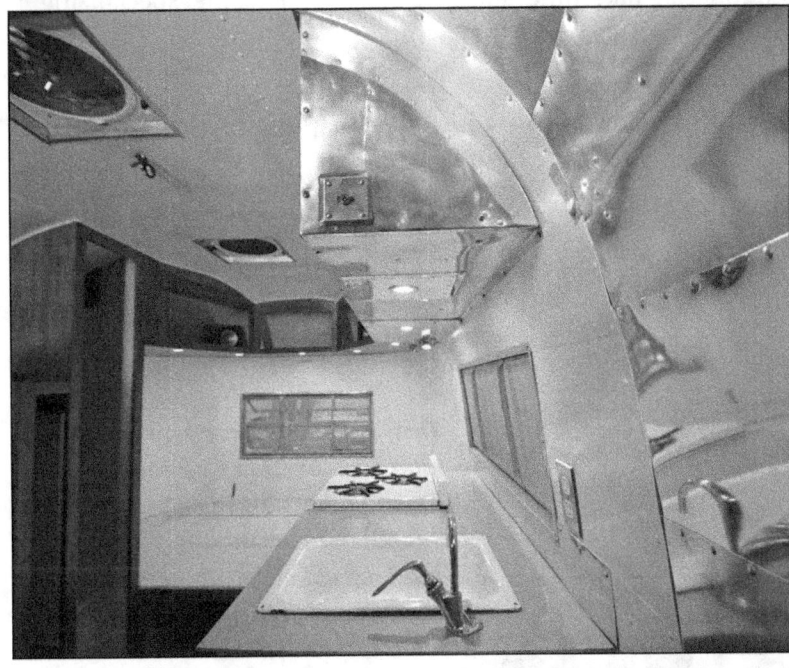

Prior to the countertop install, the Cruisette's interior is coming together here. Still to be installed are the doors and drawers, a gas lantern on the closet, and final plumbing with the countertop mounting.

The owner chose the Cruisette's interior colors, including the walnut cabinets, floor, locker doors, upholstery, and interior accessories.

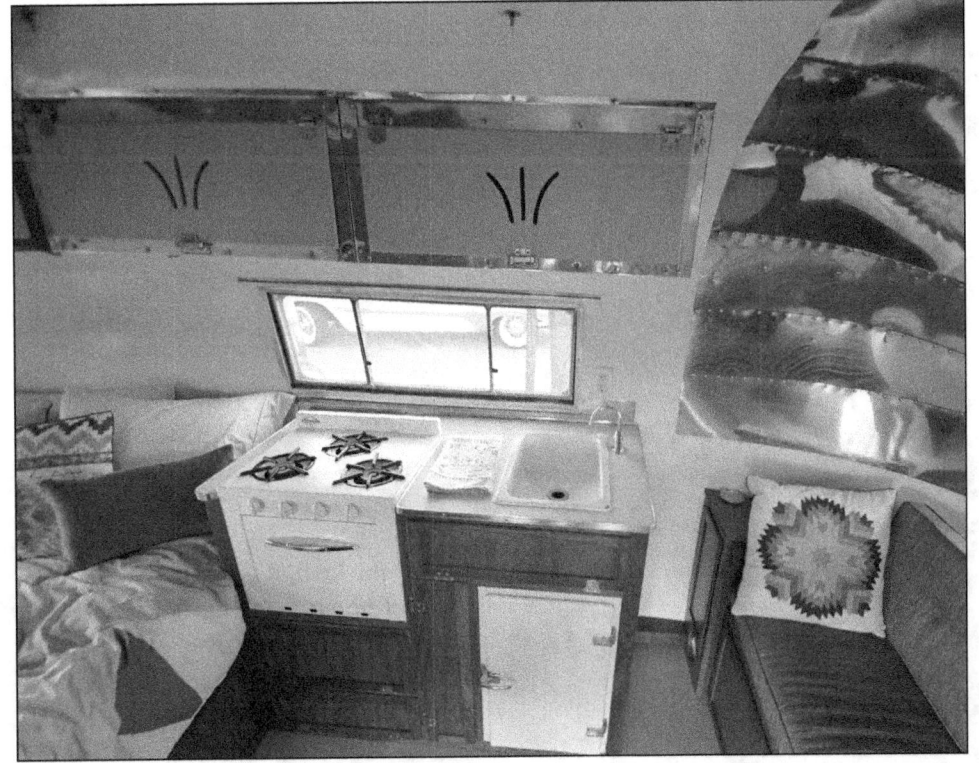

The interior is complete. You can see the color palette coordination.

project for the company contracted to do the job. It uses simple rectangles and does not need to convert into a bed. This isn't always the case in vintage camper interiors. A lounge with compound curves and a couch/dinette that converts into a bed, for example, can be difficult projects.

Also, finding the correct fabric for a restoration can take time and diligence; it is a vital factor to the camper as a whole. And this holds true for accessories such as curtains and rugs. There are many fabric outlets that provide a wide variety of options, with some specializing in vintage reproductions.

This late-1970s Airstream Sovereign now features a custom lounge, among other unique interior features. There are many ways and styles to produce upholstery for this interior, from waterfall to piped edges, and the choice of material and stitching, to name a few variables. The end product comes down to your taste and the upholsterer's ability.

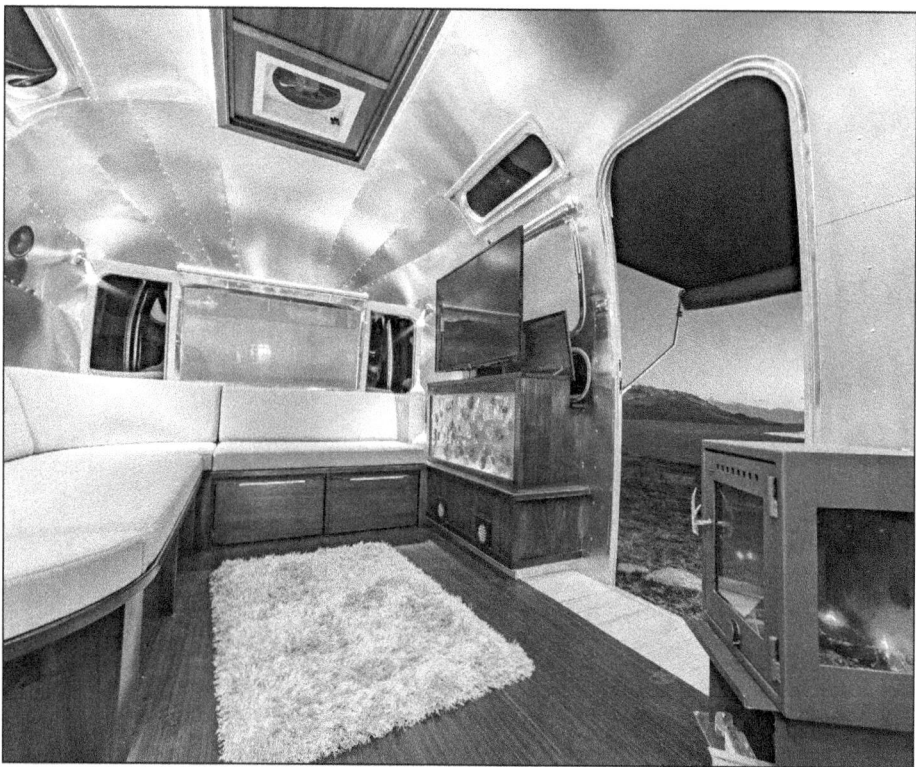

With the lounge upholstered, this Sovereign interior now takes on a new feel. Some highlights of this build are a hidden TV cabinet with art glass, hi-fi audio, custom walnut cabinetry, and wood-burning stove.

CHAPTER 11

APPLIANCES

Essential components to the camper restoration process are the appliances. And just like the camper itself, stoves, fridges, and heaters all end up taking some sort of abuse and damage from decades of use. These items can use a good portion of the restoration budget due to time and materials, whether you pay someone to do it or roll your sleeves up and do it yourself.

In addition to a range, fridge, heater and ice chest, many other appliances, some vintage and some modern, can be added to a camper. For example, I've installed washers, dryers, and microwaves in vintage campers but hid them in cabinetry.

On that note, these mechanical items can be a great way to hone your restoration skills before you

This 1950s Modernaire range is a perfect period-correct appliance for the Cruisette. It just needs a full restoration before it is ready for the small Airstream.

From the 1950s, like the range and Cruisette itself, this ice chest complements the vintage camper nicely. Its brown finish, lack of insulation, and rust, however, do not work with this build.

STREAMLINE ALUMINUM TRAILERS: RESTORATION AND MODIFICATION

CHAPTER 11

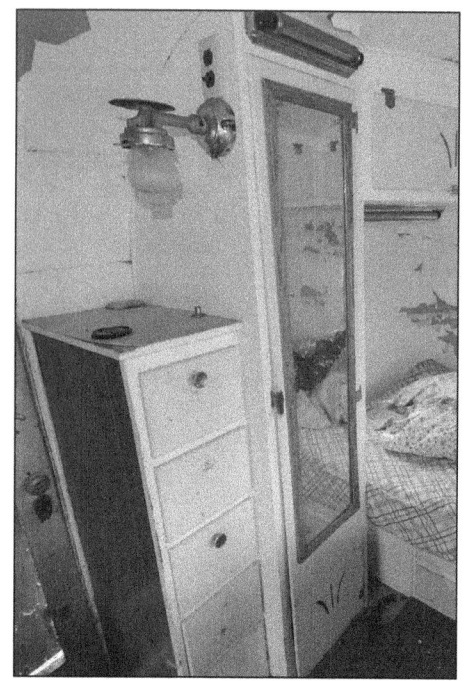

Although not necessarily an appliance, the gas lamp is an essential fixture in any vintage camper.

The backside of the stove shows damage from transit. Although disappointing, this takes only a little tweaking to straighten. Most important, the stove must sit level in the galley.

Finding a period-correct appliance for your camper can be a journey in itself. Many companies specialize in dismantling and reselling camper components. Be ready to add the cost of the appliance and the cost of restoring it to your budget.

To begin the restoration process, all appliances must be washed to remove all grime, dirt, cobwebs, and debris. A degreaser such as Simple Green and a detergent such as dish soap work great with a scrub brush and a little elbow grease. Be sure that the brush isn't too stiff to avoid scratching surfaces if you plan to save the original finish. If you're repainting or coating, this is less of a concern.

Heater

If your camper's original heater is long gone, finding a suitable replacement isn't impossible, but depending on your goals and budget, a contemporary stand-in might be the way to go. Sometimes a vintage heater can be bulky, particularly early catalyst-style versions. The Cruisette's heat comes from the Dometic trucker cab A/C unit, which runs on 110-volt, so I did not have to worry about an LP heater.

Although fairly simple to fix, often the thermocouple doesn't work or a line is clogged. Vintage heaters are a roll of the dice when it comes to safety and efficiency. Contemporary catalytic heaters are nice in their quietness and efficiency, but they do not look very vintage.

One solution is an LP quick-connect line hidden inside a cabinet. The small heaters can stand on special feet and are placed in the camper when needed and stored out of site when unnecessary. With some

This galley features a contemporary sink, faucet, and range (the hand pump is original). Despite the modern convenience and not having to restore or locate originals, these appliances do not take away from this 1950s camper's charm. When selecting a modern replacement, attention to style can go a long way.

dive head first into a full-size project. The practices are the same as for a camper, just on a smaller scale. This means less damage to the wallet or ego if things don't go as planned. If you can successfully restore a vintage range, heater, or fridge, moving on to larger-scale operations should go more smoothly.

The owner of the Cruisette selected an ice chest and range that felt best suited the tiny Airstream; the gas lamp was original to the camper.

APPLIANCES

Across from the galley is a modern Dometic three-way fridge. A custom wood insert, which matches the wall panels, helps this modern feature blend into a vintage camper.

The stove's components arrived packaged well enough in plastic bags and newspaper (bubble wrap would have been better suited). But it still suffered from the typical carrier abuse on top of the expected toll over 60 years.

layouts, the heater can be mounted inside a cabinet door, and when you need to heat the room, you simply open the door. Water heaters or pumps are hidden and should be replaced if they no longer work.

Stove

During shipping, the Cruisette's new stove took a pretty good hit to the rear corner. I was able to straighten it, and it was hidden, being in the back. The stove was in pretty rough shape, with its fair share of rust, scratches, and dings.

Because both the stove and ice chest were in rough shape, I planned to refinish all surfaces. The stove was white with a yellow top and back splash. The ice chest was brown. To tie them together, I planned to finish them in appliance white. This created some issues with the stove, as the new finish must resist the high temperatures.

Originally, stoves were coated with porcelain or high-temperature enamel; unfortunately, this process is difficult to reproduce due to health and environmental concerns. Some restoration specialists perform porcelain coating for originality. However, shipping costs to a specialist can add up quickly, and you should plan to pay a premium for a specialty service like this.

To avoid this issue, I asked a local plating company to recommend a high-temperature powder coating for the stove. Because it had to be special ordered in a set quantity, I also had the ice chest coated. It ended up costing the same amount as if I had finished the ice chest myself. If refinishing your stove with a powder coater is out of your budget or skillset, you can use a high-temperature enamel.

Inside the stove, where I noticed some rust, I used a high-temperature paint after removing the rust. (Most automotive stores or hardware stores stock a high-temperature paint for engines and grilles.) This included the door return spring and levers.

To prep the stove and ice chest for powder coating, they were completely disassembled. (The ice chest is pretty straightforward. Its front frame is wood with aluminum skin, much like a canned ham–style camper.)

To help ensure that the stove fits its location in the galley, the dimensions were clearly marked for easy reference. When there are many people working on a restoration, information should be readily available or things can go awry very easily.

STREAMLINE ALUMINUM TRAILERS: RESTORATION AND MODIFICATION

CHAPTER 11

The top of the stove is a good indication of the state of things. Here, you can see the main line going to the manifold and the slotted screws that hold the burners in place. These thread into simple clips that often rust. Finding new clips is easy; they are available at most automotive parts stores.

The burners are not physically fixed to the manifold; they simply slide over their respective orifice. The main gas line coming in and the one that feeds the stove are threaded onto the manifold. Be careful not to strip threads or fasteners, as repairing the casting or soft brass nuts is difficult. All the burners and the stove line are disconnected.

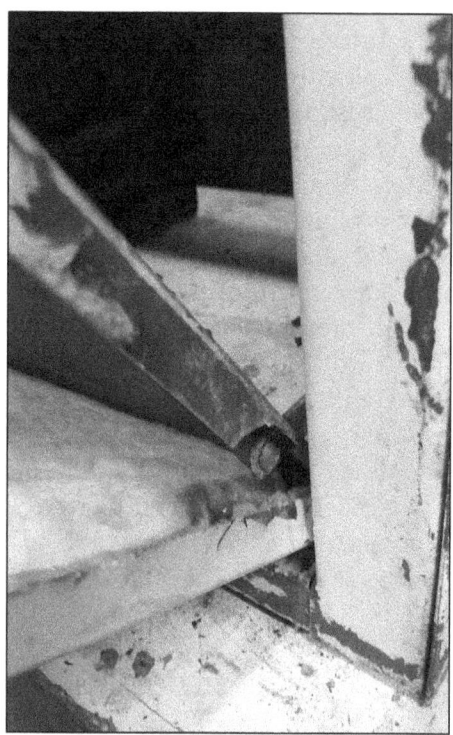

To find this screw hidden in the oven door, the handle needed to be removed. There are many screws in these appliances, so be sure to keep track of where they go to ease the reassembly process. Some batt insulation was used in the door. Use proper safety precautions when disposing of it, and replace it with a high-temperature alternative.

After the return spring was freed, the rest of the door was removed. Two screws hold the hinge pin in place. A good friend once said, in regard to rebuilding carburetors, "They can only go together one way." I always think of this quote when disassembling but still try to record the process to remove the guesswork.

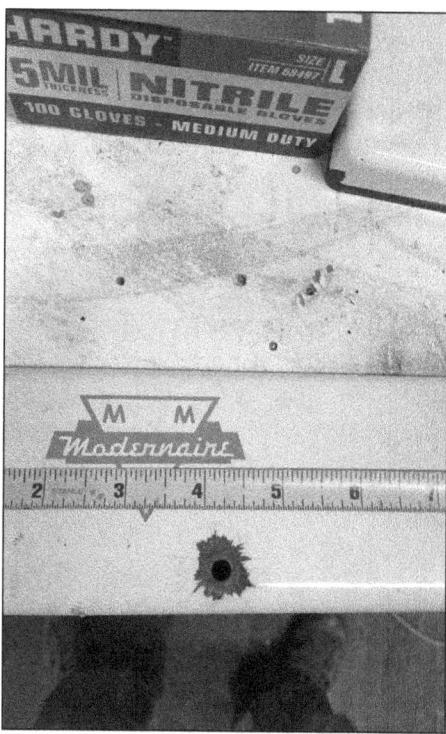

The original Modernaire decal, unfortunately, will not survive the coating process. To compensate, I enlisted the help of a decal professional. By taking photos with measurements, they were able to re-create the logo. Modernaire was a popular manufacturer of RV appliances during the 1950s and 1960s and is still in business today but now specializes in home and commercial hoods.

APPLIANCES

After the coating process and reassembly, the stove now looks like this. The final detail is to apply the decal.

The reproduction decal has been installed. The artist who reproduced it sent a couple of extras, which helped to reduce the pressure of properly aligning the decal on the first try.

Ice Chest

Be sure to document the disassembly process and mark where the hinges, latches, and other parts, such as the ice tray, go. This helps with reassembly. The wood frame to the ice chest was in rough shape, so I used the old sticks as a guide and cut new lumber. In addition, the aluminum was pretty hammered, so I shaped some new sheet metal on the brake.

Restoring an Ice Chest

1 *This ice chest had been installed in a couple of campers, judging from the various holes and nails. Also, you can see how hard and brittle the door gasket has become. Adding to the problems is a healthy dose of tin worm.*

2 *The door latch catch has spacers to provide the proper positioning. If missed during reassembly, it could create a headache.*

3 The face of the ice chest is aluminum over wood, which is held together with screws and nails. Disassembly is with a screwdriver, small crowbar, and hammer. The wood was rotted, as expected, and was replaced. Likewise, the damaged aluminum was reproduced rather than salvaged.

4 Rivets are used to fasten the two door skins together, and they capture the door seal. To coat the two pieces and to replace the seal, they are drilled out.

5 The two door pieces were separated after the rivets were removed. It was originally insulated with fiberglass batt, which I removed. The old insulation will be replaced with bubble foil, which will also be used on the ice chest's exterior.

6 After returning from the metal-coating shop, the ice chest was reassembled. I insulated it with bubble foil (see Chapter 8 for details). From the factory, these were insulated with fiberglass batt.

APPLIANCES

7 Be sure to clean all surfaces to remove any oils and dust from assembly before applying adhesive. Ice chests were originally insulated with fiberglass batt and foam boards in later years. Ice chests are a nice alternative to vintage fridges, which are often bulky and heavy.

8 A new rubber hose is fitted to drain the ice tray. This is routed out the bottom of the camper. Also visible is the new rubber door seal. If you want the vintage look and prefer the smaller size of an ice chest, several manufacturers provide a 12-volt refrigerator conversion kit.

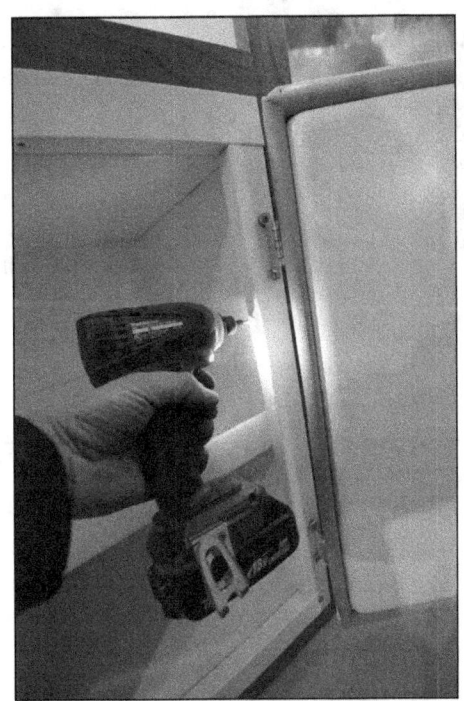

9 Rather than pound nails into the Cruisette's black-walnut galley framing, I opted for stainless screws. Regardless of your fastening system, be sure to pre-drill the holes to avoid splitting the wood framing.

10 As components are restored, they start to accumulate. Here, you can see many of the pieces to the Cruisette awaiting their turn to be fastened to the vintage camper.

STREAMLINE ALUMINUM TRAILERS: RESTORATION AND MODIFICATION

CHAPTER 11

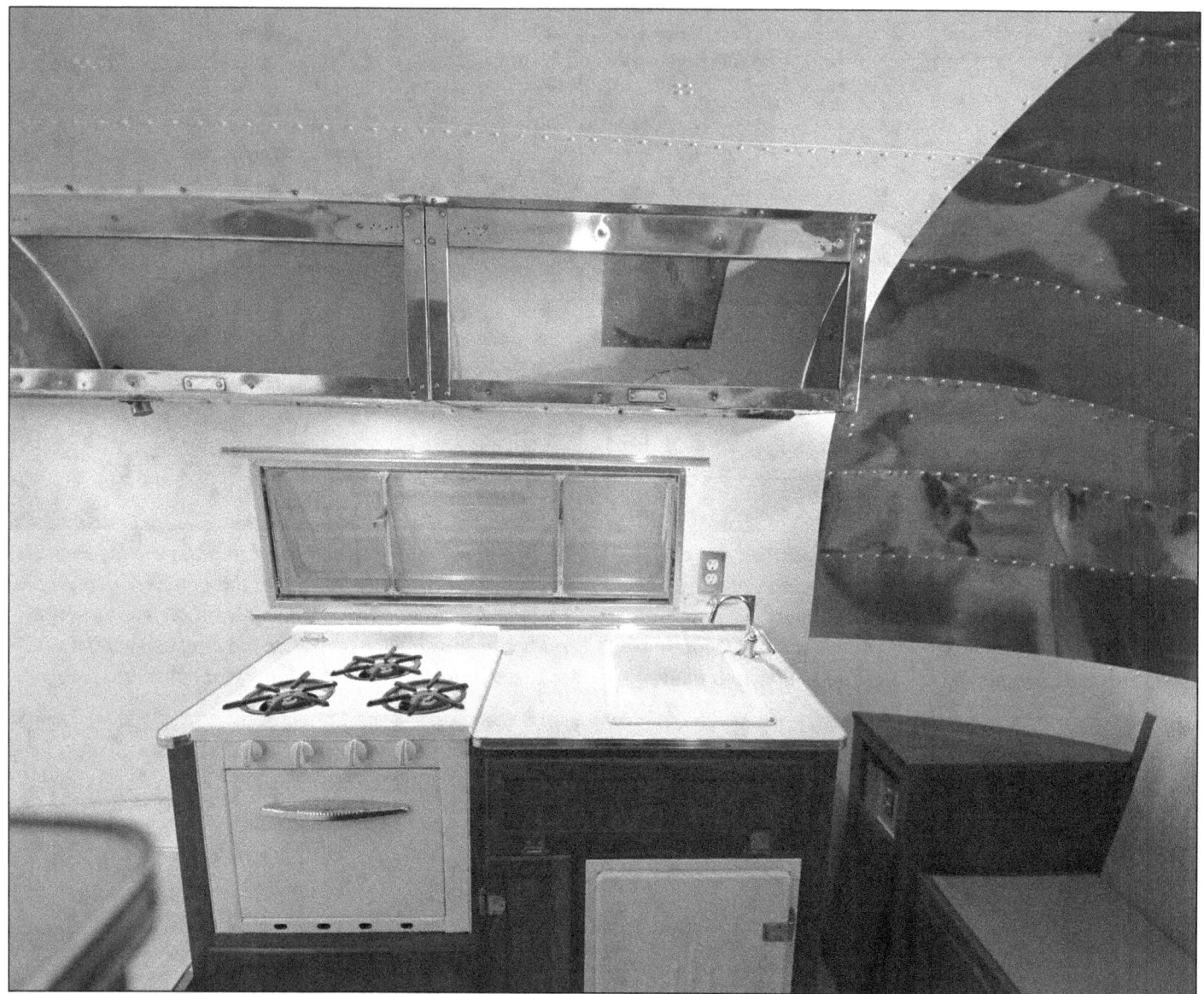

11 *A completed galley with all appliances installed. Arriving at this point took a fair amount of persistence and attention to detail, but the end result is worth it.*

Door Seal

You can request samples of rubber gaskets to avoid issues. Finding parts for something that's been out of production for decades can turn into a time and money pit, such as trying to replace a long-defunct door seal on a 1950s ice chest. I was lucky in that a neighboring business specialized in commercial refrigeration. I showed them a sample of the rubber seal, and they gave me the number of their custom seal guy.

One day the tech showed up, took a look at the gasket, and said he'd take it out to his van and be right back. Twenty minutes later he gave me a new gasket cut and welded to fit the door. Turns out he had rubber seal tooling in the van and makes gaskets on the spot.

Moral of the story? If you need to replace the gasket on a 60-year-old ice chest, start by consulting a local commercial refrigeration repair business.

Gas Lamp

The Humphrey gas lamp in the Cruisette was a popular option for campers in the 1950s and 1960s; other manufacturers such as Sun-Lite and Coleman produced gas lamps, too. Their popularity was because battery power and 12-volt lights were not a very efficient option to illuminate a camper at the time, but every camper already came equipped with an LP tank.

APPLIANCES

Restoring a Gas Lamp

1 The glass globe in a gas lamp is held in place with a retaining spring. Simply squeeze the tabs together and the globe releases.

2 After the globe was removed, I found that the gas lamp was missing its original ceramic burner nose and had a piece of threaded pipe in its place.

3 The threaded pipe has been removed and a proper ceramic burner nose was installed. Burner noses can loosen and fall out when traveling, so replacing them is a common occurrence. I did not try to light the threaded pipe and do not endorse it, but I imagine it would work in a pinch.

CHAPTER 11

4 *Before committing time to polishing, plating, and brightening, I bench tested the gas lamp by attaching it to a secure location, connected the liquid propane, and installed a mantel. After the lamp ran for a few hours, deeming it safe and functional, I dismantled it and cleaned it (see Chapter 14 for details).*

5 *Here's the gas lamp cleaned up and working. It provides a little warmth and light, but most important it adds to the Cruisette's vintage charm.*

In addition to providing adequate light, a gas lamp also provides a little warmth and helps dry the air in humid environments. They are pretty simple in design and rely on a mantel exactly like those found in Coleman lanterns. Other than that, there's a heat shield, glass globe, cast body, needle valve, and tin base.

The gas lamp's pot-metal frame and tin base were in decent condition and cleaned up nicely with some elbow grease. Typical of any restoration, you're never sure what you'll run into until you start taking things apart. When the gas lamp's globe was removed, I found a threaded pipe where a burner nose should reside. Although it would probably work in a pinch, this was not an acceptable fix for the long term.

Burner noses can loosen when traveling down the road until they fall out, and because they were made of ceramic, they also occasionally broke. Vintagetrailersupply.com stocks a variety of burner noses to keep these vintage lamps going. It also carries mantles and globes, as these parts are fragile and often break, too.

Rather than order new, I was able to find a vintage ceramic burner nose in some old parts from other restorations. For the glass globe, the owner chose a different one than what the camper originally came with, again from my parts collection. The mantel was found at a local camping outlet store; they tend to be found at most outdoor and hardware stores.

CHAPTER 12

PLUMBING AND LIQUID PROPANE

I have covered quite a few of the components in a camper, such as windows, doors, chassis, appliances, and electrical. In this chapter, I discuss systems that deal with the flow of liquids and gases. In a camper restoration, you must deal with plumbing in the form of liquid propane and water, including both fresh and waste.

Plumbing

The bigger the camper, the more plumbing it has. In the case of the Cruisette, the water plumbing is pretty simple: two holding tanks (a gray and fresh) and a vintage hand pump. Considering that some larger campers may have a galley, shower, vanity, toilet, water heater, and multiple storage tanks, including fresh (potable water), gray (sink/shower), and black (toilet), this was a nice change of pace.

Because of the small body and because a fairly large HVAC unit is hidden under the settee, I went with tanks mounted inside the frame. It is common to mount tanks on larger campers but not so common on smaller units. Due to the added cost, many camper manufacturers simply mount tanks inside the camper's cabinets.

Usually they're found up front, forward of the axles. For safety reasons, large fresh-water tanks are rarely mounted at the back. Tongue weight is a serious consideration when designing a trailer that tows safely. In general, any trailer with less than 10 percent of its weight on the tongue tends to sway when towing. Adding water to a tank mounted far behind the rear axles, due to the fulcrum over the rear wheels, causes the tongue to lose a significant amount of weight. Also, water sloshing around at the rear of a camper amplifies the effects of road sway.

Some manufacturers mounted water tanks on the side, forward of the rear axle, in the galley. To help

Of course, vintage camper galleys are smaller than household ones, so plumbing often involves working in impossibly small spaces. Here, you can see white PEX (cross-linked polyethylene) water lines (currently capped off), and black ABS (acrylonitrile butadiene styrene) waste pipes. The plumber is taking a measurement through the cabinet holes to cut a length of pipe in a galley.

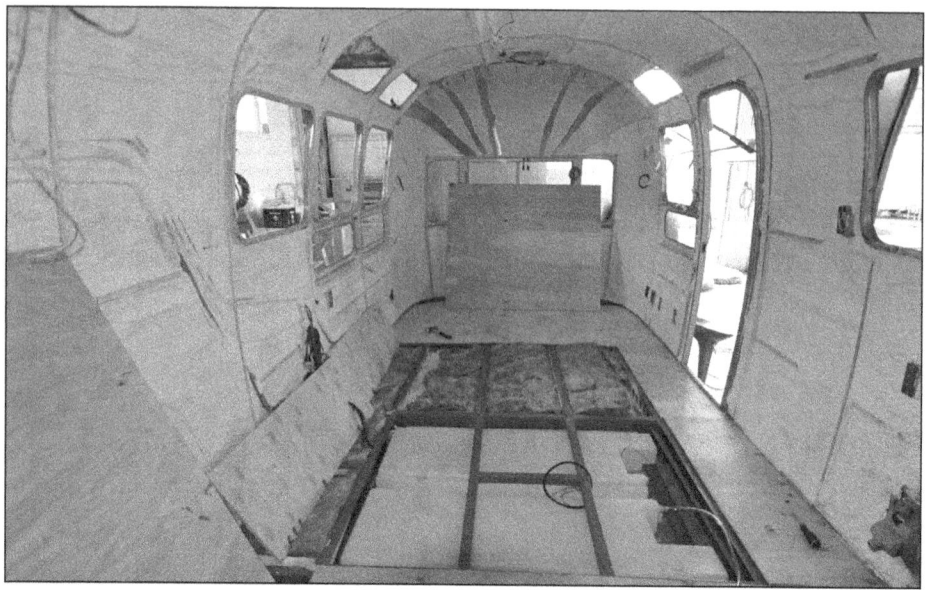

The fresh-water tank is mounted in the dinette of this vintage camper. Typically these are mounted to the same side as the galley to simplify plumbing. The corrugated gravity fill hose and a city water hook-up (the hole to the left of the bench) are yet to be installed.

This chassis-mounted fresh-water tank is nestled in the lowest position, just forward of the rear axle for good weight distribution during towing. This placement provides the least amount of sway when on the road. The protruding wires are for heating pads on the underside; to the tank's right are wires for the tank sensor.

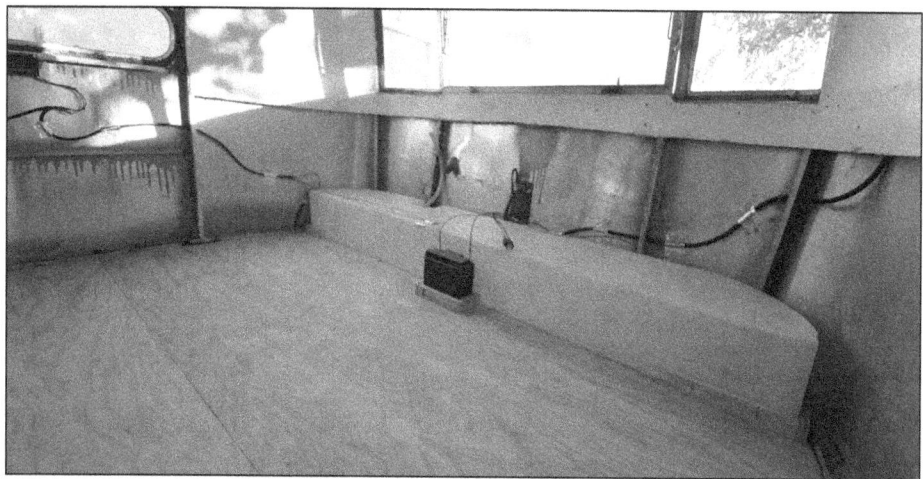

This fresh-water tank is shaped to sit flush at the front of many Airstreams. When a chassis-mounted tank is out of the budget, this is a good option to safely place the weight of a water tank centered in an Airstream. The little battery is only temporary for transit; the tank is not securely mounted yet.

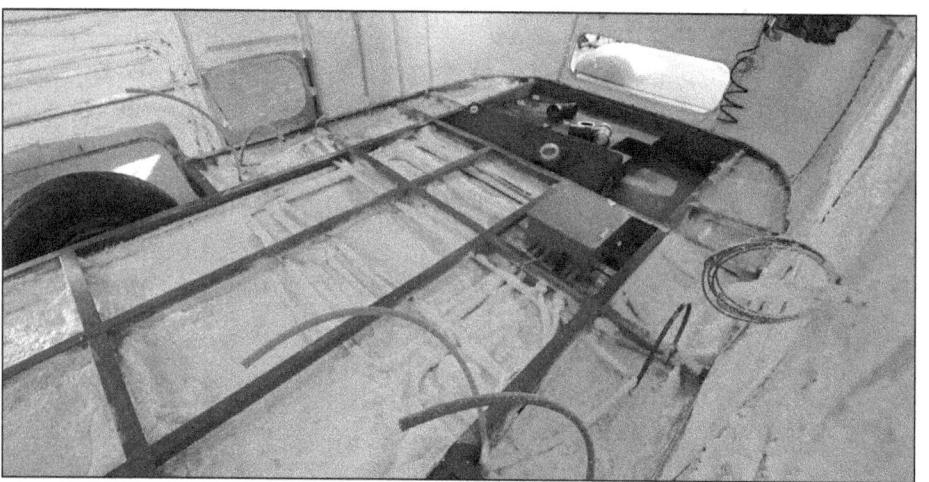

Black- and gray-water tanks are often mounted at the rear, under the subfloor. The black-water tank is distinguished by its large opening for the toilet to mount (neither of these tanks are in their final mounting locations). In this interior layout, the shower and vanity are split by the hallway; you can see both the hot and cold PEX lines that feed the shower and vanity.

offset the weight of a galley and water tank on one side, these manufacturers added leaves to one side of the camper so it rode level. Although this worked, it's not the best scenario. If possible, it is best to mount your tank in the front or in the frame ahead of the axle.

Black- and Gray-Water Tanks

Airstream and other manufacturers mount the black- and gray-water tanks behind the axles of larger units (in the frame, for a lower center of gravity), but these campers have sway control (tongue-mounted), dual axles, and a significant tongue weight. Also, the gray- and black-water tanks are typically smaller than the fresh-water tanks. When figuring out where to mount a water tank in a camper, consideration to position is very important to how the camper tows.

Water Pump

Not that much different than household plumbing, camper plumbing provides a source of fresh water when off the grid. This system includes holding tanks and a 12-volt water pump to feed the faucet, shower, and toilet. The pump is actuated by a switch, then it automatically turns on to build water pressure. It's important to turn off the power to the switch when not in use to avoid draining the battery.

In addition, cutting the power when storing a camper is vital; if it's left on and a line bursts, the pump fills the coach with water, causing major damage. Likewise, city water should be turned off when storing to avoid the same issue. The water pump should be mounted as low as possible in the pluming to assist with purging the air. To increase the life of a pump, you can install an air-accumulator

Any camper build requires countless trips in and out of the coach to take measurements and make cuts. Besides interior skin and cabinetry, a major contributor to the running in and out is plumbing. There are so many sizes and fittings and twists and turns that camper plumbing requires patience and forethought. Of this pile of ABS elbows, only a small number will make its way into the camper.

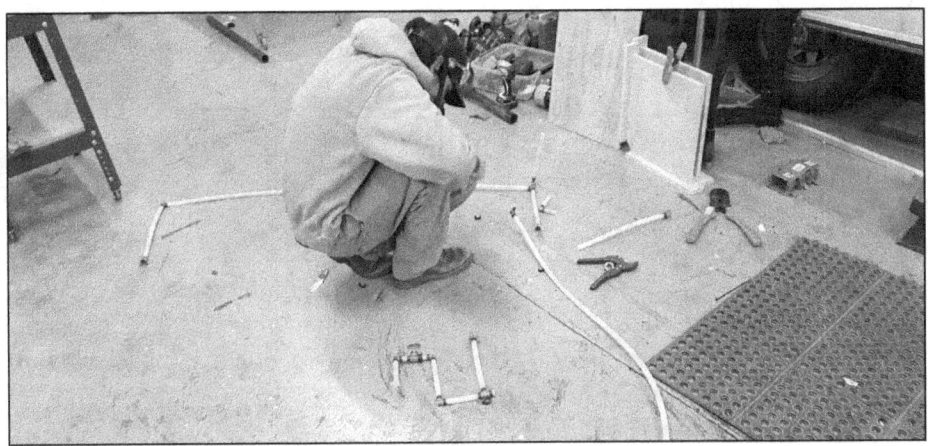

Sometimes it's easier to attach portions of plumbing outside the camper so that you don't have to work with tools in small spaces. The blue ratchet cutter is for slicing the PEX tubing and the orange crimper is for the PEX rings.

There are a few ways to cut PVC and ABS tubing. If it's small enough, a ratchet cutter works; however, larger tubing is difficult to slice and varies with fatiguing. For speed and accuracy, a miter saw is the best option. For quickness, a reciprocating saw makes swift work but leaves a jagged edge.

tank. This keeps the pump from cycling too frequently and provides consistent water pressure.

Water-Pressure Regulator

When hooked up to city water, the pressures can vary widely, which could cause problems for fittings. To prevent over-pressuring your system, install a water-pressure regulator in line with the city hookup. This keeps line pressure consistent and helps avoid a burst line.

A city water system works with holding tanks by using one-way valves. The holding tank is typically filled with a gravity-feed system; then it's plumbed to the pump. The city water inlet does not fill the tanks if a one-way valve is placed in-line after the pump. It allows water to flow from the pump to the fixtures but stops the water from the city hookup from flowing into the tank. This allows the city water system to pressurize and send water to the fixtures.

Water Valve

Likewise, there needs to be a one-way valve mounted at the city water inlet that lets water flow from the city into the camper but does not allow water from the pump to flow out of the city water hookup. There are many ways to plumb a camper. Originally, copper tubing was used. If you're going for a period-correct restoration, you can still find the correct-diameter and wall-thickness tubing and brass fasteners to restore a vintage water system. However, this requires more time and patience to complete, as a watertight seal is most difficult to achieve with threaded fittings, even with pipe dope and tape. For most restorations, I use a PEX system.

In this 1990s Airstream, two fresh-water PEX lines and an ABS pipe are exiting the gray-water tank. This ties into the galley sink drain and black-water tank venting. The sheet-metal pipe protruding is tied into the forced-air system to provide heat and prevent freezing. This is often eliminated on newer campers in favor of electric tank heating.

Running the drainpipe to the gray-water tank involves cutting holes with a drill-mounted hole saw. Like household drainpipe, camper drain piping needs to provide adequate rise over the run to allow good water flow.

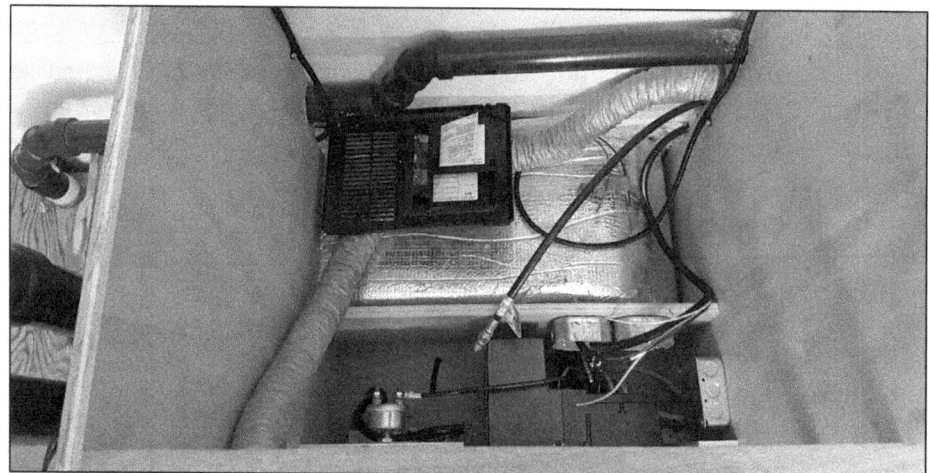

The number of turns and changes in direction of plumbing in a camper is determined by many factors. This drainpipe drops significantly to provide more space in the closet next to this cabinet.

PLUMBING AND LIQUID PROPANE

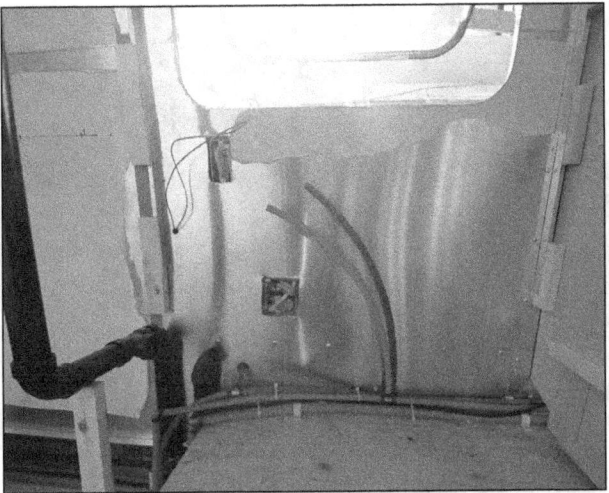

This camper build does not use a black-water tank, but its composting toilet needs to be vented to the outside. It will be connected to the gray-water tank vent at the "T." The blue and red PEX lines, secured with plastic guides screwed to the plywood, feed the vanity sink; the other lines feed the heating system.

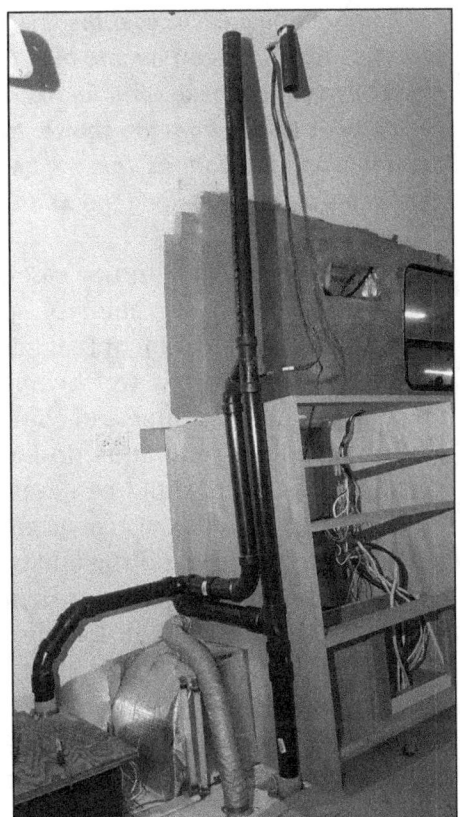

The sink drain runs along the camper wall, then turns inward to clear the wheelwell (these often bring an additional step to plumbing) before connecting to a "T." This leads to a vent that exits to the roof, which is also shared with the black-water vent. The vent piping still needs to be connected at the top.

The finished vanity with composting toilet. The vent plumbing is hidden in a false wall and the PEX is accessible inside the cabinet.

PEX Upgrades

A PEX system consists of plastic tubing that is joined in a few different ways, usually with either barbs and crimped metal rings or "push" connectors that do not require a crimping tool. The tubing comes in red, blue, and white to help distinguish hot and cold tubing. This can come in handy when you have multiple fixtures in a camper.

PEX comes in 1/2- and 3/8-inch diameters. There are many adapters and fittings to choose from, so you can almost always run PEX to

This PEX tubing feeds a heat exchanger to warm the coach.

STREAMLINE ALUMINUM TRAILERS: RESTORATION AND MODIFICATION 145

A 12-volt fan pushes air over the tiny radiators to force warm air into the room through the mesh vent. An ABS drainpipe is visible from the shower to the left, along the bottom. This will be hidden inside a trunk along the wall.

vintage faucets. In most cases, plumbing is hidden in cabinetry, so using a modern replacement that has a good track record is a worthwhile upgrade. After all the time and effort you've put into a restoration, losing it to water damage would be devastating. Another advantage of using PEX is that you can stub the end of the tubing and pressurize the system with air to check for leaks before running water through it.

For the Cruisette, I did not need to run PEX for the plumbing. Due to the simple nature of a single hand pump, I needed only 3/8-inch vinyl tubing, barb fittings, and hose clamps. Some 1½-inch corrugated hose is used to fill the gravity-feed fresh-water tank. A special barb, a large diameter NPT male to a large 1½-inch hose, was needed to successfully connect the hose to the tank (it seems every plumbing job requires a couple of trips to a local plumbing supplier to complete).

Water Drainage

Because of the Cruisette's compact galley, a low-profile P-trap found at a camper supply store made good use of the limited space. Rather than a traditional J-bend drain, these only protrude a few inches below the sink. Their primary function is for tent

Once the water tanks are mounted, it's hard to relocate fittings. During any restoration or remodel, drastic changes can cause headaches later without proper forethought. If you want a certain layout, it's best to find a model that's closest to what you want, rather than move bathrooms and galleys.

The corrugated drain hose and acrylic hand-pump hose are connected and fed to the countertop. The hand-pump hose needs to be connected to the lowest tank fitting for it to draw water.

PLUMBING AND LIQUID PROPANE

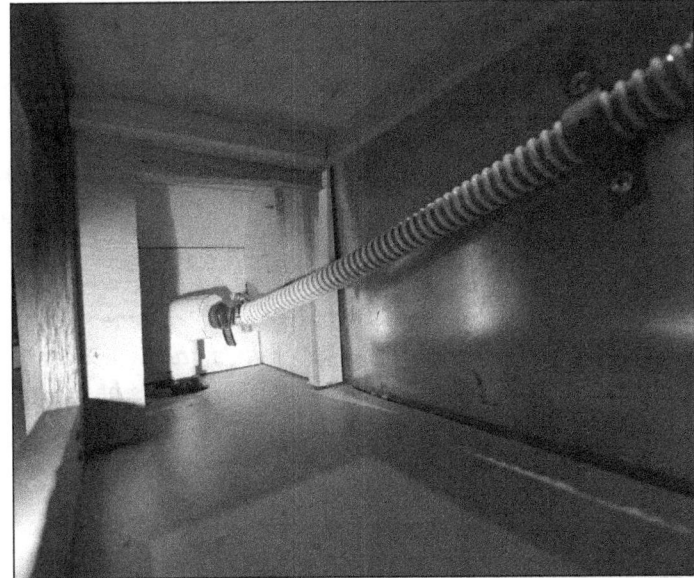

The Cruisette's diminutive size made a standard camper P-trap difficult to fit. The solution was a compact unit that uses a hose, which is smaller than the planned 1¼-inch corrugated hose. The smaller-diameter hose needed to connect to the 1½-inch gray-water tank. After checking about a half-dozen plumbing supply stores, I found the proper fittings.

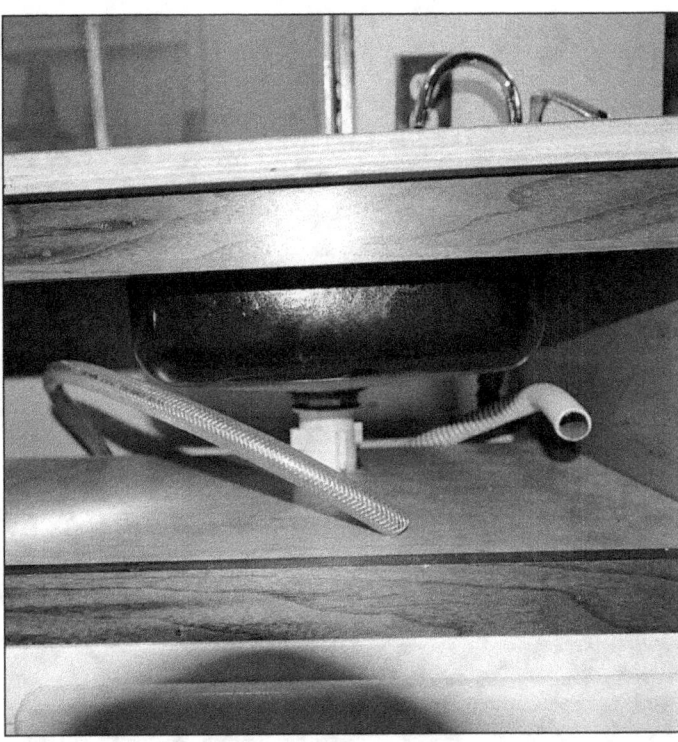

Notice how close the top of the ice chest is to the bottom of the sink. The P-trap is attached directly to the bottom of the sink drain.

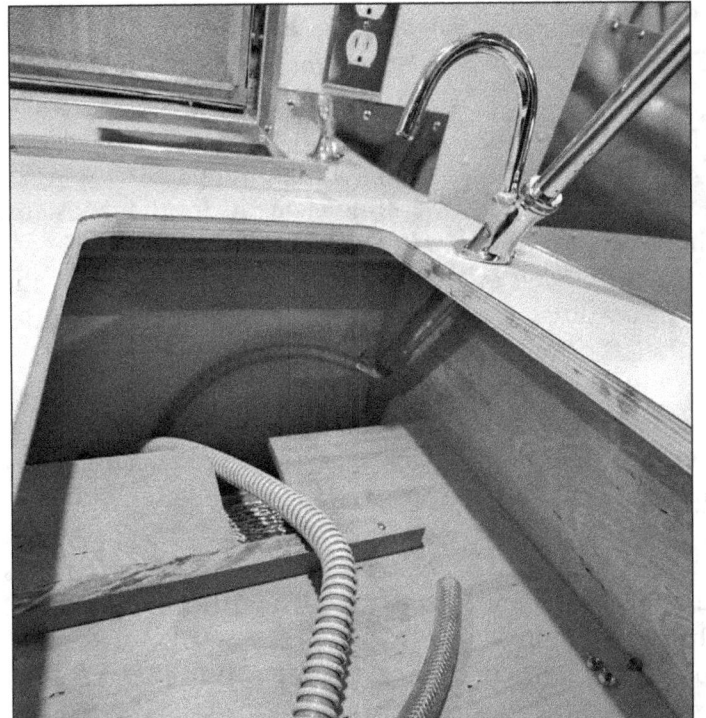

The hand pump is connected with an NPT and barb fitting. To clear the P-trap, the shelving needed to be cut away. You can see how close the insulation for the ice chest is to the bottom of the sink.

The gravity fill is connected here and run to a period-correct exterior fixture. The smaller drain hose is fastened in place with strapping. The hand pump is tested (water droplets in the sink) and installed with some caulk to prevent water damage to the countertop.

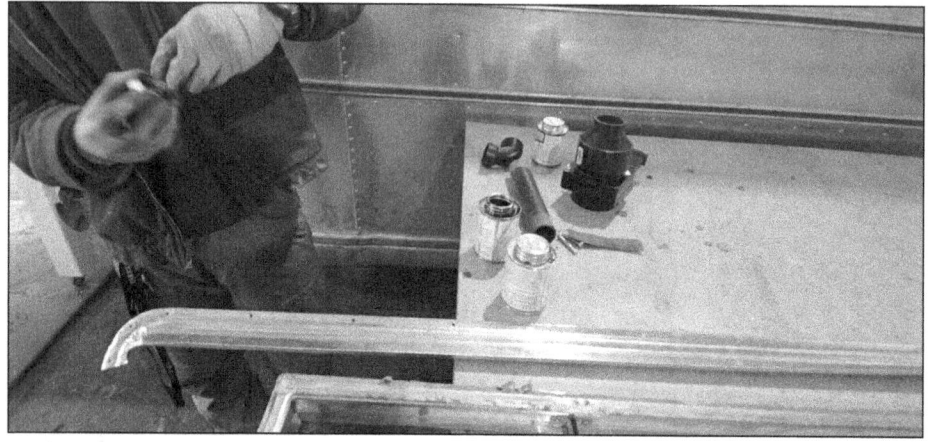

Specific adhesives are used for connecting ABS and PVC pipes. Here, the Cruisette's gray-water tank drain valve and plumbing is being assembled.

To securely mount the valve, a custom aluminum flange was fabricated and fastened to the belly pan.

trailers, where galley space is even more of a priority.

For draining into the gray-water tank, the Cruisette also uses corrugated hose connected to a large barb fitting. On larger campers, traditional ABS (acrylonitrile butadiene styrene) and PVC (polyvinyl chloride) tubing is used. Black ABS is used for sewer and waste; PVC is commonly used for fresh water. Both PVC and ABS tubing and glue can be found at most hardware stores or RV supply outlets. You can join ABS to PVC with appropriate glues or couplers, but the results are not always favorable. In a mobile application, durability is priority.

In addition to drainpipes to the gray-water tank, as in houses, campers need the black- and gray-water tanks to be ventilated. This maintains neutral air pressure, allowing free flow of water and sewage. Many stack covers and vent pipe covers are available for RVs and campers that attach to exterior skins with rivets or screws and appropriate sealants.

Besides the additional fresh-water tank plumbing and pump involved with a camper water system, tank monitoring and anti-freezing measures also differentiate RV plumbing from household plumbing. Because there's a risk of freezing in campers, lines can burst and cause major damage. To prevent this, and to enable cold-climate camping, you can add components to prevent the freezing of holding tanks and water lines.

Heating pads and supply hoses run on the 12-volt 110-volt systems to prevent freezing. It's important to ensure that your camper's electrical system can support the draw of warming elements for the tanks and water lines. Finally, because tanks are often buried in cabinetry or in the frame, monitoring their capacities needs to be done with sensors.

These sensors tie into the 12-volt system and use a strip that attaches to the side of tanks to quantify tank capacity. An electronic readout is placed within the coach, usually with other important information such as battery health and thermostat reading.

Propane

Besides water plumbing, another major component to camper systems is LP. The Cruisette relies on propane only for the stove and gas lamp, but

PLUMBING AND LIQUID PROPANE

This "T" splits the propane tubing to feed the stove on the non-curbside and the gas lamp on the curbside of the Cruisette. Here, leak detectors are being applied to ensure that no propane is leaking under the camper.

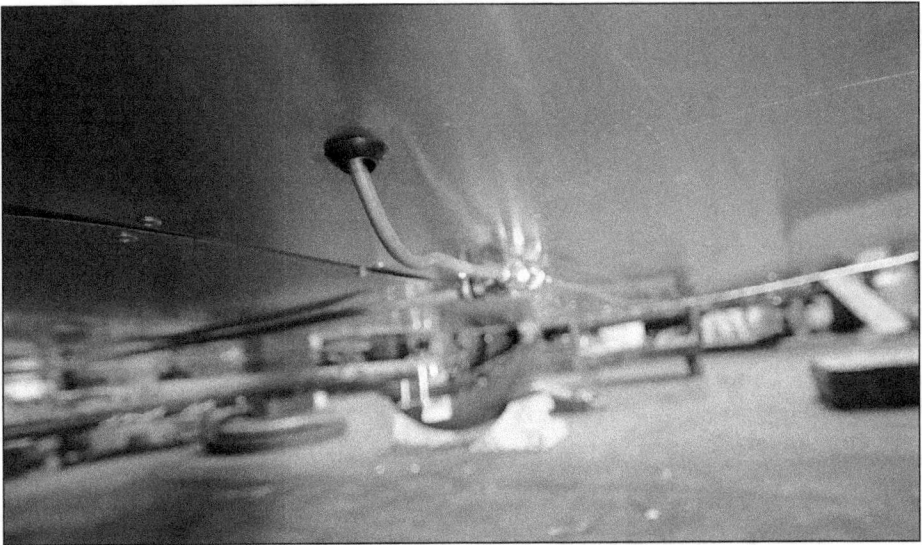

Like electrical wires, propane tubing needs to pass through sheet-metal grommets to avoid damage. Here, a propane line enters the Cruisette through the belly pan. Rubber-coated clamps are a good way to fasten copper tubing.

This typical, dual-propane tank rack is readily available from any RV store. The T-bracket clamps the tanks in place for safe travel; a wing nut makes changing tanks easy. The rack can be attached to the tongue by welding, clamping, or screwing.

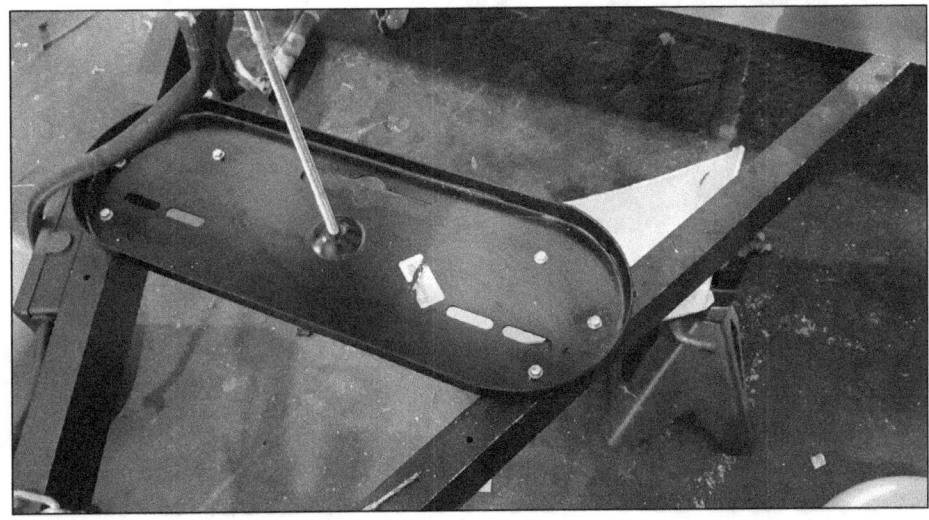

This propane rack is fastened with No. 12 self-tapping hardware. Even though they are self-tapping metal screws, pre-drilling the holes saves you much headache for fastening the rack to a camper.

CHAPTER 12

Plumbing in campers involves crawling into impossibly tight spaces. Here, a flare tool is being used to run propane tubing. Fitting your hands into this space, setting up the tool, and spinning the lever takes a certain amount of patience, contortion, and luck.

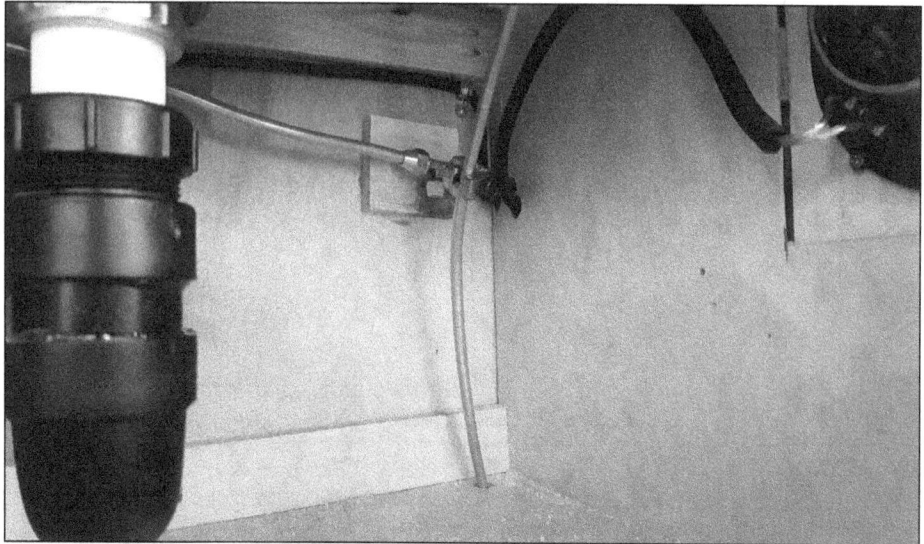

Once the flare fitting is fastened, the feed line needs to be cut to length (shown) and another fitting installed. A common mistake is to make the flare before installing the nut. If you do this, you need to cut off the flare and hope there's enough tubing to make another one.

After all the lines are connected, a leak detector is used to ensure that propane is not escaping into the cabin. If bubbles form, you need to tighten the nuts until no LP escapes.

larger campers also use propane for water heating, cabin heat, and refrigeration. This can require a network of copper LP lines to run through a camper.

Propane is a gas at ambient temperature and pressure, but it becomes a liquid when compressed, which allows relatively small storage requirements, given its energy content. This makes it a favorable means to power some camper accessories. For safety, propane is artificially made with an odor to avoid undetected exposure and bodily harm.

If your camper uses any LP, it's best to install an LP detector. Most of these alarms combine carbon monoxide (CO) and propane to alert against asphyxiation. Rather than rely on independent batteries (AA, AAA, etc.), they are tied into the camper's 12-volt circuitry so when the camper is on, the detector is on. These detectors also typically have a five-year lifespan. In planning the interior of a vintage camper, placement of a modern piece of equipment like an LP detector can be important. A black or white plastic CO/LP detector can look out of place in a 1950s camper.

The propane line pressure is controlled by a regulator; in campers, this is a two-stage version. The first stage acts as a filter to make sure the gas is pure. If the propane is tainted, a black liquid with the consistency of honey leaks out of a small port in the regulator. The second stage controls the line pressure.

Once a regulator fails, it needs to be replaced.

LP Regulator

If you're going for a period-correct restoration, you might want to upgrade the LP regulator. In most cases, regulators tend to last three to five years. Many sizes of propane tanks are available.

Most commonly the tanks are vertically mounted, but horizontal tanks are a nice choice if space is an issue. Vertical tanks cannot be used horizontally, and horizontal tanks can't be used vertically. The safety mechanism to prevent overfilling is designed for either horizontal or vertical use; it does not work if the tank is mounted improperly.

Propane Tank

The Cruisette's tongue needed to hold a spare tire (originally it sat inside the camper's baggage compartment; and the other alternative, a bumper-mounted spare, would block the luggage door). Along with the spare tire, a propane tank needed to be mounted. After some research, I found a tank that was the perfect fit.

If your camper has an original vintage tank and you want to use it, it can be recertified by a qualified service center. The tanks have a certification date stamped on them, which lasts 12 years. After 12 years, a fill station will not fill a tank until it is recertified. Most Airstreams came with aluminum propane tanks that do not rust and are lighter weight.

These tanks can be polished to a mirror finish, just like the exterior (see Chapter 13 for details). In fact, propane tanks are an item that you can tie into your camper's overall theme with a little paint. Working with propane tubing can be rewarding but also challenging.

Copper Pipe Bending

Copper is pretty soft, so it is easy to shape. It's also easy to overdo it and collapse the pipe. When this happens, all you have to do is cut out the compromised portion and add a coupling. If the tubing is visible, however, you may want an all-new line. Vintage campers usually use 1/4- and 3/8-inch copper tubing and assorted flared fittings.

These fittings require a special flaring tool available at most hardware stores. It takes a couple of tries to get the hang of the tool, and it's a bit awkward to use in tight spaces.

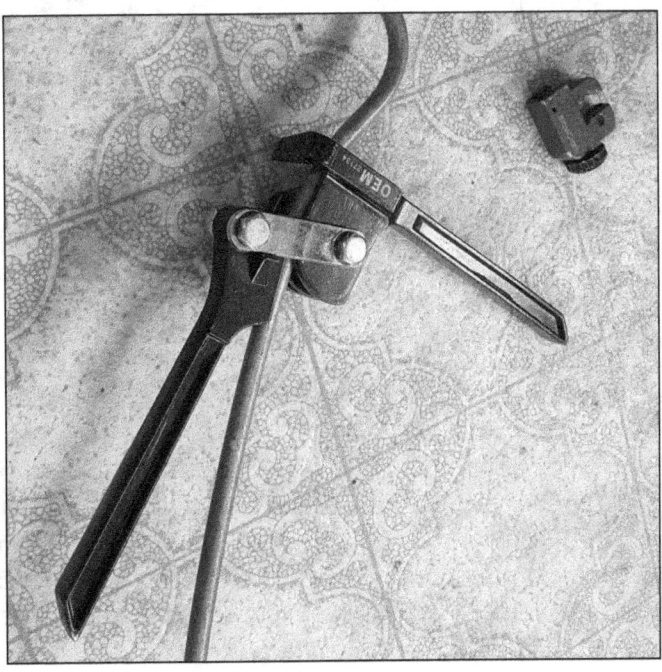

To avoid crimping copper tubing on tight bends, a brake-like bending tool from an auto parts store helps make smooth bends. Although flare fittings are not needed, some plumbers put it on the threads to prevent binding. Also, a little grease on the threads can help with torqueing them down.

The flare tool can be used on many sizes of copper tubing. The diameter you use is determined by the number of appliances and their required LP flow. As with electricity, larger-gauge wires are needed to supply multiple electrical components.

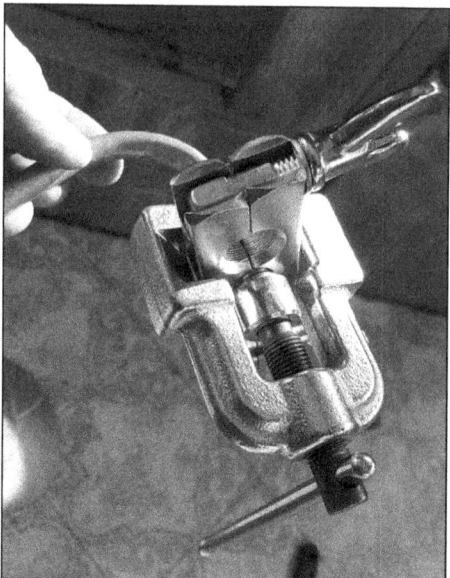

The flaring cone provides uniform-flare walls without galling the copper. To prolong tool life and provide a better flare, a drop of oil on the cone makes things go more smoothly. Just do not get oil on the clamping portion, to avoid slipping. This causes a poor flare and potential leaking.

With practice, you'll be making secure connections in no time.

Propane Testing

To safety-check your work, pressurize the system once all connections are made. You want to bleed the system of air. Turn the valve on the tank counterclockwise to release propane into your gas lines. Then light a stovetop burner. When the stovetop flame burns steadily, the gas lines are properly primed. Turn off the burner.

With the tank still open, you can check for leaks. Leak detectors are available from hardware stores that come with an applicator swab. Start at the tank's connections and work your way along the lines until you've checked them all. If any bubbles form, you want to give the flare nut another turn and check for the leak again.

To bleed newly installed propane tubing, you light the stove first. Because it draws the most LP and is usually the highest point, it purges the air. It's always satisfying to light a restored appliance for the first time, much like starting a rebuilt engine.

CHAPTER 13

POLISHING AND BRIGHTWORK

There are Airstreams, and then there are *polished* Airstreams. When an owner takes great pride in his or her American-made aluminum travel trailer, it can be polished to a mirror finish. And, although Airstream might be the first brand that comes to mind when talking polished campers, many others, including Barth, Silver Streak, Westwood, and Boles Aero, can polish up just as shiny.

In addition to a polished exterior, many components to a camper's interior benefit from brightwork polishing or plating. After decades of use, light fixtures, galley trim, and cabinet hardware show their age. Many of these components have been coated with a surface treatment for decorative purposes, including brass, nickel, and copper.

In this chapter, I look at both the small-scale polishing processes, along with having cabinet hardware re-plated, and the large-scale (a whole camper exterior) polishing process. I also discuss the basics, practices, and theories behind polishing.

Most important, I recommend proper protective equipment, including a respirator and goggles or face shield. Full-coverage clothing and a head sock are also necessary if you do not want to be covered in polishing dust.

Polishing is often unappreciated; a spinning wheel kicks up dust that's a dirty combination of surface material, buffer pad, and compound. It's almost sooty in appearance. The resulting layer of shadowy dust from every buffing step can spread like an invasive species, transferring from tools, to hydration containers, to door handles, and back to tools. If coarse-cut debris makes its way to your fine-cut equipment, you're going to have a hard time achieving a scratch-free finish.

Detailed cleaning between steps is best. Similar to high-end automotive paintwork, polishing requires specific steps and extreme cleanliness to achieve above-par results.

Prepping your workspace is also necessary. You want to cover with drop cloths any nearby shelving and any items in the same space that you do not want to spend time cleaning.

A polished Airstream, such as this 1960s Safari, embodies the rich history of American ingenuity and craftsmanship.

STREAMLINE ALUMINUM TRAILERS: RESTORATION AND MODIFICATION 153

CHAPTER 13

Other than the grinder and protective equipment, this polishing kit includes everything needed for a small- to medium-scale polishing job: a box of assorted pads, cleaning solvent, cleaning rags, pneumatic sander and buffer, various-grit sandpaper, and polishing compounds.

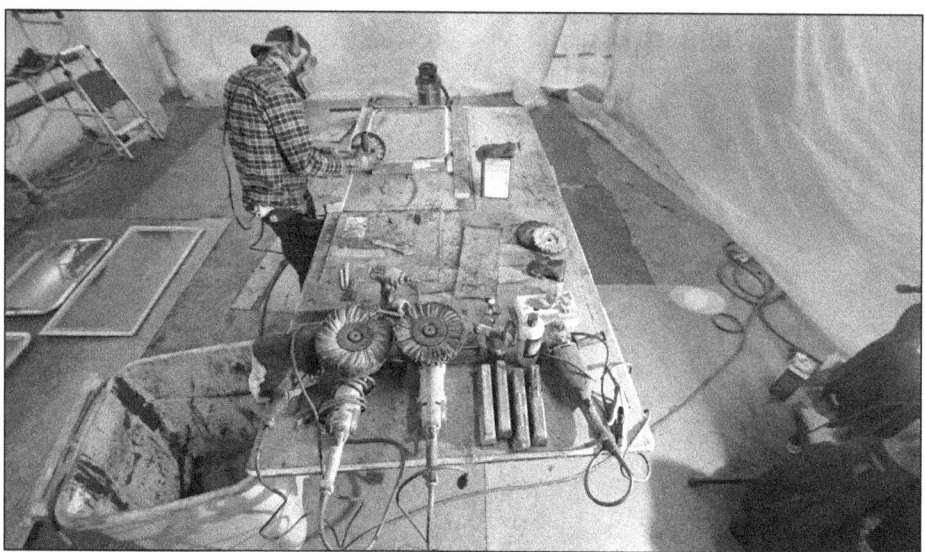

This equipment is ideal for a large-scale polishing job. On the table from left to right are a variable-speed polisher without a wheel, a variable-speed polisher with a white Domet flannel wheel for final blend, a variable-speed polisher with a smooth-cut wheel (purple) for first and second steps, four Zephyr bars (Blue Moon for blending, Moss Green for the coloring step, Brown Tripoli for a heavy cut, and stainless for heavy cutting), and The Cyclo with pro 40 liquid for a final buff.

A face shield and respirator are necessary for large-scale polishing jobs, along with full-coverage clothing and gloves. A buffing wheel kicks up black soot that tends to travel everywhere.

POLISHING AND BRIGHTWORK

After plating, these original cabinet latches and drawer pulls bring the camper's interior to life. Most times this is the more expensive route to take, but the end results speak for themselves.

A polishing wheel kicks the debris into the air and it gets everywhere!

Another avenue is DIY electroplating kits. Plenty of tutorials are available online, and a couple of manufacturers provide turn-key kits for nickel, copper, and many other materials. The initial investment may be high, depending on the products and technique, but you'll be able to use the kit and equipment on other projects.

Sometimes original hardware and latches can go missing. Dismantlers sell vintage hardware and fixtures, but it's a crapshoot when trying to find a specific match. The reproductions that are available can be a good substitute, but they tend to be cheaply made overseas (i.e., lighter tin stampings and plastics). And while a decent match, they never match the originals to a "T."

Polishing Tools

The basics to polishing are pretty simple; you essentially work surface irregularities down to their smallest possible size through a series of abrasive steps. The less-simple part to polishing is the balance of art and science. Once you understand the science of it, mastering the art takes practice. An important thing to consider is that not all manufacturers' polishing products are compatible, and differences in compound mixtures and variances in color-coding for abrasives can create difficulties in achieving a quality finish.

To start a polishing project, you use a cleaning solvent, found at automotive parts stores, that's used to remove wax, grease, silicone, dirt, tar, insect remnants, road film, and pinstripe adhesive. You also need to decide if sanding is necessary. A good rule of thumb is that if your fingernail can detect a scratch, the piece needs to be sanded. From there, polishing is similar to a "choose your own adventure" book.

Bench Grinder

When working with interior trim and fixtures, a bench grinder can be equipped with various polishing wheels for small items such as latches and handles. If you do not have a bench grinder, a vise can be used to hold a drill or grinder with polishing attachments, including a rubber-backed pad and polishing

Polishing with a handheld grinder and polishing wheel takes practice to achieve a desirable finish. It also requires experience to handle a rotating, heavy tool and not damage the surface or cause too much fatigue.

wheel. Simply screw the polishing wheel onto the rubber backup pad and slip the attachment into the drill chuck.

Be sure to tighten the chuck firmly, as it can loosen from vibration; the last thing you want is the wheel taking flight. The worst case probably won't do you bodily harm, but you don't want a dented panel or the polishing wheel to land on a dirty shop floor. A wheel contaminated with dust and dirt can stop a project if you do not have a clean backup.

Polishing metal requires being very careful to prevent cross-contamination as you work through steps to cut the surface finer and finer. If you get a coarse compound on your fine buffing equipment, you end up falling back to the coarse-cut step and have to work forward from there again, or else you have visible surface gouges.

Most drills and grinders have a trigger lock, so when clamped in a vise, both your hands are free. When applying polishing compound, simply bring it into contact with the rotating wheel for a few seconds. When grasping an object, use both hands and maintain a firm grip. A rotating wheel exerts a surprising amount of pull and yanks loosely held parts that may damage items or harm someone. You want to consider the rotation of the wheel when working the piece to prevent it from grabbing the piece.

Small-Scale Polishing

Small objects such as cabinet clasps can be carefully held with a pair of pliers to prevent surface damage; you simply wrap the jaws with masking tape. The aluminum window interior trim found on vintage campers is a common item that reacts positively to polishing. Giving these a good cleaning, cut, and polish helps to brighten the interior.

Instead of using a bench-mounted polishing setup, mounting the components to a sacrificial piece of wood (it's going to become dirty and contaminated with compound) is a good method. Conversely, I found that polishing windows in place can be a good time-saving strategy. However, you make a mess of interior components. If you gut the interior first and do not plan to save the interior skin, this is an option. Keep in mind that the amount of time cleaning could easily outweigh the time spent tooling up for polishing windows on a dedicated bench.

This brings up another point mentioned earlier: Building a stand-alone table with saw horses and plywood is a great way to expand your workshop. If you prefer to avoid making a mess of the tools and equipment on your workbench (black polishing debris find its way into all the nooks and crannies and works its way into doors and drawers), building a dedicated polishing zone offsets the time needed to clean up after a polishing job.

Trim and Fixtures

Before diving into polishing interior trim and fixtures, you should test polishing compounds in places that are not visible. This way you can experiment and make sure that you're not going to do any damage. On solid aluminum trim, this is less of a concern. On plated light fixtures or cabinet hardware, testing your polishing techniques first is critical.

If you don't do a test run, you may end up polishing through plating and require the component to be replated. In some cases, depending on job size and desired finish, it might be easier to take plated items to a professional plater. The cost might be offset by the time spent cleaning and prepping the originals, and the result will probably be better if you have a quality plater nearby.

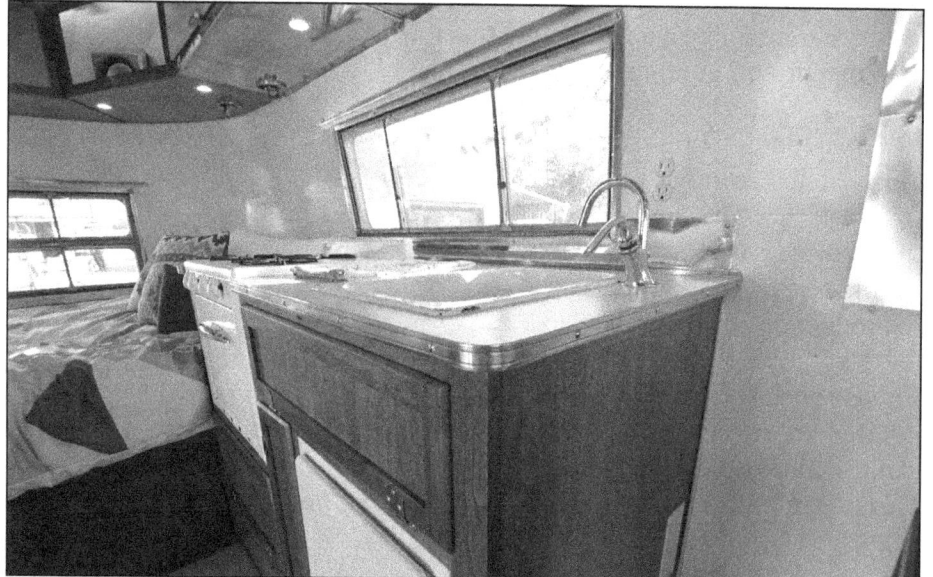

The polished trim helps bring the Cruisette's interior together. The reproduction trim comes with a satin anodized finish that needs to be sanded off to achieve this cohesive look.

POLISHING AND BRIGHTWORK

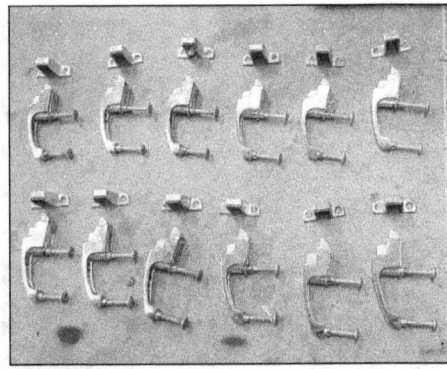

Rather than replace or polish these cabinet latches and drawer pulls, they will go to the plater for a fresh coat of brass. At the same time, I will have the interior screws coated.

Along with polished trim, the Cruisette features a polished endcap and original overhead locker, all achieved with the practices covered in this chapter.

Polishing a Propane Tank

1 This horizontal propane tank is mounted on the tongue of the Cruisette. To make this Airstream stand out, I plan to polish the aluminum tank to a mirror finish. The first step is to remove all stickers and give it a good cleaning to remove any dirt and dust.

2 To address any surface scratches, I started sanding at 240 grit with a random orbital sander. Depending on the scratch depth, you can start with a paper coarser than 240, such as 80, 120, or 220.

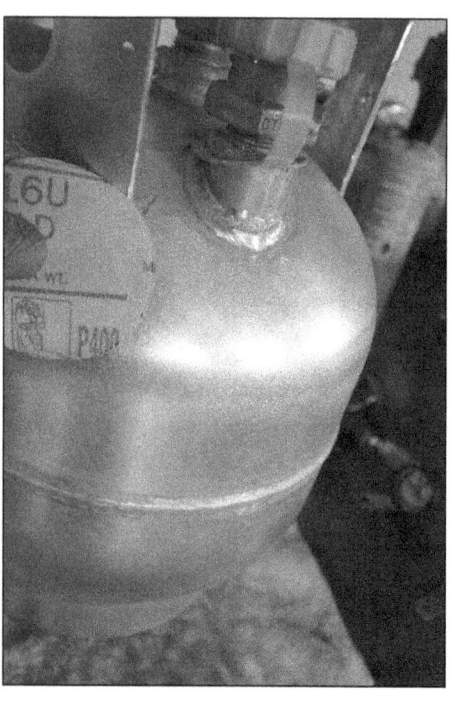

3 After the 240-grit sanding, a 300-grit pass is followed by a 400. It's important to wipe down the surface between sanding passes to avoid the buildup of larger dust particles that could contaminate and leave behind swirl marks.

4 As the sanding process works through 500, 600, 700, and 800 grit, you want to achieve an even, satin finish. Some people stop at 1000 grit, but you can take it all the way to 2000 if you desire.

5 The LP tank is ready for its first polishing pass. This coarse compound knocks down the surface irregularities and takes the finish from satin to shiny.

6 Here, you can see the blackened compound from removing surface debris and anomalies. Polishing is a dirty job that requires cleanliness for the best results. A pneumatic grinder with a small wheel (shown) cuts the compound in.

POLISHING AND BRIGHTWORK

7 After the coarse- and medium-compound passes with appropriately stiff buffing wheels, a final-detail pass is performed with a fine compound. Now the LP tank is ready to install.

8 Mounted on the coupler with the spare tire, the polished propane tank complements the Cruisette nicely. Going the extra mile, I also polished the copper LP line.

Sanding

If you've determined that sanding is necessary, work from the coarsest applicable paper to the finest. The coarsest paper necessary is dependent on the depth of the surface scratches you need to remove, typically 150 or 220 is sufficient.

For the best result, sand in a consistent motion and avoid cross-hatching. If the metal's grain is visible, follow it. Between paper grits, clean the surface (and tooling, i.e., sander and block) and change gloves to help prevent larger dust particles from making it to the next step.

Work through the grits of sandpaper until you've reached 1,000. Your stopping point is determined by how aggressive the first polishing compound is. Remember that polishing-compound grades and colors are not consistent among manufacturers. You need to decide what works best for your application.

Wet sanding can be a useful technique to keep the paper and working piece clean. Sandpaper grit can go all the way to 2,000; above about 800 or so, wet sanding is recommended. Some people recommend dipping the paper in a cutting oil instead of water. It all comes down to your experience and expected outcome.

Buffing

For the first pass, you want to work with a stiffer buffing wheel. Cotton wheels have more stitches to create a firmer wheel. On the other hand, with synthetic wheels it is harder to determine their rating. Color-coding comes in handy here, but color codes are not universal across manufacturers, so due diligence is essential.

When you've selected a buffing wheel, and chosen the coarsest applicable polishing compound (every manufacturer should have a polishing compound chart), coat the buffing wheel by lightly spinning it against the polishing compound. If you're not using a solid bar but a creamy, liquid-style compound, you want to distribute it equally around

This buffing wheel is loaded with dirty compound, indicated by the metallic shine from the removal of aluminum surface irregularities. If you kept using this wheel, it would overheat the metal and result in a poor surface shine.

CHAPTER 13

After a trip through a "rake," the wheel is cleaned of the dirty compound and ready to continue for a smooth, even luster. Keep in mind to avoid a rake that's been used with different compounds without a cleaning. If some coarse compound gets on a fine-cut wheel, you end up back stepping.

the working area sparingly. With practice, you'll find the sweet spot.

When working the polish onto the surface, best results are obtained at 3,000 rpm or less. Higher than that can overheat the surface and negatively affect the compound's ability to properly work. Another important note is to have the appropriate pressure. Just as too much wheel speed can overheat the compound, too much pressure does the same.

Slight pressure is best; when you notice a residue (a black soot) coming off, you're in the sweet spot. Remember to let the buffing wheel and compound do the work; you don't want to exert excess energy, as you'll fatigue faster and the results won't be as good.

Be sure to reapply compound when necessary, which comes with practice. A dry surface generates unwanted heat, and too much compound is messy. Once you're done with a particular step, it's best to clean the surface with mineral spirits to remove any larger dust particles and use a new buffing pad.

If your budget is tight, you can remove a previous compound by "raking" the wheel. This is done by carefully spinning the buffing wheel against a sharp, rake-shaped metal edge to remove the residue. Although not ideal, this is one route to take.

The polishing, cleaning, and prep process is repeated with finer and finer compounds until you reach the final finish compound. To achieve a mirror-like finish, apply the final compound with a single-stitch cotton wheel or softest synthetic available. On the final passes, use very light pressure.

Final cleaning needs to be completed with soft terrycloth or a chamois to avoid scratches: the last thing you want to see after all that work. Warm soapy water is a good cleaner at this time.

Large-Scale Polishing

Early Airstreams were delivered with a polished finish but slowly gave way to oxidation. To keep them looking good longer, by the mid-1960s Airstream was shipping trailers with a clear coat. While it provided a shiny exterior longer, clear coat starts to lift eventually, and oxidation works its way onto the surface of the aluminum.

To address a failing clear coat on an aluminum camper, you need to remove it using a paint stripper, a process similar to removing Zolatone from interior skin (see Chapter 2). Be sure to tape off all windows and items you do not want the stripper to contact, including lights, fans, etc. Follow the manufacturer instructions then give the exterior a good

Before installing the galley, all trim was polished outside the Cruisette to keep the sooty dust from contaminating the camper's interior.

POLISHING AND BRIGHTWORK

Polishing a vintage camper exterior takes extensive knowledge of the necessary products and tools. It also takes finesse and attention to detail to achieve a swirl-free mirror finish.

cleaning once the clear coat is removed; you don't want any chemical residue contaminating your polishing compounds or wheels.

Alclad

A common topcoat applied during the manufacturing process is Alclad. This is a corrosion-resistant surface layer of high-purity aluminum metallurgically bonded to the sheet of aluminum. It can be common for trailer repair shops to use this type of aluminum when making repairs; it was the prevalent aluminum used on Airstreams prior to 1968. This can create a few issues, depending on the vintage of the camper.

A pre–late-1960s Airstream polishes to a bright shine due to the

The surface of this 1970s Overlander shows what happens when clear coat goes bad. Before this exterior can be polished, it needs to be treated with an automotive paint stripper.

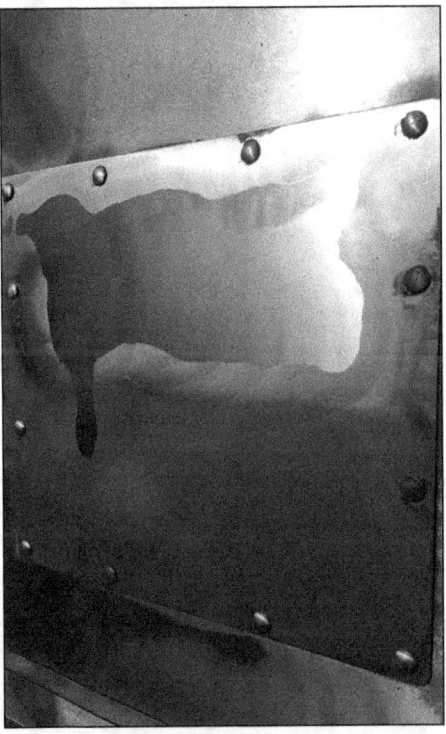

This patch has an Alclad coating on the sheet aluminum. Unlike clear coat, this top coating is bonded to the surface and requires an aggressive cut to remove. In this case, stainless rouge and a heavy back cut are used.

CHAPTER 13

Essential equipment for polishing a camper are quality ladders and scaffolding. Safety is a priority, of course, but also worthy of consideration is the damage potential to the exterior if you're working with unstable equipment.

pure aluminum coat (if it hasn't been sanded through). However, a later-model Airstream that's been patched with Alclad-coated aluminum does not match up. As with a clear coat, the Alclad needs to be removed to achieve a consistent exterior shine.

Buffing Passes

After any topcoat issues are addressed, all bodywork should be completed before polishing begins. As discussed in Chapter 5, you want to replace and/or smooth any deep scratches and dents prior to polishing.

Two types of buffing motions are used: cut (or blending) and detail (or color). The detail pass always follows the cut pass.

The cut pass is applied with a medium to hard pressure, moving the buffer against its rotation. The result should be a semi-bright and uniform surface finish. For the detail (or color) pass, you to use a medium to light pressure and move the wheel with the rotation. The result is a clean, bright, and shiny surface finish.

It's important to rake the pad between these passes to avoid

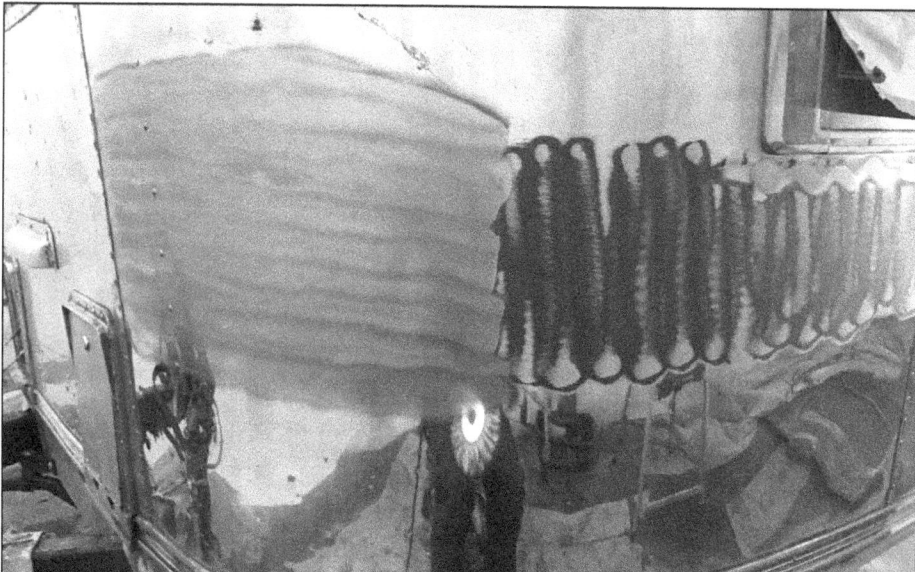

This front quarter panel shows an application step on the right and the initial back cut on the left. Working on curved panels like this can make applying even pressure difficult, but practice makes perfect.

The keystone panel on this Airstream is showing some ghosting from its Wally Caravan Club International membership number and decal. Also, the sealant residue for the running lights needs to be cleaned before polishing.

STREAMLINE ALUMINUM TRAILERS: RESTORATION AND MODIFICATION

POLISHING AND BRIGHTWORK

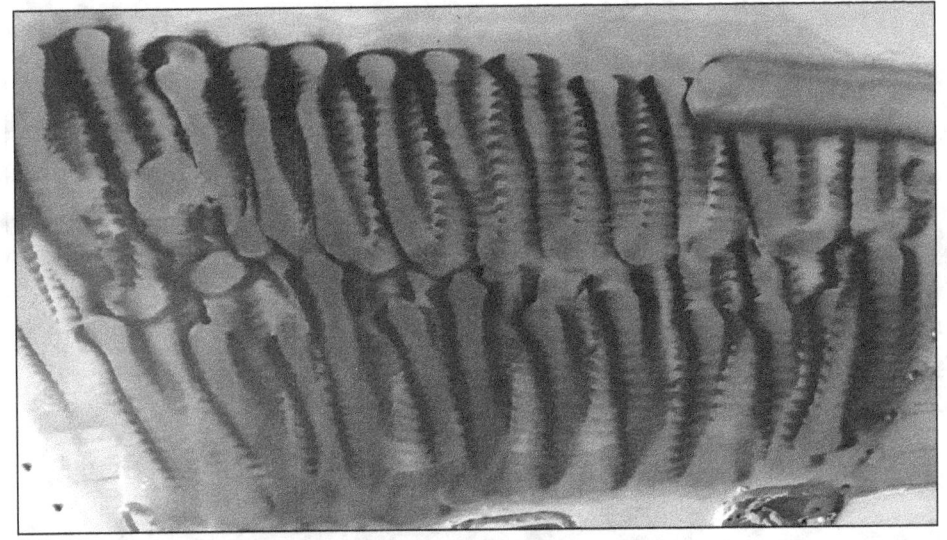

The first application step is followed with a back cut (medium to hard pressure, avoiding too much heat) to remove oxidation and the number ghosting. Before moving to the next compound, a detail cut is made with light pressure, moving with the rotation of the wheel, and the remaining compound is removed.

swirling from accumulated aluminum mud. Also important is your buffer's wheel speed. Around 6,000 rpm is a good speed for the first cut, and about 3,000 rpm is ideal for the finer second and third passes. For the final stages, 1,000 to 2,000 rpm provides the best results.

Of course, there are variables to consider when choosing a buffing wheel speed, and it's best to reference the polishing compound manufacturers' suggestions for best results.

Mastering Your Polishing

This is where the "art" portion of polishing comes into play. It takes a practiced hand to master the preferred pressures, and you can use a grinder's angular momentum (forces from a spinning object) to your advantage. Working with a 13-pound tool in your hands that's spinning from 1,000 to 6,000 rpm is fatiguing. If you're working against the grinder's natural force vectors and applying too much pressure, you're going to tire quickly.

Likewise, working on an unstable ladder or scaffolding can be hazardous. Make sure your footing is solid

After a medium-compound pass, the numbers are no longer visible. Because the top of the trailer is rarely seen, this finish is blended upward to save time and money.

Here, the aluminum is approaching a true mirror finish. It's worth noting that one panel is being worked on at a time. This helps keep track of what's finished and what needs attention next.

CHAPTER 13

Applying even application of the polishing compound from the wheel to the surface achieves better results. It takes a bit of practice to get it right. Here, it's thicker on the left than the right, which is understandable, as the wheel loses compound as you spread it across the panel.

After the initial application, the compound is worked into the surface with a back cut. You can see a nice, even distribution of the compound due to applying even pressure with the pad. Working with a large spinning wheel takes practice to get this result.

The start of the detail cut (blending) includes a clean wheel and lighter pressure. Moving in the motion of the wheel is used to buff off the remaining compound and provide an even luster.

A solvent such as mineral spirits is used with a soft rag to clean off remaining compound before the next step. All the remaining panels need to reach this state of finish. As you can imagine, polishing a large trailer correctly can be a major undertaking.

POLISHING AND BRIGHTWORK

Many areas on a trailer are not flat panels. Achieving an even distribution of compound takes finesse and experience by managing the rotational forces when operating a large grinder with a buffing wheel attached.

when polishing, and that there are no tripping hazards such as loose cords. If you drop the grinder against the aluminum exterior, or drag tooling across the surface due to a tumble, you will need to redo work. Scaffolding is available from most equipment rental yards, if you prefer not to purchase it.

Indoor Polishing

The location where you polish the trailer affects the outcome. Of course, inside is the best as it will be climate controlled. Polishing outside in the sun isn't the best scenario because the heat generated negatively affects the polishing compounds so that it "cooks" onto the surface. Keeping the compound in a state where it allows the buffing wheel to glide is essential to achieving a swirl-free finish. If the compound hardens from overheating, you end up with ghosting in the finish. Another contributor to a poor finish is a wheel that's not raked often. The buildup of aluminum in the buffer creates friction and overheats the surface.

The steps to reduce microscopic surface mountains and valleys are the same for small-scale items (discussed earlier). You work the surface

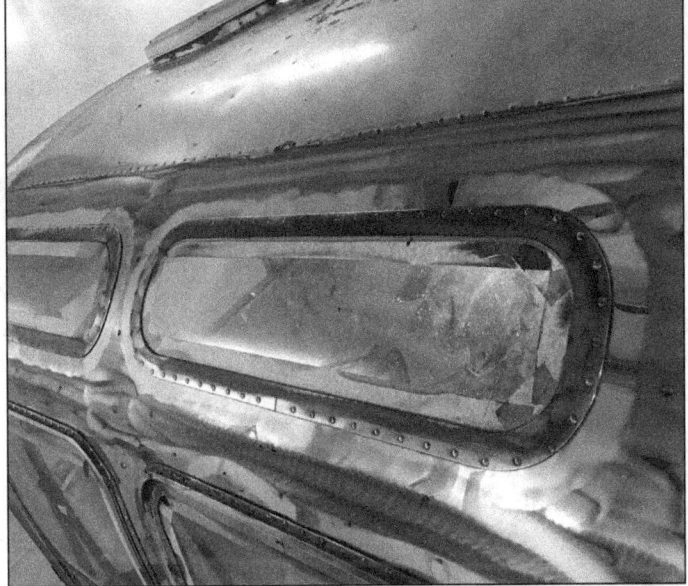

From trim to drip rails, there are many hazards to consider when polishing. A spinning, buffing wheel in inattentive hands could grab items, such as this drip rail, and bend and/ or rip them off. After the back cut, these Airstream stack windows are receiving their first detail cut.

Ready for a final buff with a finish compound, this Airstream aluminum has the desired even sheen. After any residue compound is removed, this area will be ready for a final, detail compound with the softest wheel.

If you use a creamy compound, rather than a bar, apply it evenly by hand instead of using a wheel to transfer the compound to the surface.

Prior to delivery, the Cruisette receives a final buff using soft microfiber cloths and a dual-head orbital buffer. This final stage brings the Cruisette's exterior to a nearly mirror finish.

irregularities until they're smaller and smaller, using various buffing wheels and compounds suited to the stage of the surface finish.

As mentioned earlier, always use due diligence to ensure that the compounds and various buffing wheels do not become contaminated with a coarser compound or dust/mud. This leads to swirl marks and scratches. If you leave a polishing job for a few days, make sure there is no accumulated dust (especially if working outside) that can work its way into the polishing products and tools.

Preserving Your Work

Once you achieve a satisfactory exterior finish, you want to preserve all the hard work that went into it; it usually takes about three to four years for a shine to lose its luster. It isn't difficult to give the exterior a fresh pass with a soft wheel and fine compound to bring back the shine. Because you've already cut the exterior to a high-quality surface finish, maintaining it is less involved than restoring a luster from step one.

If you don't want to polish again, products are available to seal the exterior, but this, too, needs to be re-applied periodically. Sealers are typically applied by hand with a soft rag.

A third option is to have the exterior clear coated by a trusted body shop, but the cost could easily outweigh a yearly or biannual fine polish or seal procedure.

Washing a Polished Trailer

To wash a polished camper, a simple detergent-based car wash solution works the best. Be sure to avoid products with waxes or special solvent cleaners. Before washing, rinse off any dust then apply the car wash solution. This prevents the dust from scratching the surface.

A soft washing pad at the end of an extension pole loosens dirt and grime. Be sure to dip the pad in a warm bucket often to release any accumulated dirt. After scrubbing with the wash pad, rinse the camper and dry it with terrycloth towels. If you let the water dry on the trailer, it develops noticeable water spots.

The curb appeal of a well-polished and buffed Airstream is hard to deny. The amount of work that goes into achieving this level of finish is difficult for some people to comprehend, but nearly everyone is drawn to shiny things.

This Airstream Overlander not only features a mirror exterior, it has a service window cut into the original exterior skin for use as a food-vending unit.

CHAPTER 14

Traveling with Your Trailer

Now that your camper is back to showroom condition, you're going to want to take it on the road and share it with others. Using a pre-travel checklist helps ensure that the experience goes smoothly. Every camper is different and each one needs its own checklist.

After going through your checklist, always give the camper a walk around to look for anything that is out of place. A luggage door may not be latched all the way or a wheel chuck could have been forgotten, to name a few possibilities.

Empty the Tanks

If you're leaving a campground, drain the tanks at a dumping station. Empty holding tanks mean better fuel mileage and better towing dynamics at highway speed.

Empty the black-water tank first, then the gray. This way the gray water flushes out the effluent from the black tank. If there is still water in the fresh tank, you can run it into the black and gray tanks to flush them a second time.

Not every dump station has a garden hose for rinsing, so it's a good idea to keep one in the camper. This

Towing a camper that you've put your heart and soul into can be a little nerve-racking. To ease the tension, having a set pre-trip routine helps. With experience on the road, you quickly build confidence with your camper's capability, and towing becomes second nature.

TRAVELING WITH YOUR TRAILER

Travel Checklist

Here's a sample list that can be adjusted according to the needs of your trailer and your trip.

Torque lug nuts; typically 90 to 120 ft-lbs for 15/16-inch wheels
Check tire air pressure
Turn off LP tanks
Turn off camper 12-volt power system
Lower antennas and secure the TV
Fasten doors and drawers
Close windows

Close roof vents
Stow loose items
Lock down the awning
Check running, brake, and turn signals
Check safety chains (crossed, not parallel)
Remove foot or wheel from jack
Check torque on hitch ball nut
Test the brakes before approaching any major roadways

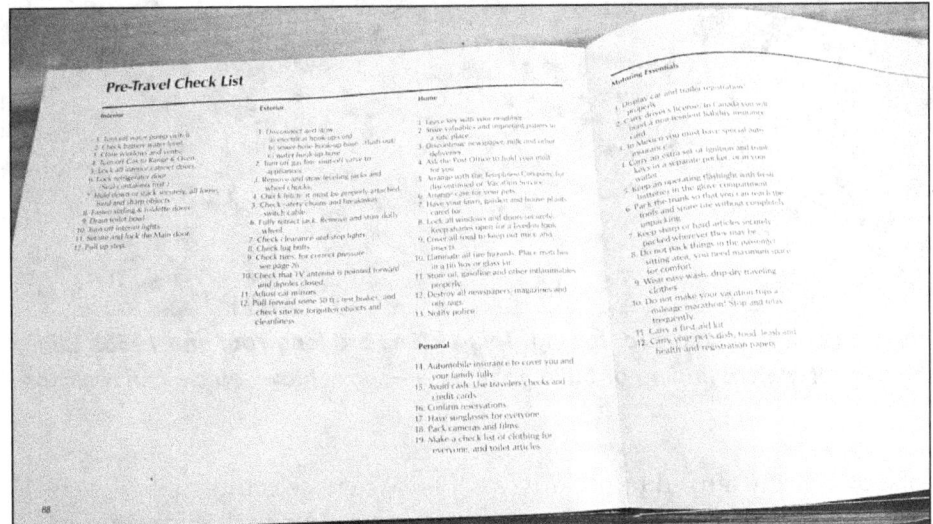

This factory Airstream checklist from the 1970s is very extensive, even covering essentials such as enjoying the trip. Going through a checklist should be routine for every trip, and other members of your entourage should have knowledge and access to it for additional sets of eyes.

hose, however, should never be stored in the same space as the fresh-water hose. The bumper on most Airstreams is designed to hold a sewer hose and is a good space to stash some rubber gloves and a rinse hose.

Towing Preparation

Towing a camper is often a two-person affair, as having a spotter makes maneuvering much easier. If you're both new to towing, it's a good idea to practice in an open lot. The spotter must be visible to the driver at all times. Even with a spotter, the driver should get out and check the surroundings to note any

Backing up a trailer is much easier with an extra set of eyes. The spotter needs to be in constant view of the operator and must have a hand communication system worked out before attempting to park a camper.

CHAPTER 14

Before the popularity of the SUV, the station wagon was a staple for towing. This 1970s Ford long-roof and 1950s Clipper are a couple of decades from being the perfect match; finding or building a period-correct tow vehicle can really tie things together.

hazards such as trees before attempting a maneuver.

Hand signals are vital to communication when backing up, as it is difficult to hear inside the tow rig. Even with hand signals it's a good idea to roll down all the windows.

When selecting a proper towing rig, there are many factors to consider. One is the Gross Vehicle Weight Rating (GVWR) the total allowable weight for the vehicle, including fluids, occupants, cargo, and trailer hitch weight. You want to make sure the vehicle can haul the loaded camper.

The maximum tow rating is the manufacturer's weight limit for towed loads. For conventional trailers, this normally includes a hitch-weight limit as well. The GVWR for all motor vehicles is listed on the data plate, typically affixed to the driver's doorframe, fuel door, glove box, or other easy-to-access location.

All contemporary trailers should have a weight sticker, typically found in an interior cabinet, that lists the trailer's unloaded weight (empty tanks, no gear). However, there's a good chance this information is missing from a vintage camper. To find out what your camper weighs, you can take it to a public truck scale.

Besides the unloaded weight, which most manufacturers list, you also need to know the loaded weight of the camper. So, before heading to the scales, fill the trailer with everything that you take with you on the road. On the scale, the total weight includes the hitch weight and the axle weight.

When selecting a tow vehicle, you want one with a tow rating that exceeds the camper's GVWR.

Remember that although you can modify a tow vehicle's suspension, drivetrain, and engine to increase its towing capacity, it's still the law to operate within the vehicle's manufacturer-issued specifications. If you're in an incident and a law officer finds your tow vehicle was overloaded based on the GVWR, you could be cited and possibly responsible for the damages.

Another consideration is the axle ratio of the towing vehicle. A low ratio (4.10:1) provides better acceleration but poorer fuel mileage than a higher ratio (3.73:1). If the vehicle manufacturer offers a towing package, it's best to purchase a vehicle

The red numbers on this Airstream represent its previous owner's WBCCI club numbers. A new owner can re-register these numbers with the club. Many clubs include vintage campers, and they are a great source for model data, camping locations, and other valuable information.

equipped with it, as the cost to add the items later often outweighs the manufacturer's cost.

Hitching Up

Given the amount of time and resources spent on your poject, making sure that you have the proper hitch is necessary for on-road safety.

Hitch Classes

If your current vehicle has a GVWR and tow rating that are adequate for your camper needs but does not have a tow hitch, you can add the required equipment. Be sure to investigate the specific hitch classes designed for specific trailer weight ranges.

Class 1 is for lightweight duty, maxing out at a 2,000-pound gross and a 200-pound tongue weight. This receiver uses a 1¼-inch-square opening and is adequate for small tent campers, jet skis, and bike racks.

A Class 2 receiver has either a 1¼- or 2-inch-square opening with a 3,500-pound gross and 300-pound tongue-weight rating. This safely pulls small campers and boats and is typically a bumper mount on light-duty trucks or a frame mount on crossovers and automobiles.

A Class 3 hitch uses a 2-inch-square receiver, a gross weight up to 6,000 pounds, and a 600-pound tongue weight. These attach to vehicle frames only, and it's important to know if the hitch is a weight-distributing model.

A weight-distributing system increases the hitch tow rating to 10,000 pounds gross and 1,000-pound hitch weight. This system requires a specific ball and hitch mount that works to distribute weight from the tongue to the other axles. Usually, if your trailer weighs more than 50 percent of the towing vehicle's weight, you need one of these hitches.

A Class 4 hitch starts at 10,000 pounds gross and a 1,000-pound tongue weight. With a weight-distribution system, those numbers jump to 14,000 pounds gross and a 1,400-pound tongue.

A Class 5 hitch is 12,000 pounds gross and a 1,200-pound tongue. The gross jumps to 17,000 pounds with a weight-distribution system. Class 5

This could be a Class 2 or Class 3 receiver; both use a 2-inch-square design. Often, the class is marked on the receiver, but the labeling can be difficult to read, be missing, or nonexistent (as here). You can always check the vehicle manufacturer's tow rating to ensure that you're not overloading the receiver.

CHAPTER 14

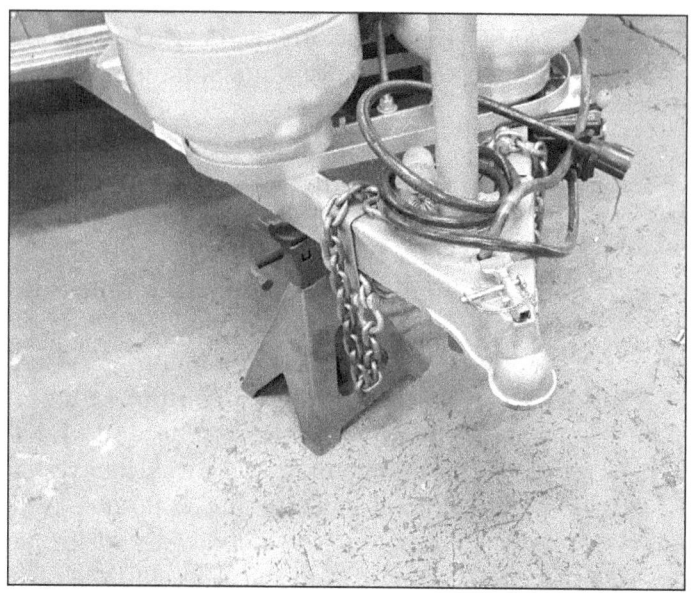 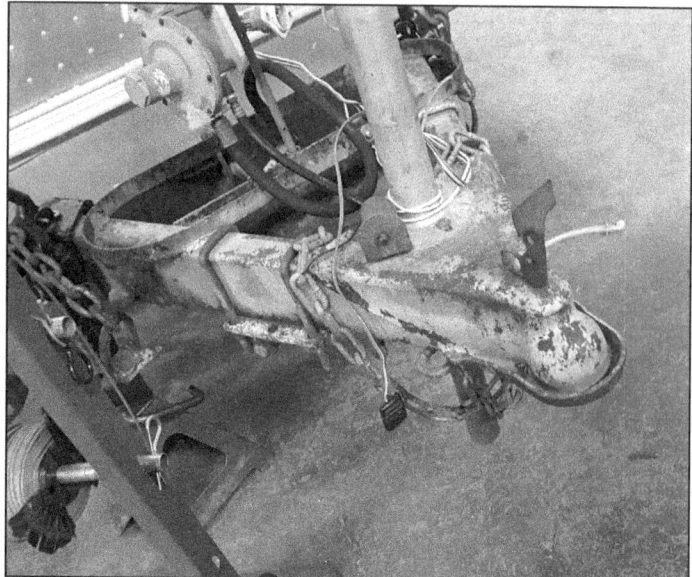

The left coupler is a 2-inch for a 1960s Caravel; the right one is a 2 5/16-inch for a 1970s Sovereign. You can't put a 2 5/16-inch ball in a 2-inch coupler, but you can put a 2-inch ball in a 2 5/16-inch coupler. If you do, it leads to dire results, especially if you haven't crossed the safety chains to catch the coupler when it bounces off the ball. Ball size is marked on the coupler, but often it's rubbed off or rusted over.

hitches use a 2½-inch-square receiver and are for the largest campers short of a fifth-wheel rig.

Ball Sizes and Mounts

As with class hitches, ball sizes correspond to the trailer coupler and hitch. Be sure to choose your hitch ball appropriately.

The ball's shank is another important factor. Depending on your receiver's shank size, the ball's shank needs to protrude enough so that the nut fully threads onto the ball. These nuts can loosen if improperly torqued and should be periodically checked.

Ball mounts come in many lengths and drop to suit the vehicle and trailer ride height. Ideally, the trailer and vehicle should ride level independent of each other's ride height. This can take some experimentation with different hitch drops because a vehicle "sags" into the suspension differently with various tongue weights and many other factors.

Airbags

A vehicle that is improperly weighted and hooked up is a hazard on the road. Poor handling, unwanted

This Boles Aero is sitting level with its tow vehicle. A combination of correct hitch drop and proper suspension sag is key to achieving this. (Photo Courtesy Joe Roberts, Abaci Photos)

Airbags are a great way to help level a tow load; however, they do not increase your vehicle's tow rating. Airbags are used in addition to the factory leaf springs to help offset the trailer tongue weight and add stability. A nice option is to have a vehicle-mounted compressor and cab controls. The compressor can also be used to top off tires with a quick-connect and air hose.

When building a camper for show, details are important, such as the correct-year black plate and correct glass-lensed taillights on the Cruisette.

sway, reduced braking, and headlights aimed at the sky or oncoming traffic create a dangerous situation.

To counter suspension sag, air bags are often an easy add-on to a tow vehicle. They can be adjusted to offset differing trailer tongue weights. Typically, a Schrader valve (common tire valve) mounted to the bumper is used to fill the bags. For ultimate convenience, a vehicle-mounted compressor and cab controls allow you to easily and quickly adjust the tow vehicle's ride height.

Choose a Destination

Once you're ready for the road, finding a destination is the next step. There are many clubs and vintage camper rallies if you'd like to show your restoration. These are also a good destination if you're unsure of what kind of camper to purchase. The wide variety and enthusiastic owners are always willing to offer advice and to show their camper's layout.

Sisters on the Fly is an all-female club that, as of writing, has accumulated more than 8,000 registered members. They sponsor many outdoor activities like fly-fishing and are very involved with vintage campers.

Tin Can Tourists is another good club for vintage campers. They hold rallies across the continental United States, and their website is a great resource for both manufacturer and specific model information.

Vintage Camper Trailers magazine is dedicated to restoring and rallying.

Finally, the Wally Byam Caravan Club, WBCCI, dates back to the early 1950s. It is a large Airstream club with rallies in many states.

A period-correct cooler, awning, and tasteful lawn furniture help give the Cruisette presence at a vintage camper rally in Palm Springs. It's easy to imagine how striking the Cruisette would be hooked up to that Desoto in the background.

CHAPTER 14

To show off the A/C unit and belly pan, a mirror was placed to give people a view of the Cruisette's underside.

When showing a camper, people like to see the process. A binder with photos is a good way to share the trials and tribulations of a restoration. In our digital world, a tablet loaded with images can also tell the story. Editing (simple things like rotation, leveling, and cropping) and reducing photos to a manageable number helps with impact.

Cleaning before Settling Down

During the journey to a vintage camper rally or show, your camper acquires dirt. Finding a DIY car wash is a good way to clean the camper before setting it up for the show. Although convenient, these car washes can be rough on a finely finished exterior polish or paint. It's best to avoid using the brushes provided by the car wash and instead bring your own.

The brushes are always abused, dirty, and worn thin by use on undercarriages or dropped on the ground. And they're on the stiffer scale of washing equipment. Soft car-wash mitts from the auto parts store and a good detergent remove the road grime and leave a nice shine. Toss all the wash equipment in a bucket for easy transport.

Good washing practice is to always start from the top and work down; be sure to use a stepladder or stool for reaching the top.

Accessorizing

Staging at camper rallies is an essential part of the fun. Having period-correct items such as cookware, sporting goods, or lawn/camp furniture brings conversation and banter to your camper. A working portable vintage tube radio is a great way to break the silence. If vintage electronics at that level is not on your hobby radar, a nonfunctioning radio from your camper's vintage could be gutted to hold a small Bluetooth radio.

Another fairly easy-to-find camping accessory is a vintage cooler.

Setting up a camper takes days, weeks, and months to find all the right stuff. At this point, the Cruisette still needs curtains.

A camper rally is an all-day affair. From setup, to showing, to meandering, you'll be busy. The reactions from people are empowering and make all the hard work worthwhile.

They're often in poor condition but can be restored with the same skills used to restore a camper.

Many campers in the 1950s, 1960s, and 1970s were used for outdoor recreation. From fishing gear such as poles, tackle, and waders to watercraft such as canoes and small boats, accessorizing your camper can become extensive.

To get around during a large camper gathering, a vintage bicycle is an easy way to travel in style. In many cases, the colors, designs, and engineering reflect that of the campers of the same era.

When it comes to sustenance, there are many vintage cookware items (watch out for pre-1970s radioactive Fiestaware!) to tie into your camper and make it a favorite at rallies. Dutch oven cooking is a classic standby; likewise a vintage cast-iron waffle maker can make both a dessert or breakfast winner. And when it comes to hydration, vintage pitchers and cocktail accessories add to any camper's theme.

This 1940s Westwood camper and Schwinn bicycle share a similar, unrestored patina and were produced in the same year. Finding period-correct accessories for your camper can be just as rewarding as the restoration process.

EPILOGUE

From personal experience with restoring campers and teaching a three-day class about what a camper restoration entails, I found people often feel intimidated by all the details and hard work involved in a restoration.

The skills necessary in the automotive world to maintain and preserve vehicles include auto-body specialists, engine technicians, and suspension tuners, to name a few. You know that it's rare for upholsterers to grab a wrench and rebuild an engine; likewise, an engine tech probably isn't going to jump on a Singer to stitch up a leather interior. The same is true in household construction and maintenance: specific trades, ranging from plumbing to interior design, don't often intermingle.

A vintage camper restoration requires skills and methods used in both the automotive and housing industries and, in the case of riveted campers like Airstream, aviation construction. That's a lot of ground to cover. And much of it is often covered by a single person, the owner.

I hope this book has helped you narrow your camper restoration skill-set, so that you can focus on your strengths and look for professional assistance where it will be more economical and practical. Like a "choose your own adventure" novel, camper restoration can be a journey through many possible avenues. You should now have some idea as to which road you want to take to complete your project.

Happy camping!

www.ingramcontent.com/pod-product-compliance
Lightning Source LLC
Chambersburg PA
CBHW081447070526
44586CB00019B/2259